Napa Stories

"A tavola non s'invecchia mai."

"At the table, no one gets old."

Napa Stories

PROFILES, REFLECTIONS & RECIPES FROM THE NAPA VALLEY

Michael Chiarello

with Janet Fletcher

Photographs by Steven Rothfeld

stewart, tabori & chang
new york

Design by Barbara Vick

Published in 2001 by

Stewart, Tabori & Chang

A Company of La Martinière Groupe

115 West 18th Street

New York, NY 10011

Library of Congress Cataloging-in-Publication Data

Chiarello, Michael.

    Napa Stories: profiles, reflections, and recipes from the Napa Valley/

    Michael Chiarello with Janet Fletcher; photography by Steven Rothfeld.

      p.cm.

    ISBN 1-58479-116-0

     1. Wine and wine making—California—Napa Valley.

     I. Fletcher, Janet Kessel. II. Title.

    TP557 .C43 2001

    641.2'2'0979419—dc21   2001031470

Printed in England

10 9 8 7 6 5 4 3 2 1

First Printing

To Belle and Barney Rhodes, who have touched my heart
and career in the most extraordinary way.
You will always be a guiding light wherever my life leads.

Contents

Growth

Renewal

A B C D E F G H J K L M N O

1 2 3 4 5 6 7

Chateau Montelena

Araujo

Calistoga

Schramsberg

Turley

Rombauer
Duckhorn

Charles Krug

Spring
Mtn.

St. Helena

Joseph Phelps

Howell
Mtn.

Chiles
Valley

Harrison

Pope
Street

Zinfandel
Lane

Rutherford Road

St. Helena

Rutherford

Beaulieu

Oakville Cross Road

Staglin

Bella Oaks
Robert Mondavi

Oakville

Yountville

Stag's
Leap

Shafer

Harlan

Yountville Cross
Road

Stag's
Leap
Wine
Cellars

District

Yountville

Mount
Veeder

Trefethen

Highway 29   Etude

Carneros

A Bird's Eye View
of the
NAPA
VALLEY
APPELLATIONS

3   5

When I moved to the Napa Valley at the age of twenty-four to take a chef's job at Tra Vigne, a St. Helena restaurant, I didn't realize I had made a decision that would change my life. I had been looking for a good place to settle for awhile with my growing family, but I didn't know that this picturesque wine valley would become the home I never wanted to leave.

Over the next few years, Napa Valley embraced me, taught me, encouraged me. I had grown up with wine—my parents are southern Italian, from Calabria—but now I was meeting the people who actually make it. I was cooking for them (and sometimes with them), sharing wine with them, hearing their stories, feeding their children. Napa was unveiling itself to me in a human and personal way. The more time I spent with vintners and growers, the better I understood and appreciated the wines they made.

Wine critics like to talk about *terroir*—all the physical elements that characterize a vineyard, from sun, soil, and slope, to the way the wind comes up in the evening. They say the best wines are those that express the uniqueness of their terroir. But I think that definition misses something. With due respect for the critics, I've come to believe that wine is much more than just grapes, soil, and weather.

The Napa Valley wines I like best have some essence of the winemakers in them, some hint of their character and spark. When I drink Schramsberg sparkling wine, I always picture Jamie Davies and her late husband, Jack. I remember the stories they told me about struggling to restore their run-down property, and how hard they worked to create an audience for fine American sparkling wine. I remember hearing how Jack and Jamie led the fight to keep a highway from running right through the valley. And I remember Jamie's stories about taking all her employees to the White House so they could see where Schramsberg wines are poured. When I taste their wine, all these memories come rushing back.

When others drink Napa Valley wine, I want them to taste more than just the fruit, oak, and tannin. I hope they will taste the history and the effort that has shaped every glass. That's why I have collected these stories, told to me by some of the most prominent people in the valley—with names like Mondavi, Trefethen, and Duckhorn—as well as by some essential Napa characters whose names rarely reach the public. These personal stories reflect the modern history of Napa wine, from the early contributions of André Tchelistcheff, perhaps the most influential wine consultant ever, to the current views and achievements of such winemaking stars as Larry Turley and Tony Soter.

I don't think the term 'pH' appears very often in this book. You won't find detailed tasting notes or the play-by-play for each vintage, nor will you see much about ratings and scores—who's up and who's down. Instead, we chose to discuss risk-taking, winemaking philosophy, career highs and lows. I heard some fascinating personal histories and some touching anecdotes about helpful competitors, harvest crises, self-doubt and triumph. I also heard concerns about some difficult issues facing the valley— mostly environmental controversies relating to growth, hillside development, and water use. Although you will read only the vintners' perspectives here, I'm well aware that there are differing points of view on these significant matters.

I didn't want these conversations to get bogged down in technical details, but I did want every read-er, even the aficionado, to more fully understand how wine is made. I've often thought of the wine-making process as a series of decisions, from where and how to plant the grapes, to how long to age the wine in the barrel, up to the final decisions about whether to fine and filter the wine before bottling.

Vintners make different decisions every step of the way, which explains why no two wines are alike. Many of the vignettes in this collection describe a critical decision in the winemaking process, and I've asked a winemaker—or sometimes two—to share with me how he or she confronts each choice. These aren't "right" answers or even necessarily the mainstream approach. Some of these winemakers are taking a new or unconventional path.

Napa Valley is indisputably wine country, but Napa's appeal goes beyond wine for me. Its physical beauty, architectural richness, multicultural heritage, and the local passion for good food, art, and music are among the other reasons why I'll never leave. I've tried to highlight some of these cultural and culinary contributions to the valley's way of life in another series of vignettes, accompanied by Steven Rothfeld's lovely images.

Today, Napa Valley is an international symbol of high-quality wine and respect for the good life. But that image didn't happen overnight—it was consciously created by many strong-willed people, some of whose stories are told here. When you know these stories, every glass of Napa wine reveals more richness, complexity, and pleasure.

I was brought up in a family that believed in sharing stories as a way of preserving heritage and memory. I hope that when you enjoy these vintners' wines, you will share their stories and help me keep their legacy alive.

Roots

*I*n 1935, a couple of years after Prohibition ended, an Italian immigrant named Cesare Mondavi visited his oldest son at Stanford University to inquire about his son's career plans. Cesare, a home winemaker, had profited from Prohibition by shipping wine grapes from California to the Italian home winemakers he knew back East. (The law allowed heads of families to make two hundred gallons of fruit juice at home, and a good share of that juice became wine.) Cesare saw even more potential in the aftermath of Prohibition, and he urged his son Robert to think about a future in the wine industry.

It took a visionary to see the promise of Napa Valley then. Fine wine grapes had been replaced during Prohibition with mediocre varieties that would stand up to long-distance shipping. The American public was accustomed to poor-quality sweet wines and had little enthusiasm for dry table wine.

Nevertheless, the Mondavi family—Cesare, Robert, and Robert's brother Peter—bought the Charles Krug property in St. Helena in 1943 and began to build a market for bottled wine from Napa Valley. They had few competitors apart from Inglenook, Beringer, and Beaulieu Vineyard. At Beaulieu, the brilliant Russian enologist André Tchelistcheff was producing most of the standard-setting wines of the Valley.

Despite the growing profile of the Charles Krug property, few other wine pioneers followed. By 1960, Napa Valley had only thirty wineries—half as many as when Prohibition ended. There were fewer than four hundred acres of Cabernet Sauvignon in the Valley (compared to twelve thousand now) and so little Chardonnay that it wasn't even listed in the annual grape report.

Who can say what turned the tide? Maybe it was the presence of John and Jackie Kennedy in the White House, and their obvious enjoyment of French wine. Whatever the cause, the 1960s saw the launch of a boom in Napa Valley that has never really slowed.

Belle and Barney Rhodes foreshadowed the revolution when, in 1959, they bought and planted the Oakville plot that became "Martha's Vineyard." Jack and Jamie Davies followed, buying the decrepit Schramsberg property in 1965 with the ambitious dream of making fine sparkling wine. A year later, Robert Mondavi unveiled the Robert Mondavi Winery, the first new Napa Valley winery in more than twenty-five years (except for the tiny Stony Hill). In 1968, demonstrating the vision that marked his business career, Gene Trefethen bought six hundred acres in Napa; growing wine grapes was his idea of retirement. Gene's sister-in-law, Barbara Eisele, and her husband, Milton, thought they would beat the Trefethens to Napa, but it took them another year to find their dream vineyard—now a Napa icon.

Their reminiscences follow: remarkable stories of passion and adventure, risk and reward. These dreamers and others planted the roots of the modern Napa Valley.

Belle and Barney

Rhodes

If America had royalty, Barney and Belle Rhodes would be the duke and duchess of Napa Valley. They are admired on so many fronts: as proprietors of Bella Oaks Vineyard, one of the Valley's top Cabernet Sauvignon vineyards; as wine collectors with an internationally renowned cellar; as generous philanthropists; as tireless promoters of Napa Valley; and as superb hosts. Belle is one of the Valley's most accomplished home cooks, and every dinner I've been to at their Rutherford home has been a dream come true. My absolute best memories are of times I've spent with Belle and Barney.

Over the fifty-plus years of their marriage, this remarkable couple has traveled the world and they have a huge network of international friendships. They would never think of letting you go off to London or Bangkok without letters of introduction to their friends. Both of them are from the South, and they have these lovely Old South manners that are definitely different from what I grew up with in the farming town of Turlock, California. Before you go to dinner at their house, you practically get a briefing book on the other guests so that you will have plenty to talk about.

Barney was a dermatologist who became chief operating officer of the Kaiser Foundation Health Plan. But from his early days as a doctor, his passion was wine and Belle quickly came to share that interest. Along the way, she studied cooking with a star-studded roster of instructors, including Roger Vergé, Jacques Pépin, Lorenza de' Medici, and Cecilia Chiang. One of their dearest friends says Belle and Barney are on a first-name basis with most of the great chefs of Europe and Asia.

Since I moved to Napa Valley in my twenties with my young family, this childless couple has been like parents to me. Once they traveled to Bangkok for two days to welcome me to a promotional food and wine event (one of many) that Belle set up for me with the Robert Mondavi winery at the Oriental Hotel. They don't travel as much as they used to, but they continue to be my model for gracious living. A day doesn't go by that I don't have them in my heart. Belle shares her recollections with me.

ROOTS

Barney's family had wine only on holidays, and even when he was a child, they would let him have some by the tablespoon. But his interest in wine really started when he went to medical school at Duke University. The chairman of the department was a brilliant man who had lived for a long time in London. When he was approached by Duke to come teach there, he said, "I will not go unless you move my wine cellar." This man would invite people over to enjoy wine, and if someone couldn't make it, he would let his nephew come and bring Barney.

Barney finished medical school and did his internship with the Navy because they made it sound so nice. You could make money at the same time. We met at Jacksonville Naval Hospital in Florida. I was the chief pharmacist mate in the WAVES. He was the kind of man you would look at and say, "God, he's good-looking!" We were married on October 12, 1944.

I was born in a little town in West Virginia and grew up along the Ohio River, between Wheeling and Parkersburg. It was a glass manufacturing area primarily. It turned out that the silica in the Ohio River was ideal for blowing glass. In fact, I would wager today that the greater quantity of eight-ounce wine glasses is produced in the town where I was born.

In those days, you couldn't just go to a supermarket. So if you had any little plot of land, you tilled it, and you had fruits and vegetables that you preserved. My mother was a wonderful baker and cook, especially with canning and preserving. My two older sisters didn't want to get their hands dirty, so I said, okay, you do my ironing and laundry and I'll do your kitchen work.

That's how Belle first learned to cook, but her wine education had to wait for Barney. Together they toured wine country and tasted and bought, with no intention of becoming collectors. They were living in Oakland then, and they began to make friends with people who shared their interest in good food and wine.

We used to go up to Napa Valley early on, and we would go to Charles Krug, Martini, Christian Brothers, BV [Beaulieu Vineyard], Inglenook—there were only about ten places. We had friends that we would meet and go here and there together, and it was just sort of a challenge to see how many wineries you could do over a weekend. Of course we would take some bottles home with us, and then go to the next winery and get the same varietal, so we would be able to have some idea of which was better. But we were not buying to build a cellar. We were buying to have something soothing to drink after a hard day.

After World War II, we were invited to meet a friend on sabbatical in Paris. It was great for us because we had not been abroad. I think that our being able to accept that invitation—Barney was making enough money then—was an ideal thing. Our friend had just picked up a brand new Citröen and we managed to put hundreds of miles on it going around the whole of France.

Shortly after that trip, we bought thirty acres of bare land in Napa Valley for a song—it was a green-chop alfalfa property. We planted Cabernet Sauvignon but the grapes never did well. They were too near the Napa River. We couldn't give them away.

Their next venture was only a little more successful. They bought about ten acres in St. Helena, consisting of mixed varietals, most of them undistinguished

Of course we would take bottles home, but we weren't buying to build a cellar.

by today's standards. What grapes they couldn't sell to Louis Martini they sold to the Napa Valley Co-op. Belle thinks they paid $800 an acre—absolute peanuts—but she remembers Louis's wife Elizabeth chiding them for overpaying and running up everyone's taxes.

Before long they sold that property, too, but by 1959 they were ready to try again. They bought an old prune orchard west of Oakville, ripped out the trees and planted twelve acres of Cabernet Sauvignon—literally, the two of them, on their knees. Barney was such a novice farmer that he got the tractor stuck in the barn when he forgot that you had to hand-crank it to start it and he pulled it in too far. That generated a lot of laughs around town.

A couple of years after they planted their Oakville vineyard, Belle and Barney helped launch a legend: Heitz Wine Cellars. Joe Heitz had expertise—he had studied and even taught enology—but he had no capital. So he turned to Barney and said, "You know people with deep pockets." And, in fact, Barney was able to round up ten or twelve investors, some of them fellow Kaiser physicians, to help Joe get started.

We've been investors in Heitz ever since. We just had our annual board meeting, and it's amazing how many of the Kaiser people are still shareholders. Only now, instead of getting nothing but a bottle of wine occasionally, you get a nice little check.

By 1963, Barney began to tire of the long commute to his Oakland office. He was rising fast in the Kaiser organization, and he was spending too much time on the road. When a real estate agent dropped by unannounced one evening and said he had a couple looking for a farmhouse and vineyard just like theirs, Belle invited them all to come back the next day for breakfast. So before the Rhodeses even harvested the first crop off their new Oakville vineyard, they sold it to Tom and Martha May, who later christened it "Martha's Vineyard."

We became extremely friendly with the Mays, and it was just one of those marriages made in heaven. When we sold them the house, we put a half-dozen bottles of wine in the fridge for them—Heitz, of course—and from that point on, they became shareholders in Heitz and still are. It was like we became honorary parents to them.

Belle and Barney never regretted their decision to sell what became one of California's most famous vineyards. But just a few years later, they were back in the Valley. They bought yet another prune orchard, this one west of Rutherford, and planted what became the Bella Oaks Vineyard. From the start, the grapes have gone to Heitz, whose Bella Oaks Cabernet Sauvignon is a California classic.

After their initial trip to France, Belle and Barney continued to travel to Europe often—tasting, tasting, tasting. They became close to Michael Broadbent, an auctioneer at Christie's, who advised them on their purchases at London wine auctions. Gradually, they built up a world-class wine cellar, filled with the best wines of Bordeaux and Burgundy, the finest German bottlings, and exceptional Ports and Madeiras. In 1997, when they decided to part with some of them, "wines from the collection of Belle and Barney Rhodes" were the highlight of a major New York wine auction.

But they weren't just Europe-focused. They also loved California wines; in fact, they introduced Michael Broadbent to the best ones. For many years, they selected the California wines for Cathay Pacific Airways, a plum assignment that took them to Hong Kong often. But although they bought more wine than any couple could ever drink, they were never speculators.

What's the point in having it if you're not going to consume it? That wasn't our thing. We were doing it so we would have balance for all kinds of entertaining, a big diversity of style and country. I suppose we had fifteen thousand bottles at one point. But we had it to share. Wine consumed by yourself is just not proper.

Barney is a famously good wine taster—the kind who can identify the shipper and vintage when the Port is passed around. But Belle has a good palate, too, and strong opinions:

I've never liked wines that are thin. I think wine has to have some guts to it. You take a sip and the thing's saying, "Hey, look at me!" You don't have to have flowery speeches about it, but if it talks to you and you want another glass and you say, "I'm going to go out and buy some of that before it's all gone," that's good wine.

At home they have a cellar of wines that are ready to drink and another cellar for bottles that need more aging. It's not at all obvious how the collection is organized, but Belle insists that Barney knows just where everything is. He used to spend an inordinate amount of time picking wines for a dinner party. He would get the menu and guest list from her, and then he would disappear in the cellar for hours.

Belle is an incurable pack rat who keeps detailed records of all her luncheons and dinner parties in spiralbound notebooks: the guest list, the seating chart, the menu, notes on food preparation and presentation—even the thank-you notes. Their New Year's Day parties were marathons, with Belle preparing eight or more courses, from caviar mousse to macadamia nut tart, and Barney opening up to fifteen different German wines.

It's not easy to get Belle to talk about how she makes a menu. She has thirty-five hundred cookbooks, so maybe she never knows what will inspire her. One thing I've noticed is that meals at the Rhodeses almost always end with warm pistachios and a round-bottomed Port decanter that you have to keep passing because it won't stand on its own. Usually Barney is taking little naps between sips at this point.

If it sounds like the Rhodeses do nothing but travel and give dinner parties, that's a false impression. They are major, active donors to many causes. Barney generously supports Duke University, and Belle looks for ways to help young people. She has pledged her cookbook collection to Napa Valley College, which named a teaching kitchen in her honor. She also spearheaded the fundraising for a scholarship fund for culinary students at Napa Valley College. If you visit the Culinary Institute of America at Greystone in St. Helena, you'll notice a room named for Belle and Barney, who rarely say no if the issue is food or wine education. Their patronage, encouragement, and promotion of the culinary arts have helped make Napa Valley a wonderful place to visit and live.

Belle and Barney

rarely say no

if the issue is food

or wine education.

A Cantinetta Dinner for Belle and Barney

```
POTATO GNOCCHI with MUSHROOM SUGO
CRUCIFIED QUAIL VÉRONIQUE
ROASTED WINTER SQUASH AGRODOLCE
ORANGES with LEMON CURD AND BROKEN BISCOTTI
WARM PISTACHIOS AND PORT
```

I've never known any people who entertain as much or as beautifully as Belle and Barney Rhodes. Their luncheons and dinner parties are legendary, and when they began to cut back on their entertaining at home, they simply moved the party elsewhere. Often "elsewhere" is the Cantinetta at Tra Vigne—our small store and wine bar, which we happily open in the evenings for their dinner parties.

Well in advance, Belle will send the annotated guest list and a list of the wines Barney will be bringing from his cellar. Then there will be some fussing over the menu until we get it just right. More often than not, quail is on it. Belle adores quail, especially this Quail Véronique, with its fragrant spice rub and warm grape sauce.

I don't know if I have ever served this exact menu at a Rhodes dinner, but it's full of their favorites so I know they would approve.

Flour makes gnocchi heavy; potato keeps them light. That's why I bake the potatoes for gnocchi instead of boiling them, so the dough will need less flour. For this amount of sauce, you'll only need half the gnocchi you make. Freeze the remaining gnocchi, uncooked, to have a head start on another meal. Boil them directly from the freezer.

For the gnocchi:

2 pounds russet potatoes

Coarse salt

4 egg yolks

½ cup freshly grated Parmesan cheese

½ teaspoon salt

Pinch freshly ground pepper

Pinch freshly grated nutmeg

1 to 1¼ cups unbleached all-purpose flour, plus more for dusting

For the sugo:

⅓ cup extra virgin olive oil

4 cups finely chopped, mixed wild mushrooms

1 tablespoon chopped garlic

1 tablespoon minced shallot

1 tablespoon minced parsley

1 teaspoon minced fresh rosemary

¼ cup red wine

½ cup tomato puree (from fresh peeled tomato)

½ cup chicken broth or water

Sea salt, preferably gray salt (see Note)

Freshly ground pepper

1 generous tablespoon unsalted butter

Parmesan cheese for grating

Make the gnocchi: Preheat oven to 375° F. Bake potatoes until very soft on a bed of coarse salt in a baking dish. (The salt keeps the potatoes from touching the dish and developing a hard spot.) Cool potatoes until warm, then halve lengthwise and scoop out the flesh. Pass the flesh through a food mill or ricer, or push it through a coarse sieve, or grate it. You should have about 4 cups.

In a bowl, combine potato, egg yolks, cheese, salt, pepper, and nutmeg. Work the mixture with a wooden spoon until smooth. Add the 1 cup flour and knead very gently, patting and pressing the dough with your hands until all the flour is incorporated. Add some or all of the additional ¼ cup flour if the dough feels too moist. Transfer dough to a work surface and roll into a log about 3 inches in diameter. Cut the log into eight equal pieces.

Give each piece a quarter-turn so that you are rolling the dough in a different direction, then roll into ropes a generous ½-inch in diameter, as if making breadsticks. Flour the ropes generously, then cut crosswise at ½-inch intervals. You can shape the gnocchi on a ridged butter paddle (see *The Tra Vigne Cookbook,* Chronicle Books, 1999, for detailed directions), or you can cook them as is. Let them dry at room temperature for at least 20 minutes.

Make the sugo: Heat a large sauté pan over high heat. When hot, add oil, then sprinkle in the mushrooms. Don't stir! Let the mushrooms sizzle and caramelize for 7 to 8 minutes, then add the garlic and cook, stirring, for about a minute to release its fragrance. Add the shallot and cook for about a minute, then add the parsley and rosemary. Cook briefly to release their fragrance, then add the wine and simmer until almost evaporated. Add tomato, then broth. Simmer until lightly reduced, 4 to 5 minutes. Season to taste with salt and pepper. Remove from heat and stir in the butter.

Bring a large pot of salted water to a boil. Add half the gnocchi. They are usually done about 2 minutes after they float to the surface, but test one to be sure. Lift them out with a skimmer and transfer to the sauce. Return the pan to heat and cook the gnocchi briefly in the sauce to coat them well, then divide among four warm bowls. Grate Parmesan cheese over each serving.

Note: Gray salt from France's Brittany coast is my favorite salt for most uses. It is moist and chunky and full of flavor from minerals found in the ocean. To make it easier to use for everyday seasoning, I dry large quantities of it in a 200° F oven for 1 hour, then pound it or grind it in a spice grinder until medium-coarse.

SERVES 4 AS AN APPETIZER

The method of readying these quail for the grill with two crossed skewers always makes me think of Saint Andrea. According to the stories I learned as a child, he was crucified on an X-shaped cross. We "crucify" the quail to encourage the breast and leg meat to cook evenly. Véronique—as in "filet of sole Véronique"—indicates that the dish contains grapes.

For the toasted spice rub:

¼ cup fennel seed

1 tablespoon coriander seed

1 tablespoon peppercorns

1½ teaspoons red pepper flakes

¼ cup mild chili powder

2 tablespoons kosher salt

2 tablespoons ground cinnamon

Make the spice rub: Toast the fennel seed, coriander seed, and peppercorns in a small, heavy skillet over moderate heat. When the fennel begins to color, turn on the exhaust fan. Working quickly, add the red pepper flakes and toss briskly. Transfer mixture to a plate to cool. In a blender, grind toasted seasonings with chili powder, salt, and cinnamon until fine. Alternatively, you can grind the toasted seasonings in a spice grinder or coffee mill, then place in a bowl and stir in the remaining ingredients.

8 whole boneless quail

16 eight-inch wooden skewers

Extra virgin olive oil for rubbing the quail, plus 1
   tablespoon

1 tablespoon thinly sliced shallot

1 tablespoon minced fresh rosemary

1½ cups white grape juice

Sea salt, preferably gray salt (see Note on page 26)

2 cups chicken stock

1 cup seedless red grapes, halved

Thread a skewer through each quail from the right wing through the body and into the left leg. Then run a second skewer the opposite way: through the left wing, then the body, then the right leg. The two skewers will form an X and the quail will be flattened and fully supported by the skewers.

Brush a little olive oil on each quail, then season generously with spice rub.

Prepare a medium-hot charcoal grill. When coals are covered with gray ash, place quail on grate directly over the coals and cook on both sides, 5 to 6 minutes total. Remove to a warm platter and let them rest while you make the sauce.

Heat 1 tablespoon olive oil in a 12-inch skillet over moderate heat. Add shallot and sauté until lightly colored. Add rosemary, grape juice, and a pinch of salt. Raise heat to high and reduce to a syrup, then add chicken stock. Continue simmering until you have 1 cup sauce. Add red grapes and let them heat through and become glazed with the sauce. Spoon over the quail.

SERVES 4

Oranges with Lemon Curd and Broken Biscotti

I'm not much of a fan of gooey, sticky desserts—I'd rather have something with texture and a balance of sweet and tart. And because I'm a better cook than baker, I love desserts I can make on the fly. This one is a true "cook's dessert." You can use storebought biscotti (plain, not chocolate or choco-late-dipped), and you can substitute berries for the oranges in summer. Note that you will need a small blowtorch to carmelize the sugar on top of the curd; most broilers are not hot enough.

lemon curd:

⅓ cup sugar

9 large egg yolks, room temperature

⅓ cup freshly squeezed lemon juice

1 tablespoon grated lemon zest

3 tablespoons unsalted butter, in small pieces and at room temperature

1⅓ cups crumbled biscotti

1⅓ cups skinless orange segments

4 tablespoons orange juice

4 teaspoons superfine sugar

Make the lemon curd: In the top of a double boiler, whisk the sugar and the egg yolks until sugar has dissolved and mixture is pale yellow, then whisk in lemon juice and zest. Set the bowl over simmering water and whisk constantly until mixture reaches 145° F; it will visibly thicken but don't let it get too hot or the eggs will curdle. Remove the bowl from the heat and add the butter a little at a time, whisking until each addition is incorporated and the curd becomes thick. Transfer to a bowl, cool, then refrigerate until well chilled.

In each of four 10-ounce ramekins, put ⅓ cup crumbled biscotti. Toss the orange segments with the orange juice and divide them among the ramekins. Put a dollop of lemon curd on top of the oranges and sprinkle the curd in each ramekin with 1 teaspoon sugar. Just before serving, use a blowtorch to caramelize the top of each portion. Cool briefly to solidify the sugar top, then serve.

SERVES 4

ROOTS

Right Grape, Right Place

If Napa Valley vintners have learned anything since the 1970s, it's the value of planting the right grape in the right place. Growers and winemakers now have a better sense of the climate and soil needs of each grape variety, and they've mapped the many microclimates of Napa Valley. Such information helps them avoid planting Chardonnay in an area too warm for it, or planting Cabernet Sauvignon in a cool pocket where it might not get fully ripe.

University of California researchers helped clarify some of these planting decisions when they divided California into growing regions based on "degree days"—the cumulative number of hours that the temperature is above 50° F during the period between bud break (typically mid-April) and October 31. Region one is the coolest, suitable for Pinot Noir, Riesling, and other early-ripening varieties. Region five, the hottest—encompassing parts of the San Joaquin Valley—is a more challenging area for fine wine grapes. Napa Valley ranges from region one in Carneros to region three around Calistoga.

"The system has some merit," says Mary Hall, a vineyard manager and viticulturist whose clients include Etude and Acacia Winery. "On the other hand, it can be easily skewed. If it was a cool year that turned hot at the end, but you picked before the hot weather, then it was still a cool year for you. Or maybe it was a cool year except for two days when it was 113° F for five hours. It doesn't show you the specifics that can really affect a vintage."

So while degree days offer some guidance to vineyard owners trying to decide what to plant, they're not the deciding factor. For one thing, the Valley includes many "gray" areas, where it may or may not be too hot for Pinot Noir, too cold for Zinfandel. In the end, the decision may rest on how badly a vintner wants to grow a particular grape, and how willing he or she is to challenge Mother Nature.

"It boils down to people's gut feeling and personality and experience and accumulated knowledge," says Hall, "and sometimes science gets thrown out the window a little bit."

Confounding even the growers, some varieties perform well in a wide range of climates. Syrah, for example, thrives both at Araujo Estate in warm Calistoga and at Truchard Vineyards in cool Carneros. "Both are beautiful wines, and you think, how can that be?" says Hall.

Nevertheless, you can't discount the impact of climate. Pinot Noir grown in a hot region will typically ripen too quickly, developing sugar before it develops flavor. Hot-climate Pinot Noir lacks color, acid, and flavor—it tends to taste washed-out, notes Hall. In contrast, Zinfandel grown in a cool region may never develop the rich, ripe, spice and berry flavors that Zinfandel lovers crave.

Along with climate, soils determine the options for vineyard owners making planting decisions, but conventional wisdom about soils has changed dramatically. In the seventies, the county encouraged people to plant in the Valley's most fertile areas. "Anything on Howell Mountain, on the bordering hills, or in Carneros was frowned upon because there was minimal soil," says Hall. "It might be good for grazing, but it wouldn't be very productive. Now we've learned that a lot of these soils are the really desirable ones for high-quality grapes."

Today's viticulturists analyze soils minutely before planting anything. Based on the analysis, a single thirty-acre vineyard might be divided into five different blocks, each with its own rootstock, grape clone, trellising system, and irrigation, to take advantage of soil differences. "Micro-managers" may be scorned in business, but they're admired in the vineyard.

New Life for a Landmark

I've always taken pleasure in finding new uses for old things, or using new objects in unexpected ways. When I was growing up, nothing was ever wasted or thrown away. Now, at my house, my grandfather's old plow is a piece of garden sculpture. Old wooden picking boxes became nightstands when I stacked them beside my bed.

So you can imagine how pleased I was when one of Napa Valley's oldest wineries, an endangered architectural landmark, found new life as a cooking school. Greystone Cellars in St. Helena, long used by the Christian Brothers to make sparkling wine, is now the continuing-education campus of the Culinary Institute of America. Since 1995, chefs and other food and wine professionals from around the world have come here for advanced training and a taste of Napa.

The Greystone story had a happy ending, but it was touch-and-go for awhile. When Heublein, the beverage giant, bought the Christian Brothers brand in 1989, they inherited Greystone but didn't want it. The building needed millions of dollars worth of earthquake reinforcement, so they put Greystone on the block.

Naturally, the community worried about what would become of this architectural treasure. When it was built in 1888, Greystone was the largest stone winery in the world. The wealthy businessman who commissioned it, William Bourn, planned to operate it as a cooperative, where Napa Valley growers could bring their grapes to be made into wine. It was designed as a gravity-flow operation: Grapes would be delivered to the top floor for crushing and fermenting. The wine would then be sent to the middle floor for aging, and finally to the bottom floor for bottling. The phylloxera epidemic of the 1890s altered Bourn's plans. He never opened his cooperative. Instead, he sold the building and it passed through many hands before the Christian Brothers bought it in 1950. When Heublein began looking for buyers in 1991, the community demanded to have its say.

What uses could be made of Greystone that would enhance the Valley? How could it be put to profitable use without bringing more congestion to St. Helena? Who could possibly afford to buy and repair this massive building?

When executives from the Culinary Institute of America in Hyde Park, New York, looked at Greystone, they saw its potential immediately. But they also knew they couldn't afford to buy the property *and* do the repairs.

In the end, Heublein donated most of the cost of the building. The institute undertook a $15 million renovation, adding a restaurant, teaching kitchens, a retail store, a demonstration auditorium, and organic gardens. To keep traffic and commotion at a minimum, the community prohibited the school from holding public events or from advertising its restaurant or store.

That hasn't kept the CIA Greystone from becoming hugely successful. Professionals come from around the world to take advanced classes in bread baking, pastry, food and wine pairing, or food writing. The restaurant and store are thriving, and despite the initial concerns about traffic congestion, I never hear locals complaining about this addition to our community. It's a winner for everyone. Students' hearts and minds are opened once they're exposed to the beautiful gardens and vineyards; chefs from all over the world get a taste of our wines and our style of life; and they take a positive impression of Napa Valley, and maybe a few bottles, home with them.

Robert and Margrit Biever

Mondavi

How do you begin to talk about what Bob Mondavi means to the Napa Valley? There is no more tireless promoter of California wine, no better example of vision. With Margrit, he has helped make the valley a mecca for art and music, as well as for wine and food.

Bob eats at Tra Vigne frequently, and he has never hesitated to march back into the kitchen and tell me when something's not right, but I know he'll be back the next week. Often I spot Bob and Margrit having dinner by the window in the evening, watching the rain and looking like newlyweds.

In the fall of 2001, Copia: The American Center for Wine, Food, and the Arts will welcome its first visitors to Napa. This great cultural center on the banks of the Napa River, at the gateway to Napa Valley, is the longtime dream of Robert Mondavi. He and Margrit are its major benefactors, although many others, including many of the Valley's vintners, have followed their lead.

What is Copia? A museum. An exhibit space. A performance space. A venue for cooking demonstrations and wine lectures, for classroom and garden activities for kids. A place that will tell the world about American contributions to food, wine, and the arts, as Bob Mondavi has done for years.

Bob: As a child, I wanted to excel at anything I did. I didn't care whether it was football or marbles. I would look at my competition first to see whether I physically could do that or was smart enough. I knew I only had average intelligence so I had to work at whatever I did. But I knew that people were lazy and would not work as hard or be as dedicated, so all I had to do was be determined and stay with it. And the other people would drop off, you know. They would give up. And I had all the patience in the world.

That's why, later, I traveled the world over, to find out what my competition was. No other wine people traveled then. But I was traveling to learn.

Robert spent his early years in Virginia, Minnesota, where his Italian immigrant parents had settled. (See interview with Peter Mondavi, page 80, for more details.) His father, Cesare, worked in the iron mines, then opened a wholesale grocery business; his mother, Rosa, opened their house to boarders, cooking and cleaning for Italian immigrant men. Rosa was a famous cook, and her skills in the kitchen played a big role when Cesare went into the grape-shipping business.

Bob: My mother loved cooking for people who ate. The more you ate, the more she loved you. But I didn't realize then what a good cook she was. My dad would bring home the banker or the growers if he wanted to cut a deal, and my mother's cooking would firm everything up. What did they come for? My mother, not my father. She would see to it that they would go home with a lot of homegrown vegetables.

My father was just the opposite of my mother. Very, very quiet. He never praised any of us, but he gave me a lot of leeway. I was always anxious to do things, and the fact that he let you do things was his form of approval. But he didn't say "you did a good job" or things like that.

They were all Swedes and Norwegians in Minnesota at that time, and they looked down on the Italians. I wanted to learn to speak English very rapidly. My mother would speak to me in Italian but I'd always answer in English because we were ridiculed in Minnesota.

Bob's Old World upbringing shaped his lifelong attitudes about wine. He has always believed and preached that it is the most natural and wholesome of beverages and that children should be introduced to it at the family table.

Bob: When I was growing up, we'd have leftover chicken for breakfast, or my mother would make oatmeal with tomatoes, and we would have coffee with red wine and sugar and I developed a taste for that.

My mother fed me wine and water when I was three or four years old. Wine was considered a liquid food. Never have I seen my mother, father, two sisters, or brother ever abuse it. Yet when I went to school at Stanford, I went on a beer bust. They would drink beer, Scotch, bourbon, brandy, but no wine, and they would get plastered. And I thought, oh my God, these people aren't civilized. And that's why I wanted to create Copia: The American Center for Wine, Food, and the Arts.

I want to educate children, adults, and our legislature that, in moderation, for most people, wine is good for you. Wine has been with us for seven thousand years and it's going to be here as long as man exists, so we have to teach each other how to consume it.

In 1921, Cesare moved the family to California so he could go into the grape-shipping business. Throughout Prohibition, he supplied wine grapes to the home winemakers back East. And he did well enough to send both Bob and his younger brother Peter to Stanford. In fact, Bob was at Stanford when Prohibition ended, and Cesare saw an opportunity.

Bob: In 1935, a little over a year after Repeal, he came to me and asked what I was going to do upon graduating. And I said I was going to be either a businessman or a lawyer. And he said, "Bobby, I feel there's going to be a

Page 35: Robert and Margrit Biever Mondavi dance the day away at Napa's unfinished Copia: The American Center for Wine, Food, and the Arts, which they helped to found.

Pet llamas enjoy
the view from the
Mondavis' hilltop
estate in Napa.
Terra cotta figurines
(opposite) inside their
art-filled home are
mostly pre-Columbian,
collected during the
couple's wide travels.

future in the wine business." And I thought, well, why not go into a young industry and grow with it? So I took chemistry in my senior year at Stanford. Then I was tutored by a professor who was teaching enology at the University of California at Berkeley at that time. I'd spend two or three hours with him about three or four days a week—a short course on winemaking. And that's the only formal training I had.

At first Bob worked at the Sunny St. Helena Winery, a bulk wine producer that was his father's first venture in the Napa Valley. In 1943, he joined his dad at the Charles Krug Winery they had just purchased. After returning from the war, Peter made the wines, and Bob's natural talents as a salesman and marketer helped the winery flourish. But after their father died, the brothers had different ideas on how the winery should grow.

Bob: When my dad was living, he was the boss of the family and there was no doubt about what would take place. I don't think my mother stepped into the winery twice. I got along with my father very well and I was much more aggressive than my brother. Peter was much more conservative. He didn't want to spend. I wanted to get the finest equipment that money could buy. I was always looking for what I could do to improve winemaking, and Peter was more content to continue to do what they did before and work hard at that.

In 1965 he broke with his brother, who objected to how freely Bob spent company money. Their mother sided with Peter. Bob was told to take a leave of absence, and it was made clear that there wouldn't be a job for Bob's older son Michael at Charles Krug Winery.

Bob: I went to my mother and said, "Mother, when we built the winery here with Dad, the whole idea was that the family would take part. You pass it from one generation to the other." But she was given advice from a consulting firm not to bring Michael in. I said, "Mother, Michael is going to go someplace else. He has always wanted to be in the wine business." So I left Krug and built the Robert Mondavi Winery. My brother was very upset. He said, "You know that's competition."

When Bob, with two local investors, built his winery in 1966, it was the first major new winery in Napa Valley since Prohibition. In the years since then, the company has become an international leader, with partnerships in wineries in California, Chile, and Italy, and exports to eighty countries. But one of their biggest contributions to the wine world is their emphasis on research and their willingness to share what they learn.

Bob: From the beginning, I knew our wine should be very natural and so I didn't even filter it. Our wines were tannic in the beginning. We didn't pick our grapes as carefully as we pick them now. Now we want to be sure that our grapes are beautifully ripe so the tannins are soft. They've become more gentle, much more friendly, much more velvety in character.

We did a lot of experimental work, and we're still learning. We were the first to have satellite pictures taken of our Carneros vineyard. And then we saw how much more fertile certain parts of the vineyard were, so we began to make our wine in special lots according to the vigor of the vines. We're now using different rootstocks, and we're planting our vines closer together (see page 77). Different grape varieties require different spacing because of the vigor of the vines. But it's taken years, many years, to learn these things.

In addition to promoting his own winery, Bob never stops boasting about Napa Valley. He is a world ambassador for wine, California wine more specifically and Napa Valley wine in particular. Everywhere I go in the world, I meet winemakers who know and revere Robert Mondavi.

Bob: A revolution took place in food and wine in the last forty or fifty years, and what California has contributed is amazing. Even though people have been making wine in Europe for many, many years, they weren't really willing to do any new research work. The French and Italians just did what their forefathers did, and if you did anything different, you were a rabble-rouser. You were upsetting the apple cart. The revolution really started in Napa Valley.

We could not sell our wine in New York thirty or forty years ago. I remember when my daughter Marcia came to work for us. She went around to the various restaurants in New York and they slammed the door. Napa Valley wines—forget it!

It's hard to underestimate Bob Mondavi's courage and leadership. When neo-Prohibitionists were attacking alcohol and advocating warning labels and "sin taxes" on it in the late 1980s, Bob led the effort to promote wine's health benefits and its contribution to civilized life. Every bottle of Mondavi wine began to carry a mission statement about the benefits of wine in moderation.

Bob: Wineries were afraid of public liability lawsuits. The doctors were afraid of malpractice lawsuits. That's why we came out with the Mission program in the 1980s. The Wine Institute said, "They're going to sue you, Bob, and it could be awful." And I said, "I'm not afraid of telling the truth." Throughout history, for most people, wine in moderation was healthy and good for you. And that's all we were showing. Yet we could be sued, and that's why the big wineries from the Central Valley wanted no part of it.

Today, Bob is chairman of the board but his children make the decisions. Michael is president, Tim is head of winemaking, and Marcia is a member of the board of directors who represents the company at events in New York and around the world. Robert Mondavi is a publicly traded company now, although the family has half the equity and the majority of the votes.

Bob talks a lot in public speeches about "the good life." Although he has many material comforts, I don't think his definition of good living has much to do with possessions. It has more to do with simple pleasures—with celebrating daily around the table with people you love and making time in your life to appreciate beauty.

Bob: Appreciating wine, food, and the arts together is the good life. When you eat good food, you're happier. When you drink wine, if you don't do it in excess, it lifts the spirit. And if you put your whole heart and soul into what you're doing, how much better life is. Too many people aren't passionate. Take a job that you like and you never have to work a day in your life.

I think Margrit, Bob's wife, has helped open his eyes to the richness that the arts add to life. Due to Margrit's influence as vice president of cultural affairs, Robert Mondavi Winery has been a leading supporter of the arts in Napa Valley. Their summer concerts on the lawn are always sold out.

Margrit: I remember early on when I asked him if we could have an art show, and he said, "Sure, if it doesn't cost anything." Then, when we built the Vineyard Room, I said, "Can I do a concert?" And he said, "Sure, if it doesn't cost anything." So we borrowed the stage from the high school, the chairs from the church, and the piano I took in my Volkswagen bus from home. It was a benefit for the Napa Valley Symphony, and people came! Then the next year it just broke loose.

Margrit also is the force behind the Great Chefs cooking school at the winery, which has helped bring so many world-famous French chefs to Napa and spread the good news about Napa Valley wines. The program started in the mid-1970s and is still going strong, although today it often showcases American chefs.

From their philanthropy in the Valley (they're major supporters of the campaign to revive the opera house and the lead donors to Copia, among many other gifts) to their openness about winery research, they're an inspiring example for the wine industry worldwide.

Bob: We want to be helpful to everyone, and I feel that very strongly. It's better to give than to receive. I had to work like the devil to get in the position where I could give, and yet by giving, you get more in return. In the long run, you'll get more in return.

Christmas Dinner for the Mondavi Family

CAPPELLETTI IN HEN BRODO *with*
WILD MUSTARD GREENS

ROSA MONDAVI'S PASTASCIUTTA

ROAST CHICKEN *with* FENNEL AND SAGE

ROAST CREAMER POTATOES

BOB'S BRAISED FENNEL

FORNI-BROWN FIELD LETTUCES *with* NEW OIL

WARM BISCOTTI *with* FRESCOBALDI VIN SANTO

When I was asked to cook the Christmas dinner for the Robert Mondavi Winery, I wanted to create a menu that reflected the family's heritage. I never met Rosa Mondavi, Bob's mother—she passed away before I moved to the valley—but from the stories I've heard, she and my mother would have gotten along well in the kitchen. They were both naturally good cooks who never let go of the Italian traditions. If the Mondavi home was like mine, Christmas meant two pasta courses—one of them always a handmade filled pasta like cappelletti *because filled pasta takes extra work, meaning extra love.*

After the soup pasta and the sauced pasta, we served roast chicken with braised fennel, a vegetable I always associate with an Italian Christmas. Afterward, we dressed a salad of local greens with lemon juice, gray salt (see Note on page 26), and extra virgin olive oil, in this case the new-crop oil from Italy. The Mondavis have a partnership with the Frescobaldi family of Tuscany, so it seemed right to end the meal with Frescobaldi *vin santo, the luscious dessert wine.*

Plump ricotta-filled

cappelletti float in a

rich broth with fresh

greens added at

the last moment.

This method of oven-poaching is the way my mother would cook an old hen. It makes a very clear and flavorful broth. We would eat the boiled chicken along with the cappelletti, but you can save the chicken for the next day. The bigger the chicken, the better the broth.

This recipe yields more cappelletti than you need, but it's just as easy to make a lot as a few. They freeze beautifully. Place any extra on a baking sheet in the freezer. When frozen, transfer to a freezer bag. When ready to use, boil directly from the freezer.

You can make your own pasta dough, as my mother did, but storebought pasta works fine. Pass the sheets through a pasta machine to make them a little thinner.

For the brodo:

1 large free-range chicken, preferably 4 to 5 pounds, giblets removed

1 onion, peeled and halved

1 carrot, peeled and left whole

2 whole ribs celery

½ cup peeled, seeded, and very finely diced tomato

1 bay leaf

For the cappelletti filling:

14 ounces (about 2 cups) whole-milk ricotta cheese

2 egg yolks, preferably organic

¾ cup grated pecorino romano cheese

Pinch of nutmeg

Pinch of salt

½ teaspoon freshly ground black pepper

1 pound fresh egg pasta in thin sheets

Sea salt, preferably gray salt (see Note on page 26)

2 tightly packed cups of mustard greens, spinach, broccoli rabe, or dandelion greens

Parmesan cheese for grating

Freshly ground black pepper to taste

Make the brodo: Preheat oven to 300°F. Rinse chicken well. Place in deep, flameproof roasting pan with onion, carrot, celery, tomato, and bay leaf. Add enough cold water to come about two-thirds up the sides of the bird. Bring to a simmer on top of the stove, straddling two burners if necessary. Cover, place in oven, and poach 1½ hours; broth should simmer gently. Remove from oven and turn chicken breast side down to cool. Remove chicken from broth and reserve for another use. Tomato solids will have settled to the bottom. Pour the clear broth off the tomato solids and set aside.

Make the filling: Beat ricotta with a wooden spoon until smooth. Beat in egg yolks, cheese, nutmeg, salt, and pepper. Refrigerate uncovered until firm.

Lay a sheet of fresh pasta on a lightly floured work surface. Cover remaining dough to keep it from drying out. Imagine a horizontal line bisecting the sheet. Place 1 teaspoon of filling just below the imaginary line on the half nearest you, and about an inch from the left edge. Repeat, placing mounds of filling every three inches. Brush surface of dough lightly with water, then fold the top half of the dough over the bottom half to cover the filling mounds snugly. Press between and around the mounds of filling to seal the dough. Using half of a 3-inch fluted cookie cutter, cut half-circles from the stuffed pasta sheet. The folded edge should be the straight side of the half-circle. Repeat with remaining pasta and filling; you should have enough for about 50 cappelletti. Transfer them to a clean dish towel lightly dusted with flour. If possible, position a fan near the cappelletti and air-dry them for 30 minutes, turning them over after the first 5 minutes.

Season broth to taste with sea salt. Bring 1½ quarts to a simmer in a saucepan. Add 16 cappelletti and cook just below a simmer. They are done 1 to 2 minutes after they rise to the surface. Pinch the edge on one to be sure. Transfer cappelletti with a slotted spoon to four warm bowls. Add greens to broth and cook until greens are tender, then use tongs to divide the greens among the bowls. Ladle a little broth over pasta and greens. Grate Parmesan cheese over bowls and finish with a grind of fresh black pepper.

SERVES 4

Rosa conserved summer's ripe plum tomatoes in a sauce she could use for pasta all year. Depending on the rest of the menu, she might add anchovies, tuna, clams, or bits of leftover meat to the sauce. Adapted from Seasons of the Vineyard *by Robert Mondavi, Margrit Biever Mondavi, and Carolyn Dille (Simon & Schuster, 1996).*

4 tablespoons olive oil

3 garlic cloves, peeled and lightly smacked

2 cups **Rosa Mondavi's Tomato Conserva (right)**

½ cup chicken broth

1 pound fresh fettuccine

3 tablespoons chopped Italian parsley

Salt

Freshly ground pepper to taste

Freshly grated Parmesan cheese to taste

Bring 4 quarts of water to a boil. Meanwhile, heat the olive oil over moderate heat in a large skillet. Add the garlic and cook until golden, then remove the garlic. Add the tomato conserva and chicken broth and simmer gently while you cook the pasta.

Salt the boiling water well. Add the pasta and cook until al dente, then drain, reserving about ¼ cup of the cooking water. Toss the pasta with the sauce (you may not need all of it if you like your pasta lightly sauced) and parsley; if needed, add cooking water to thin. Adjust the seasoning with salt and pepper and serve immediately. Pass the Parmesan cheese.

SERVES 6 TO 8 AS A FIRST COURSE

Rosa Mondavi's Tomato Conserva

A handy basic sauce for the pantry. Use wherever tomato sauce is an important element of the dish. Once a jar is opened, refrigerate and use within 5 days.

9 pounds ripe plum tomatoes

3 carrots, peeled and chopped

3 onions, chopped

2 celery ribs, chopped

2 tablespoons salt, or to taste

7 or 8 large sprigs of basil

7 or 8 large sprigs of Italian parsley

Core the tomatoes, halve them, and place in a large nonreactive pot. Add the carrots, onions, and celery and 2 tablespoons salt.

Cover the pot and place over high heat. When the tomatoes begin to give up their juices, lower the heat and cook at a bare simmer for about an hour. Tie the basil and parsley sprigs together with kitchen string and add to the vegetables. Cook, uncovered, until the vegetables are very soft and the sauce is thick, about 1 hour more.

Meanwhile, sterilize canning jars and lids. Bring a large kettle of water to a boil.

Remove the basil and parsley from the sauce; taste and adjust the salt. Press the sauce in batches through a food mill into a bowl. Ladle the hot sauce into the hot canning jars and cover with lids and rings according to manufacturer's directions.

Place the jars in the kettle and cook in the boiling water bath for 10 minutes. Remove the jars with canning tongs and cool to room temperature. Refrigerate any jars that do not seal, and use them within 5 days. Store sealed jars in a cool, dark place. They will keep for up to a year.

MAKES ABOUT 4½ PINTS

ROOTS

I wanted to do a main course for the Mondavi Christmas party that would have meaning for Bob Mondavi. We talked about it and discovered that we both remembered harvesting wild fennel as kids. (In fact, in adulthood, I found a stand of wild fennel at the Robert Mondavi Winery that I used to raid on occasion.)

This roast chicken is seasoned generously with fennel seed, although by all means use wild fennel fronds and seeds if you have them. The halved carrots support the chicken as it cooks and eliminate the need for a rack. While the chicken cooks, prepare the potatoes and fennel for the oven so they can go in as soon as the chicken comes out. If you have two ovens, you can cook the vegetables at the same time.

1 tablespoon sea salt, preferably gray salt (see Note on page 26)

1 tablespoon toasted fennel seed

2 tablespoons finely minced fresh sage

Extra virgin olive oil

One 3-pound free-range chicken

2 carrots, halved lengthwise

Preheat oven to 450° F. Turn on the convection fan, if you have one.

Pound salt, fennel, and sage together in a mortar, or crush in a mini-chopper or with the flat side of a chef's knife. Coat your hands with olive oil and massage the bird all over. Rub the spice mixture all over the chicken, pressing it into the skin and sprinkling some inside the cavity. Truss the legs.

Line a baking sheet with aluminum foil and oil the foil lightly. Place carrots in the middle of the baking sheet, cut side down and parallel, to make a raft for the bird. Set the chicken on top of the carrots. Bake until chicken begins to color nicely, about 25 minutes, then reduce oven temperature to 375° F and continue roasting until chicken juices run clear, about 35 minutes more. Set chicken aside to rest but leave oven on. While it rests, bake the potatoes and fennel.

SERVES 4

Roast Creamer Potatoes

1½ pounds small boiling potatoes ("creamers"), about 1 inch in diameter, halved

3 tablespoons extra virgin olive oil

3 tablespoons drippings from roast chicken

20 whole fresh sage leaves

8 whole garlic cloves, unpeeled, stem end trimmed

Sea salt, preferably gray salt (see Note on page 26)

Cover potatoes with salted water and bring to a boil. Simmer uncovered until they are three-quarters done, 5 to 8 minutes, then drain.

Heat olive oil in a large ovenproof skillet over moderately high heat. When oil is hot, add the potatoes and the drippings. Turn potatoes cut side down. Let them form a good crust, tossing occasionally, then add sage leaves, garlic, and salt and toss for a minute or two. Transfer to the 375° F oven and bake until potatoes are tender when pierced, about 15 minutes.

SERVES 4

Bob's Braised Fennel

2 large bulbs fennel, sliced lengthwise ¼-inch thick

Butter for the baking dish

Sea salt, preferably gray salt (see Note on page 26)

Freshly ground black pepper

Chicken broth

Arrange sliced fennel in one layer in a flameproof buttered baking dish. (You may need two dishes.) Season with salt and pepper. Add enough broth to come halfway up the sides of the fennel. Bring to a boil on top of the stove, then cover and place in the 375° F oven. Bake until fennel is tender, about 30 minutes.

SERVES 4

Ultimate Polenta

Before Napa Valley was grape country, it was grain country. Wheat, oats, and barley carpeted the land that vines cover now. By the 1850s, when the Gold Rush created a spike in demand for flour, Napa was the second-largest wheat-producing county in California.

Over the years, I've taken my daughters to see a reminder of Napa's past at the Bale Grist Mill north of St. Helena. Built in 1846 by a colorful character named Dr. Edward Turner Bale, the mill is maintained and operated by the State Parks system today. If your timing is right, you can see the mill in operation—the thirty-six-foot water wheel powering massive grindstones from France. You can even purchase a bag of grains freshly milled on the premises. The mill's polenta is simply the best, much better than storebought. We always bring some home and cook it up that day. The last time

we did that, my seven-year-old daughter Gianna and I cooked the mill's polenta alongside a supermarket brand, and she could easily tell the difference.

Dr. Bale was a British surgeon with the Mexican army under General Mariano Vallejo. He married General Vallejo's niece and, in 1841, received a land grant of seventeen thousand acres in upper Napa Valley—a gift worth untold millions today.

Bale was apparently a difficult man. He drank heavily and was hot-tempered; during one fight, he shot Vallejo's brother. He also knew an opportunity when he saw one, building his state-of-the-art grist mill to handle the Valley's growing production of wheat.

Bale himself did not see his mill in operation for long. He headed for the Mother Lode in 1848 to look for gold and died in 1849, at the age of thirty-eight. He bequeathed his cattle to his sons and land

to his daughters; one of his daughters married Charles Krug and the couple planted some of the first wine grapes in the Valley.

The mill passed from hand to hand and eventually fell into disuse and disrepair. A picture of it in the early 1900s shows it overgrown with ivy. Eventually, it was deeded to the California State Parks system, and in the 1970s, a campaign was launched to raise funds to make the mill run again. Workers dismantled the whole structure piece by piece, then repaired and reassembled it.

Today, the water wheel turns again on weekends for the benefit of visitors, producing a few souvenir bags of ground wheat, corn, and rye. I wanted to sell the polenta at the Cantinetta, our store next to Tra Vigne, but park rules wouldn't allow it. If you ever visit Napa Valley, don't leave without a bag of this truly fresh, whole-grain polenta.

The mill's polenta

is simply the best,

much better than

storebought.

Dorothy

Tchelistcheff

I feel blessed to have known André Tchelistcheff, "the dean of American wine-makers." Ironically, he wasn't American but pure Russian, a short man with a heavy accent and the bushiest, blackest eyebrows I ever saw. His family was learned and distinguished and wealthy, but they lost everything fleeing the Bolsheviks.

His widow, Dorothy, who still lives in Napa, says that André wanted to be a doctor. Instead he became the most famous winemaker and enologist of his day. He spent thirty-five years at Beaulieu Vineyard (BV), then seventeen years as a consultant for wineries in California, Washington, and Italy. Because of those consulting years, a whole new generation of young winemakers—including Marco Cappelli at Swanson, Jill Davis at Buena Vista, and Rob Davis at Jordan—consider André their mentor.

In 1991, when he was almost ninety years old, BV asked him to come back to work, and he accepted. In typical fashion, he became close to Joel Aiken, BV's young winemaker; in fact, Joel's two boys call Dorothy "Grandma."

On his ninetieth birthday, the who's who of the wine world gathered at the Fairmont Hotel in San Francisco to salute this little giant.

He really loved the young people. He knew each young person, and for many of them, he was more or less a father figure. He consulted not only on the wine, but on all of their lives. He just didn't go and taste the wine and tell them what to do and walk out. If they had a problem, he'd come home and pick up a French enology book that he particularly liked. He'd read and read, then he'd call the winemaker and say, let's try this or that.

He himself was a "young" person. He was not set in his ways. Maybe because of his background, he was able to understand and accept change. And he always changed.

Joel remembers that when André came back in 1991, and they had their first meeting and went through the winery, André said, "Here are these same old redwood tanks that I always hated and wanted to get rid of. They're

In his thirty-five years at Beaulieu Vineyard, André Tchelistcheff made legendary Cabernet Sauvignon and Pinot Noir. Previous page: Dorothy Tchelistcheff is "grandma" to Mitchell (left) and Andrew, the sons of Beaulieu Vineyard winemaker Joel Aiken.

still here." And he turned to Joel and said, "I can change. Why don't you?" And Joel has said several times since that that's why he did change some things. Now they've got French oak in the Private Reserve.

Rob Davis tells a story about how he had this great idea about a wine, and he told André and André said, "Well, yes, I did that once. It made lousy wine. But you've got to try it." Later, when they tasted the wine, André said, "Yep, made lousy wine." But he didn't say to Rob, "Don't do it." He said, "Go ahead and try."

André had a remarkable memory. Dorothy says he "had a library in his head." Fifty years afterward, he could tell you exactly what the de Latours served at his first dinner at Beaulieu Vineyard in 1938. He remembered every detail of the food and the wines—and not from notes either. He remembered fifty years of vintages by heart—how much it rained that year, or how dusty it was.

I was the culinary director of BV when he came back to work for the winery in 1991, and I had the chance to taste some of the older wines with him. His taste memory was incredible. He never forgot a wine.

You know he smoked his whole life until the last four or five years, when he was having bronchial problems. About three weeks after he stopped, he got two cases of wine from [Château] Ste. Michelle that he was supposed to taste and evaluate. It was August and it was hot, and he was really sweating over this task, but because he had such a backlog memory, he managed. But, he told me, it was very strange. Before, when he was a smoker, tastes came to him in the shape of a pyramid. After he stopped smoking, they came to him like a fan. He said, "I'm tasting so many more things than I ever tasted before." He made that remark several times.

I remember when he came to Tra Vigne and we did some food and wine pairings for the BV people. Everybody came with big notebooks, but I said, "Put them away and give me your senses and your memory." I learned to taste by remembering the environment that I experienced a taste in. That's why asparagus tastes good to me in spring and not in January. And I remember André laughing and telling stories and everybody trying to write everything down instead of really feeling it. When you're listening from your brain to your hand, you're not recording the real experience.

André never wrote anything down, but still he never forgot. When I started to cook some of the Russian dishes, they had to look, taste, and smell just like they did seventy years before. I had some rough times.

One Easter I decided I was going to make him a *kulich*. It's Russian Easter cake, like *panettone* but richer and more moist. Well, I didn't have the right mold so I used a coffee can. He came home and I was mixing the kulich up and he looked at it and said, "What's that?" And I said, "It's kulich." "Oh, no. That's not kulich." "Well, all right. Whatever it is. I'm baking it."

So I baked it and it came out of the coffee can and of course it had brown rings around it from the indentations. He looked at it and said, "It's not kulich." I said, "Well, this is American style." Then he told me that to cool it, you needed to lay it on the pillow, but he didn't tell me you had to keep turning it on the pillow, so it had a dented back. When I brought it back to the kitchen, he said, "That's not kulich.' Okay, André. So I

André didn't think he would last a year in Napa Valley.

For all his renown,

André Tchelistcheff believed

that he made only two great

Pinot Noirs—one of them,

the 1947 Beaulieu Vineyard

Georges de Latour.

decorated it and I stood it up in our little kitchen, and he looked at it for three or four days, and finally he said, "Well, we better try it."

He admitted that it wasn't bad, but when we went to San Francisco to visit his sister the next time, she gave him his grandmother's recipe for kulich. It was all in Russian, but he said he would translate it for me. So he started: "Take two *kopecks* of yeast." And I said, "What kind of yeast and how much is two kopecks?" The recipe went back.

André was thirty-six years old, an enologist in Paris with a Russian wife and young son, when Georges de Latour, the owner of Beaulieu Vineyard, handpicked him for the winemaking job.

Beaulieu's winemaker was retiring, so Mr. de Latour went to France, to the research lab where André was working. He wanted someone with a European background for the job, and André's professor recommended him. Apparently, it was a chore to get him here because it was the Depression, and Dorothy Perkins, who was the Secretary of Labor, said we don't need extra people here and absolutely nobody is coming in. It took U.S. Senator Hiram Johnson to get him in. I still have the telegram.

He came through immigration in New York in September 1938, and made it to Napa Valley in time for the vintage. In those days, people in Rutherford still wore guns strapped on them, and they used to have big brawls on Saturday night at the local restaurant. André didn't think he would last a year. He lived right across from the winery, and he and Dimitri [his son] would walk into St. Helena every time the movie changed. He knew how to say hello and good-bye in English, and that's all.

I suppose André stayed because things were unsettled in Europe at that time, and he felt there was a future here. He'd lost so much in his life. His parents came out of Russia with nothing but two changes of clothes for the children. Besides, he was pretty stubborn. When he set his mind to something, he was going to do it.

He wasn't happy with what he found in the winery, either. Dorothy says he was most shocked by the poor sanitation he saw at BV. He also complained later about what he called "the ice of secrecy" at the winery. He thought it was counterproductive.

That secrecy at BV must have irked André, because he believed scientists should share information. In 1947, he opened the Napa Valley Enological Research Laboratory in St. Helena to do lab testing and help everyone raise the quality of their wines. About the same time, he also started the Napa Valley Wine Technical Group, to bring winemakers together to advise each other and share research results. The group is still active more than fifty years later, and it's a good symbol of how open and nurturing the Valley has become. There aren't many winemaking secrets today.

André stayed with BV until 1973, four years after Heublein, the giant beverage conglomerate, bought it, leaving behind thirty-five vintages of legendary Cabernet Sauvignons and Pinot Noirs. Although he came to believe that Pinot Noir did better in Carneros than in Rutherford (in fact, he helped pioneer Pinot Noir in Carneros), his favorite BV Pinot Noir was from Rutherford.

André was a Pinot Noir man, basically. He was known for his Cabernets, but he tried all his life to make Pinot Noir. It got him in trouble with Heublein, but he always said he made only two really great ones—the 1946 and the

*We never had
a big cellar. André
always gave all his
wines away.*

1947. In fact, he would say they really only made a vintage and a half of great Pinot Noir. The "half vintage" was because, in 1947, Dr. Maynard Amerine [the distinguished enology professor from U.C. Davis] wanted him to change his fining methods. I think André used to fine with egg white and Dr. Amerine wanted to use something else. So they made it both ways and, of course, André didn't like Dr. Amerine's half.

Those two vintages were made from a little tiny grape variety called Petit Noirien. The clusters were like little pine cones. But by 1946, the vineyard was old and only giving about a half-ton per acre. Madame de Latour would walk through and say, "Mr. Tchelistcheff, are you growing grapes or are you growing leaves?" So after 1947, he took it out. He tried to save it by planting cuttings on another BV ranch, but it was never the same.

Dorothy had been André's secretary at BV for ten years when, in 1968, the two of them—both married to others—fell in love and decided to marry. André was twenty-two years her senior, and their love story "set St. Helena on its ear," she says.

She left BV after they married, and André retired in 1973, ill at ease in the corporate structure that came in with Heublein. He started a consulting business that quickly thrived, and Dorothy says that his seventeen years of consulting—for Buena Vista, Jordan Winery, Château Ste. Michelle, Simi Winery, Swanson Vineyards, Niebaum-Coppola, Firestone, and more—were probably the happiest of his professional life. He liked being able to say exactly what he thought, without worrying about public relations.

André was always learning. He once said that he wanted his tombstone to read that he was a permanent student of the University of California.

The summer before he died, I took him to France and we were there for five weeks. We did Champagne, Alsace, Arbois, Burgundy, Bordeaux, down to Toulouse, back to Cognac, back to Paris, over to London for a tasting, back to Paris, and then home. But when we were at Romanée-Conti, André was so excited that he turned to Aubert de Villaine [the owner] and said, "I would like to return next year for a *stage* [an apprenticeship]. Will you accept me?" And he meant it. He really meant it. So they looked at me and said, "What do you think?" I said, "Well, he has trouble with stairs. If he can get up and down the stairs, it's fine with me."

The last nine days he was in the hospital, the young people would come in and he would ask, "Have we had a frost? What have you done with this wine?" And so on and so on, in the last nine days of his life! The day he died, he lectured his doctor for two hours on the Russian Orthodox religion.

I figured Dorothy must have a cellar full of old gems, but I was wrong.

We never had a big wine cellar. André always gave all his wines away. Just as an example, one day Joe Swan [of Joseph Swan Vineyards in Sonoma County]—who was pretty tight with his wine—brought six bottles to André. Joe said, "I really hate to give him this wine because I know he's going to give it away." And, you know, the young people would come over and the bottles would go out the door. I never even tasted it.

We drank tea. André was with wine all day long. Some days, he would have tasted sixty wines, so he was tired of it. So we had tea, and he had jam with his tea like the Russians.

It's not easy to sum up André Tchelistcheff's achievements, but he had a huge impact in many areas. He convinced vintners to take frost protection seriously and helped develop protection measures. He was a stickler for sanitation and made others understand its importance. He improved the quality of his own and others' white wines by advocating cold fermentation to preserve fruitiness and, for sweet wines, sterile filtration. He showed others how to control the malolactic fermentation in red wines. And on and on. But it seems to me that his greatest legacy wasn't some breakthrough in his lab, but his commitment to sharing his breakthroughs. The cooperative nature of Napa's wine industry today owes a lot to André Tchelistcheff—and to Dorothy, who stood beside him.

André was a Pinot Noir man, basically. He was known for his Cabernets, but he tried all his life to make Pinot Noir.

Choosing Rootstocks and Clones

When a grower decides to plant Pinot Noir, his or her decision making has just begun. Choosing the right clone of Pinot Noir for the scion (the fruit-bearing wood) and getting it planted on the right rootstock can make the difference between a good wine and a great one. Growers have long known that they need to graft European wine grapes (Vitis vinifera) such as Chardonnay, Merlot, and Cabernet Sauvignon onto American rootstock

because vinifera vines are susceptible to phylloxera, a devastating root louse, and American vines are resistant. In the 1970s, when many new vineyards were planted in Napa Valley, rootstock decisions were simple. Growers chose either AxR-1, a prized all-purpose rootstock, or the more vigorous St. George if they were planting on rocky hillsides.

Then California vines on AxR-1 began succumbing to phylloxera, and the Valley had to abandon this popular rootstock. By the time they replanted their stricken vineyards in the 1990s, growers had learned a lot more about rootstocks and their contribution to quality.

When today's Napa Valley winemakers have the chance to plant a new vineyard, they spend considerable time looking for rootstocks that fit their situation. Do they have gravelly soil or clay soil? Is their soil deep or shallow, rich or poor? Will they be dry-farming or irrigating? Does the vinifera variety they want to grow tend to be vigorous, producing lots of vegetative growth (leaves and canes)? Too many leaves can shade the fruit, leading to vegetal aromas and flavors in the wine. The solution? A low-vigor rootstock that keeps the vinifera scion in check.

"We're all looking for vine balance," says John Caldwell, a viticulturist and clone authority in Napa. (For more on vine balance, see page 77.) "You don't want vines overly vegetative. That can screw up your wine quicker than anything."

Grapevine nurseries now offer a wide range of rootstocks for different needs, and vintners choose them carefully. At the same time, they must choose the clones of Pinot Noir, Sauvignon Blanc or

Chardonnay they prefer, in the same way that a gardener chooses whether to plant Early Girl or Brandywine tomatoes.

A clone, by definition, is a selection that can be traced back to a single vine. Say you're a Pinot Noir grower and you find, in your vineyard, a single Pinot Noir vine that year after year produces clusters with smaller berries—a desirable trait for fine wine grapes. If you propagate more vines from cuttings of that vine, and your new vines grow well and produce a superior wine, you have a clone with some commercial potential.

Researchers in the U.S., France, and other wine-growing countries are constantly trying to develop improved clones. When they find a worthy one, it's registered with a government agency (in this country, the Foundation Plant Materials Service of the University of California), and given a number. Then commercial nurseries make it available to the trade. The process of identifying, propagating, planting out, evaluating, and registering a clone can take twelve to fifteen years, says Caldwell.

Are Napa Valley wines getting any better because of all the focus on rootstocks and clones? "No question," says Caldwell. "If you taste our 1980s wines against our 1990s wines, I personally think the nineties are much better." Some of that improvement is due to better winemaking, he admits, but choosing rootstocks wisely has boosted quality, too—even more so than choosing the right clones.

The clone is like the icing on the cake, says Caldwell. All the other elements have to be in place—a good site, the right rootstock, proper viticultural practices. "Then, if you want to get that next notch of quality, it's the clone."

Jamie

Davies

With Schramsberg, their Calistoga winery, Jamie Davies and her late husband, Jack, virtually created the market for premium California sparkling wine. Today, Schramsberg has several competitors, but most experienced tasters would say that it's among the handful that can compete head-to-head with French Champagne.

You couldn't imagine two better ambassadors for California sparkling wine. Until Jack's death in 1998, he and Jamie seemed like a fairytale couple—handsome, gracious, successful, but without a shred of pretension. Jack was an industry leader who always had time for a good cause, especially land conservation. Jamie, whose wine palate is remarkable, worked side by side with Jack, often traveling to promote the wines while he took care of the kids. Jamie is the winery president now; son Hugh is the winemaker.

Situated on 220 wooded acres, Schramsberg was the first hillside vineyard estate in the valley, established in 1862 by Jacob Schram. Its caves, where sparkling wine is now aged, were hand-dug by Chinese laborers. Robert Louis Stevenson visited Schram in 1880 and wrote about it in *Silverado Squatters*.

When Jack and I were first married, in 1960, we were very much taken by life itself. Neither one of us grew up in a wine-consuming family, but we shared a genuine enthusiasm for bringing friends together at the table and bringing wine into that experience. We were all novices, so nothing was correct or incorrect. It was more of an exploration, because wine was what people were talking about, and it occurred to us one day that there was going to be a renaissance for wine in America, and we wanted to be part of it.

Jack was director of marketing for Fibreboard Corporation. The company made paint, wallboard, gypsum, cartons—commodity wares. When they sent him to L.A. to run the southern packaging division, I think we both knew there was something else for us in life.

We got the idea that if our instincts were right and we had the smarts and a wine coach and a thought-out plan, we could change our lives. We could have an integrated family life in a rural community where we would all be together, and Jack in particular would be with us instead of going away to work every day.

In 1964, we started looking for land in Napa. We didn't know whether we were going to become grape growers or get into winemaking, but one thing became clear. We were quite taken by the historic properties, by the idea of reviving a piece of history. Virtually all of the historic wineries of Napa County were on the block at that time: Château Chevalier, Freemark Abbey, Chateau Montelena. Nobody wanted them. They were all considered white elephants, too expensive to revive. People would say, "Why would you do a stupid thing like that? You'll never sell the wine."

One day, Jerome Draper, Sr., who owned Draper Vineyards, asked us if we had ever seen the Schram property. He said, "I have the key. I'll take you up there and you can look around."

Even before she told me, I knew what made Jamie fall in love with this place. If you hike up behind the house, you come to an allée of olive trees—a wide path that's probably a hundred yards long, with huge, ancient olive trees lining both sides. It takes your breath away.

So I'm walking down the olive lane and I'm thinking, this is it. I know it, and the rest of you go away, because as it happened, one of the couples with us was Michael and Ann Stone. And the same day, they went up to Calistoga and saw the Goodenough Ranch and purchased it with Peter Newton, which was the beginning of Sterling Vineyards.

The seller of Schramsberg was Katherine Cebrian, a grande dame of San Francisco society. She once brought all the debutantes up to crush grapes, and they had oysters in the horse troughs and a cable car going up and down the hill. Society people from San Francisco still talk about that party. But mostly she neglected Schramsberg, and when it really started to crumble, she decided to sell.

So we saw this spectacular piece of property that was totally defunct. The caves were open and filled with trash. The barn had almost fallen to the ground and it had these pillars with more woodpecker holes than wood. Everything was falling down, and the neighbors were saying, "You've got to be kidding to take on a place like this."

All it needed was money—a lot of it. Jack and Jamie knew they would need enough capital to plant a vineyard, buy some grapes in the meantime, and purchase farm and winery equipment. They also knew they wouldn't have any revenue for years.

Even though they had never planted a grape and never made a bottle of wine, they found investors easily. Jack inspired confidence and he had that amazing ability to carry people along with his vision.

To Jack, with his marketing background and his Harvard MBA, it was obvious we needed a niche. What was missing in the Valley was *méthode champenoise* wine (sparkling wine made by inducing a second fermentation in the bottle) using Chardonnay and Pinot Noir. The locals considered that a waste of good grapes. At that time, the only

Jamie Davies pours herself a glass of her favorite beverage.

two producers in the country of méthode champenoise were Korbel and Kornell, but they bought wine to put through the second fermentation, rather than making the base wine themselves.

In those days, California champagne was not respected as wine. It was wedding wine—bubbles and sugar. Bring it out to launch the bride or the ship, then take it away and move on to something else. But in Europe Champagne was a beverage of choice, not just for celebrating the moment, but for the meal. So we thought there was an opportunity here, but first we had to get the grapes. There was precious little Chardonnay in the entire county at that time, and the Pinot Noir was planted mostly in the wrong places.

We were looking for five tons of Chardonnay to get started. We couldn't make the wine here because the place was a wreck. But we thought if we could locate some grapes, we could have them delivered to another winery and then pick the wine up in the spring, to go through the second fermentation in the bottle here at Schramsberg. Jerome Draper, Sr., said, "What little Chardonnay I have is committed. But I can sell you five tons of Riesling."

What winery would go along with this very small deal? It would be more of an annoyance than anything else. Well, Robert Mondavi came to our minds because he was known then, as now, as a champion for Napa wine. So we met him at a café and he listened to our plan and said, "You're going to do what? Well, you're crazier than I thought."

It was the whole méthode champenoise thing. It's so labor-intensive, and it requires a much longer aging cycle, which affects return on investment. And then there were so many ways you could mess up.

But he said, "I can see you're really serious about this, so I'll be glad to do it—because if you succeed, we all succeed. You can add some luster to the Valley."

The Davies' Victorian
home once belonged to
Jacob Schram, a German
immigrant who planted
the first hillside vines
in Napa Valley.

When Robert made the deal with the Davies in 1965, he was still a partner in Charles Krug with his brother Peter. The Riesling grapes would be delivered to Krug in the fall, and in the spring, the Davies would get back the equivalent in Chardonnay wine while Krug kept the Riesling. The Davies would bring the wine back to Schramsberg, bottle it with a little more yeast and sugar, and induce the second fermentation in the bottle.

So much for plans. By spring, Robert and Peter had parted ways, and Robert had left Charles Krug to start his own winery.

So we had to go introduce ourselves to Peter and remind him of this arrangement that he didn't know about. And, of course, he was still smarting from the experience with his brother. But he said, "If my brother made a deal, I will honor it." And that's how we made our first 250 cases.

Still, someone had to teach Jack and Jamie the rest of the process—turning a still wine into a sparkling one. They asked Dr. Maynard Amerine, a renowned enology professor, if he knew a good consultant, but in those days few people had any experience with quality sparkling wine. Dr. Amerine thought of Dimitri Tchelistcheff, whose father, André, was the eminent winemaker for Beaulieu Vineyard. Dimitri was a consultant in his own right, working in Baja California then.

Dimitri would come up four or five times a year and we'd go through the cookbook method for making wine, literally. He'd say, "Now don't you dare get off this page. You're not ready yet." The wonderful thing about Dimitri's trips was that it was an occasion for his father to join him. Dimitri rarely came without André, so we got two-for-one in effect.

The first year, the wine overflowed the tank during fermentation because we had inadvertently put in too much juice. Out of the blue, André walked in the door. "I'm just passing by. I thought I might say hello." It was like we had a guardian angel. He would often come by and bail us out in times of need.

Other neighbors were always available, accessible. If a fermentation got stuck, Jack would pick up the phone with his foot on the valve and call Warren Winiarski (the owner of Stag's Leap Wine Cellars), and Warren would lead him through the process step by step until the problem was solved.

As if launching a new brand wasn't daunting enough, Jack and Jamie dove into Napa Valley politics. In 1965, when they bought their property, the pro-growth and slow-growth forces were both gearing up for battle. The slow-growth group wanted to limit urban sprawl by creating an agricultural preserve outside the city limits. In the proposed agricultural preserve, the minimum lot size would be forty acres. So a farmer with, say, fifty acres wouldn't be able to divide his property in half for his kids, or sell half of it to a developer.

We felt from the beginning that we were stewards of this land. It wouldn't own us and we wouldn't own it. We would have the privilege and pleasure of being here for a time, and hopefully we would leave it better than we found it.

Every time we went back to L.A. there were more freeways and fewer trees, and we could see that the same thing could happen here. When we heard that a freeway route had been planned to go right through the middle of the Valley, there was nothing to do but get involved.

I guess some neighbors sensed our regard for the land and suggested we go to a meeting at Dorothy Erskine's house. (Dorothy was a founder of People for Open Space, an environmental organization.) Well, before Jack left the meeting, he was chairman of the citizens' committee to support the creation of an ag preserve.

We worked on the battle for two years. We were newcomers and, of course, we had "L.A." blazing on our foreheads. Now we were running around trying to tell long-term Valley families that they wanted an ag preserve and they might lose their rights to the use of their land. Well, flames went up, but Jack was a good spokesperson and articulate and people listened.

In a way, it was a sad time because it pitted neighbor against neighbor. It was such a monumental change being proposed, and people thought of it as life-threatening in a way. You know, "I've got four kids and I want to divide my land into four pieces." Yet some of them understood that maybe the time had come when they had to look at it a little differently.

Jack and Jamie mounted a door-to-door effort to explain the merits of the ag preserve to landowners—that it would help keep Napa rural and protect it from the kind of development that had altered Los Angeles. They kept a typewriter in the car so they could type up letters for people who couldn't make it to the hearings. Then they would show up at the hearings with mountains of letters in support of the ag preserve.

Thanks to their organizing and the efforts of many volunteers, the ag preserve was established in 1968. In 1990, Napa County voters made it even more secure.

I think everybody who admires Napa Valley's natural beauty owes a debt to Jack and Jamie Davies. They had the foresight to know what would happen if the freeway went through. Even today there are no fast food outlets, chain restaurants, shopping malls, or department stores north of the town of Napa.

For the Davies, the late 1960s brought challenges beyond the ag preserve. They had to make and market their wine, plant a vineyard, raise three small boys, and find time for the business socializing that selling wine demands. Entertaining would have been easier if there had been some good restaurants around.

The absence of them forced us all to become chefs. There was no place to dine in Napa County then. And, of course, as new vintners, we wanted to provide the right company for our wines. We didn't want to take people to the steam table at the El Real restaurant and line up for mashed potatoes.

When we heard that a freeway route had been planned to go right through the Valley, there was nothing to do but get involved.

The allée of century-old olive
trees at Schramsberg captivated
Jack and Jamie Davies and
helped persuade them to
restore the historic property.

So it became clear that there was a need to become more sophisticated about entertaining at home. When you have three babies, you can't roll out the red carpet for everyone, but you can learn how to do things simply and well. Some of us thought we should start a cooking school in the Valley so we could all learn together, which is exactly what we did (see page 92). It became a roaring success and everybody benefited, especially our husbands.

I thought that school was terrific, too, because it raised the culinary bar in the county. Everyone became more knowledgeable, and they began to demand high-quality ingredients. Now Napa has plenty of terrific restaurants, so winery owners don't have to entertain at home. As a chef, I'm grateful for the business, but I'm also sorry I missed out on those private dinner parties of earlier times.

People are too busy now. They just don't take time for it. And there's another element, I think. A lot of people moving into the Valley today have created a career before coming here. When they come to wine country, they want to do things quickly, without engaging in the details. So if you entertain, you hire someone to do it. Or if you want to plant a tree, you bring in the expert. I can't think of anything we didn't do ourselves. And I realize how different my life has been because of that, but also how rich and full. I wouldn't dream of having someone come and plant a tree without my being completely involved. This place is too important to me. It sings to me. I hear Jacob Schram up there in the sky every day, encouraging me to keep doing things the right way as opposed to just getting it done.

When Nixon took the 1969 Schramsberg Blanc de Blancs to Beijing in 1972 and it was poured in the Great Hall of China, the winery's reputation was set. Surprisingly, Jamie and Jack didn't know that was coming. The State Department had requested some wine, but they assumed it was for a State Department dinner. Then one morning, a friend telephoned and urged them to turn on their TV. There was Barbara Walters in China, holding up a bottle of Schramsberg and describing the small Napa Valley winery that made it.

Today Schramsberg champagne has been poured at so many White House events that it is hard to keep count. One high point for the Davies was attending Ronald Reagan's second inauguration and watching the president toast his wife with their wine. Out of that experience came the idea to take all their employees to the nation's capital, so that everyone could see firsthand what became of the wine. The staff toured the White House and saw some of the menus featuring Schramsberg, and they beamed with pride. Later, when a policeman tried to cite some of the women—including Jamie—for jaywalking in Georgetown, one of them pulled out her business card and said, "Sir, you can't ticket us. We make the champagne on the President's table!"

Even when your brand succeeds, you have to know when to change. For the Davies, change has meant moving beyond Napa Valley to find the best grapes for sparkling wine. In recent years, Jamie and her team have found that fruit from cooler regions, like Monterey County, Mendocino County, Marin County, and Sonoma's Russian River and Carneros areas, gives them the crisp, lean wine they need for their blends.

Jamie Davies enjoys a
few peaceful moments at
Schramsberg in the shade
of an old olive tree.

Now, with less than 85 percent of its grapes coming from Napa Valley, Schramsberg is no longer "Napa Valley champagne." But Jamie and her winemakers are convinced that this is the right step for quality.

In the wine world, you create your own plan of action and rise or fall because of it. If it doesn't work, you move on. And that was the thing about coming here. Friends, and of course our parents, were just aghast. "How could you leave your security and move up to that old place?"

The big risk for me was that we were using our friends' money, but if all else failed, we could sell the place. And we were re-employable. If you believe in yourself, there's always something else to do.

Over the years, so many people have come here and said, "Oh, we admire what you do but we couldn't do that. It's too big a risk." Well, if you want to move into exciting things, you have to be willing to take a few risks. If you're not, then stay in your banker's job or whatever it is that you don't like, but you'll never know the thrill of capturing those moments, the good and the bad. There are plenty of each, right?

Champagne is for times when you're living life to the fullest. It brings people together for their finest hours as well as sometimes the sad moments in life. But there's something about the effervescence that always gives me a lift. It says, hey, this is what life's all about. This is worth living. It makes any moment a special occasion.

ROOTS

Vines: How Far Apart?

When you plant beet seeds in a garden, you space them according to package directions so the beets have room to grow. But as you'll see when driving through Napa Valley, there's no consensus about how much room grapevines need to grow, or what vine spacing—both between the vines and between the rows—produces the best-quality fruit. Believing that good wine comes from vines that struggle a bit, many growers and wine-

makers are advocating close spacing in an effort to stress the vines. Some are planting vines as closely as meter by meter, in vineyards that might in the past have been planted seven feet by twelve feet. Others, like Doug Fletcher at Chimney Rock Winery, believe that the appropriate spacing varies from site to site, depending on the soil and rootstock.

Before you can determine spacing, says Fletcher, you need a soil analysis. How deep is the topsoil? How rich is it? Where is the water table? The answers will guide you in choosing the right rootstock. Some rootstocks are drought tolerant, for example, and can probe deeply for water in dry soils. The interaction of soil and rootstock determines how many leaves a vine will produce, a number that growers can calculate fairly accurately by weighing the pruned canes in winter.

"When a cane gets to be about four feet long, you have enough leaves to ripen the fruit," says Fletcher. "If you let a cane grow to six feet instead of four, you're wasting sugar that could have gone to the fruit. Young leaves take sugar to grow; only a mature leaf puts sugar toward the grapes. So if you have a vine that's continually growing, you're sending sugar to the wrong place. You're in the *dolmas* business instead of the grape business."

But if you know that your vines want to produce, say, two hundred leaves each, you can leave ten buds on each vine when you prune and expect that each bud will generate a cane that will produce twenty leaves and stop growing where you want it to—at about four feet. Vines managed this way are "balanced," says Fletcher. Leave too many canes and they won't produce enough leaves per cane to ripen the grapes; leave too few and they will grow too long, wasting sugar and shading the fruit.

"There's some good research that shows that for all the leaves to be in the sun, the canes have to be about two-and-a-half inches apart," says Fletcher. "So there's this sort of simultaneous equation.

You have to have so many canes and they have to be so far apart. So those two things should determine the spacing between the vines."

Close spacing may make sense in the wine-growing regions of Bordeaux and Burgundy, says Fletcher, where soils are less rich than they are in parts of the Napa Valley. But it doesn't always make sense here.

"If you try to plant vines close together in rich soil"—in other words, if you don't leave room for enough canes—"the vines want to grow all summer long," says Fletcher. "In fact, you can drive up and down the Valley and see vineyards like that. They're beautiful little square hedges because people have trimmed them all summer long. They're pretty, but they're not what you want for grape quality."

There's another reason to want the vines to stop growing, and to do so early. When vines stop producing leaves, they also stop cell division in the fruit. Fletcher wants the cells of red grapes to stop dividing early, while the berries are still small relative to the casing, because a high skin-to-juice ratio makes a more deeply colored, flavorful wine.

What about the argument that close spacing stresses the vines, enhancing quality?

"There's just no evidence to show that it does," says Fletcher. "Research shows that total leaf area is independent of grapevine spacing. If you plant your vines closer together, you're still going to have all those leaves. If there were root competition, you would expect to have fewer leaves and that's not the case."

As long as there are at least two winemakers in Napa Valley, there will be different opinions about how to grow grapes. But Fletcher is convinced that, when it comes to wine quality, vine balance is key. "It wasn't until we started using these vine balance techniques to stop the growth, get the leaves in the sun, and get some sunlight on the fruit that we started seeing better wine quality."

Stone Walls

Ours is a country that prizes things that are shiny and new, but I grew up with Italian parents who valued tradition and history. I've always loved antiques because they tell a story, and when I look at the old stone walls that snake across Napa Valley, I can almost hear their stories, too. Most of them were built by immigrant labor: first Chinese, then Italian, then Mexican. They were assembled haphazardly in some cases, with great care and artistry in others. But all of them tell a story of the land.

A stone wall is terroir represented in an enduring structure. When Napa Valley landowners cleared their property to plant vines, they turned up stones too big to leave in place. Typically, they would instruct their fieldhands to stack the rocks around the edge of the property, both to delineate their holdings and to avoid having to haul the rock away.

Instead of a winery tour, try taking a stone wall tour of the Valley sometime. On the Silverado Trail at the Oakville Cross Road is the impressive wall at Rudd Estate, most of it newly built, although you can still see some of the original wall, too. I watched for months as workers dredged up rocks from that property and slowly pieced that beauty together. You'll see lots of other walls up and down the Trail, on the cross roads and on Highway 29. There's a particularly handsome one on the south side of the Rutherford Cross Road, about halfway across the road, next to a grove of olive trees.

Dale Taylor's name is often the one that comes up when Valley people consider building a wall. Dale has been a masonry contractor here since 1960, and people say his walls are among the best. He's worked for Cakebread, Edgewood, Cardinale, Duckhorn, and a lot of other families in the Valley. Although sometimes people ask him to imitate a primitive style—as they did at Edgewood—he is really proud of the more precise work he does.

"Most people don't look at the craftsmanship," says Dale. "I can tell where a more experienced hand has worked." Unless the client specifies another style, a good mason will aim to have tight joints and mortar of even thickness, to use as few small pieces ("chinks") as possible, and to avoid clustering the largest stones cr stones of the same color. On a good wall, vertical joints are never more than two stones high. "You don't want any joint to run too far in one direction," says Dale.

For the average wall, a stonemason can lay up forty to fifty square feet a day. Tight-fitting work can take a lot longer, slowing the progress down to ten to twenty feet a day. Around my home in St. Helena is a wall built with stones from my grandfather's ranch in Mt. Shasta, in far northern California—a daily reminder of my family's foundation.

Peter

Mondavi

Being of Italian heritage myself, I feel a bond with a lot of the Italians and Italian-Americans in the Valley, but there's a special place in my heart for Peter Mondavi. Week in and week out, Peter has lunch at my restaurant, Tra Vigne, and he always

has a story—told in half-Italian, half-English—and a hug for me on the way out. Back when Napa Valley tourism was slow in the winter, we might do only a dozen lunches, but Peter's table would always have four.

Peter grew up in a family much like mine. His parents, Cesare and Rosa, were immigrants from the Marche region. They settled in Virginia, Minnesota, and ran a wholesale grocery. When Prohibition started, Cesare was appointed by the local Italian community to go to California and find some grapes to ship back for all the home winemakers. (Heads of families could make a limited amount of grape juice, which inevitably became wine.)

It didn't take long for Cesare to realize that shipping grapes could be a good business. He moved his family to Lodi, in California's Central Valley, and shipped grapes east throughout Prohibition. So arguably Cesare deserves some credit for helping keep California's vineyards alive; without the home-winemaker market, most growers would probably have pulled out their vines.

Zinfandel, Carignane, Alicante Bouschet, Muscat—any varieties that were thick-skinned and sturdy enough to survive the trip went east in ice-packed, later refrigerated, railroad cars. Both Peter and his older brother Robert remember spending much of their teenage years nailing together thousands of wooden shipping crates.

After Prohibition was repealed in 1933, Cesare got into the wine business, first in Lodi, then by buying the Sunny St. Helena Winery in St. Helena. For a period in the late 1930s, Peter ran the winery in Lodi while Robert oversaw operations at Sunny St. Helena, which shipped unbottled bulk wine.

By the early 1940s, the Mondavis sensed it was time to move into the bottled wine business. They

learned that the Charles Krug Winery was for sale—the oldest winery in Napa Valley, dating from 1861—and the sons urged their father to buy it. It was wartime, and Peter was stationed in England, but he got a leave to come home for the negotiations.

I was with Dad in San Francisco for the occasion, at one of the banks. The seller was a Mr. Moffitt, a banker in San Francisco. We went with our local banker. Of course we knew the price of the property. It was $75,000, but it wasn't a question of the price. It was a question of what it took to rehabilitate the place, and in those days, with the business such as it was, it was an expensive venture. Anyway, we had a general conversation about the winery and our interest in perpetuating it. It was only about a half-hour conversation, just talking generalities—typical of business in those days. Then Moffitt's secretary called him and said he had a telephone call, so he went into another office and took his call, then he came back and said the caller had been someone interested in the winery, but he told them it was ours, just like that. So it was all over then.

Peter had a pretty strong technical background in wine by that point. He had studied business and chemistry at Stanford, and then he went to the University of California at Berkeley to do graduate research on wine. It's widely acknowledged that he and his professors did some groundbreaking work.

The main research that I did there was on cold fermentation, and that was a big plus for our industry. We were ahead of everyone else for about ten or fifteen years. Of course, it was an expensive operation. You had to have heavy refrigeration to control the temperatures. On the red wine, it wasn't too great of an issue because you fermented at a warmer temperature to extract color and flavor. But when it came to the white wines, the colder you fermented, the better it was. We'd ferment around 45° F to 50° F.

Cold fermentation for white wines was indeed a big breakthrough. As Peter's work proved, fermenting at cold temperatures helped preserve the fruity character of white wines. California's whites improved dramatically when wineries began to adopt this practice and ferment their wines in temperature-controlled tanks. Modern tanks now have "jackets" to circulate refrigerated glycol, which keeps the juice cold while it's fermenting.

I think the young winemakers have gotten a little bit away from this. I don't know why. Take the barrel fermentation of Chardonnay. I think they're all fermenting them too warm. Maybe some are not, but most of them are losing the fruit. Have you seen the big changes in Chardonnay? All over the map, you know. All over the map.

It's true. There's a California Chardonnay for every taste these days. Some winemakers—Peter included, obviously—like the fruit-forward style that you get with cold fermentation in stainless steel, but others are going for a richer style and barrel fermentation. Ironically, Krug was one of the first California wineries to import French oak barrels.

Originally built in 1861, the Redwood Cellar at Charles Krug (below) is a registered historic landmark.

We started with French oak barrels in 1956, and over a couple of years we brought in thirteen or fourteen hundred of them. But we found that we were premature. At that time, the barrels were $35 or $40 [they're about $500 today] and at that price, you couldn't afford them. We couldn't afford to raise the price of the wine ten cents a bottle to pay for the barrel. The market wasn't there. You could buy shaved American whiskey barrels for $10. So we discontinued the French and stayed with used American barrels until wine prices firmed up.

Even after their father died and with their bottled wine business taking off at Charles Krug, the brothers continued the grape-shipping business. Peter would go down to Lodi during the harvest and oversee the shipment to the home winemakers. Maybe there was some sentimental attachment to the business because the brothers grew up on homemade wine, like I did. (And just like in my house, their mother made the wine but their father drank it and took the credit!)

I wonder how good my mother's wines would taste to me now. Few immigrants, my family included, had any real technical knowledge, much less any money for the right equipment.

We started with French oak barrels in 1956 but found that we were premature.

Well, they were good wines to start off with, but what usually happened is that they would turn a little sour because, after all, home winemakers weren't used to bottling it. You would keep it in the barrel and siphon out of the barrel. Only a few would break it down into jugs. So the barrels would be partly full longer than they should be. And I think that's typically why people in the east wanted a high-sugar grape, because they wanted high alcohol to help preserve the wine.

Peter and Robert got out of the grape-shipping business about the time White Zinfandel came into the picture.

The price of Zinfandel grapes jumped from $100 to $1,000 a ton. So there was no way you were going to ship Zinfandel to the home winemakers. The shippers that remained got involved with other produce like citrus and cherries and table grapes. But we chose the winery because that was going to be the future business.

Over the years, there were so many areas where the Charles Krug Winery was first, or among the first. Along with the Louis Martini Winery and Beaulieu Vineyard, Krug was a pioneer in Carneros (a wine-growing area at the southern tip of Napa Valley, adjoining the San Francisco Bay), recognizing that that cooler region was perfect for Pinot Noir. The Krug property in Carneros is beautiful and now quite valuable. Krug also published one of the first—perhaps *the* first—Napa Valley winery newsletter. Called *Bottles & Bins,* it was chatty and easy to read, written by a renowned bon vivant named Paco Gould. And if you wonder how the practice got started of offering tastings for the public at wineries, look to Krug. The winery's "Tastings on the Lawn"—which are still held in the summer—may have been the first public tastings in the Napa Valley. In the early days, three hundred people would show up to sample Krug wines with a little cheese. Educating the public was a necessity then, Peter says, because most people really didn't know one wine from another.

In the early 1990s, Peter turned the winemaking over to his son Marc. His younger son, Peter, Jr., runs the winery's business side. Both sons are dedicated to bringing Charles Krug into the top tier of Napa Valley wineries, and they are replanting the vineyards with the best clones of the Bordeaux varieties (Cabernet Sauvignon, Cabernet Franc, Petit Verdot, and Merlot). I think it's a relief to everybody who cares about the valley that this historic winery is in such good hands. Marc studied enology and viticulture at U.C. Davis, and Peter, Jr., has an engineering degree from Stanford and an M.B.A. I mean, as a dad with a family winery to pass on, how lucky can you get?

Peter, Sr., still comes to work every day, to an office crowded with wine bottles and dozens upon dozens of thick binders. He is the king of Standard Operating Procedures.

My role is to make sure there's a system around the place, so whoever's involved in that particular department knows the rules and regulations. In a winery, you have rules and regulations and procedures, and it's a constant challenge because every time a new person comes in, they have their own little pet system. I want to know every report that is established in this office, and who gets them. Every desk has its own book of procedures. If new people put in their own ideas that are improvements, that's fine, I'm open to that, but otherwise I want a procedure. I want a system. I'm sure you need that in the kitchen.

No kidding. I could take a lesson.

I've always loved learning from the experiences and stories of older people, and with sixty-plus years in the California wine industry, Peter Mondavi has much to relate. As his career winds down, I wonder what he wants to be remembered for.

I just want people to remember that our family has been a major factor in the industry, having gone through thick and thin here in Napa Valley, when others came and went. We stuck with it through the hard times and were able to keep our heads above water during those tough years.

That's why I purchased all the land we have outside the home property. In those early days, the big corporations would come in and outbid us and we'd lose the grapes. So I made up my mind. I said the only way we're going to survive is to have our own vineyards. So I guess I'd like to be known as a solid citizen. Not a fly-by-night. In other words: We're here to stay.

ROOTS

Pruning for Quality

Every winter, when the vines stand bare, vineyard workers undertake one of the year's most critical tasks: pruning. Vine by vine, they remove last year's growth and choose how many buds to leave for the coming year. Their actions determine what shape the vine will take and help control the size and quality of the crop. As any casual wine-country observer will notice, there's more than one way to prune a grapevine. The three principal methods—each subject to personal variation—are cordon pruning, cane pruning, and head pruning. Which method a grower chooses depends on grape variety, site, tradition, conviction, and even on such practical matters as available labor.

The dominant approach in Napa Valley today is undoubtedly cordon pruning. A cordon is a permanent cane—a cane tied to a horizontal trellis wire when young and left on the vine year after year. Some vines have one cordon, others have two, trellised in opposite directions so the vine looks like a T. New canes emerge from spurs on the cordon and, in most Napa vineyards, these canes are trained upward on catch wires to keep both leaves and grapes in the sun.

Grapevines bear fruit only on year-old wood, so workers in cordon-pruned vineyards typically remove all of last year's growth except for a couple of buds at the base of some of the year-old canes. Each of these buds will push a fruit-bearing cane.

In cane pruning, used mostly in Pinot Noir vineyards, the cordons aren't permanent. They're removed every year and replaced with one or more of the previous year's new canes, laid down on the horizontal trellis wire. The fruit-bearing canes sprout from buds on these year-old canes. This method is preferred in areas subject to late frosts because vines pruned this way don't bloom simultaneously; if there's a frost during bloom, the whole crop won't be lost.

"Cane pruning also helps you control yields," says Thomas Brown, the winemaker for Chiarello Family Vineyard and formerly assistant winemaker for Turley Wine Cellars. Compared to thick, permanent cordons, which store a lot of energy, the year-old fruiting canes in a cane-pruned vineyard are rather weak, says Brown. "They're not going to set much fruit. And the thinking seems to be that Pinot Noir, more than any other varietal, needs less crop to produce a better crop."

Head-pruned vines are less common in Napa Valley, although you still see them in older vineyards. "That was how most of the early Italian immigrants trained their Zinfandel," says Brown. If pruned right, these bushy vines typically have eight well-spaced "arms" that, when viewed from above, resemble the spokes of a wheel. The new growth isn't trained on wires but is instead allowed to sprawl. Old-school growers liked having the fruit grow close to the ground, where it could benefit from reflected heat. But the sprawling vines also shade the fruit and create the potential for unchecked mold and mildew.

Winemakers like Brown and Larry Turley, who love the character of wines made from old head-pruned vines, work hard to get air and light into the canopy of their old Zinfandel and Petite Sirah vines. After the fruiting canes emerge in the spring, they'll go through the vineyard and snap off laterals, the secondary canes coming off the primary cane, to get more air and light to the fruiting zone.

"It takes a long time per plant," says Brown. "You have to really step back occasionally and walk all the way around the plant and look at what it needs to ripen. If you let in too much sun, the fruit will burn."

Most California winemakers leave pruning to the vineyard crew, but Brown says it's a chore he enjoys. "It's the French model. You know, 'Vineyards in the spring, cellar in the fall.' It just keeps it more interesting. We have some new vines here, so I actually see them go into the ground, nurture them for three years, and then get to make wine from them. To me, that's the most rewarding part of the business."

Little Italy West

Martini, Mondavi, Solari, Trinchero. Forni, Sattui, Navone, Nichelini, Domeniconi, Bartolucci, Regusci.

The story of Napa Valley winemaking in the first half of the twentieth century is peppered with Italian surnames. Some of these names live on only in history books and memories; others grace wine bottles today. Because of my Calabrian heritage, I've always loved hearing stories about the old Italians.

Italian immigration to California mushroomed at the end of the nineteenth century, and many of those immigrants found their way to Napa Valley. Their timing wasn't great. By 1890, phylloxera was ravaging Napa's vineyards, and many wineries were struggling or closing. When the Prohibitionists began gathering steam in the early 1900s, many vineyard owners pulled up their vines and planted walnuts or prunes.

But not the Italians. Many of them believed Prohibition was so misguided that it couldn't possibly last long. They continued to tend their vines, maintain their cellars, and make the homemade wine the law allowed. When Prohibition ended, the Italians were in a good position to revive the valley's shuttered wineries.

The story of Ernie Navone and his family was pretty typical of that era. Everybody in St. Helena knows Ernie. For years he was the butcher, and later the owner, of Keller's Meat Market on Main Street. He's retired now, but his gnarled hands and thick, stubby fingers testify to a lifetime of pruning vines and cutting meat.

I was born here in St. Helena in 1922. When we grew up, there were olive trees up and down Fulton Lane. In December, my dad would be out there beating them, shaking the olives onto rugs, and we kids would pick them up. We would pick the olives up and down the street, not just our own, and we would make oil for two to three weeks. I hated that with a passion.

My mother was from Turin, my father from Asti, from a family of winemakers. He and his two brothers came to San Francisco in 1904, but he went back to Italy a few years later and met my mom. She had dreamed of coming to America since she was fourteen. At the funeral of a mutual friend, someone pointed him out to her and said he was returning to America, and she said, "Maybe that's my ticket." They were married and came to St. Helena about 1914.

By that time, my dad's cousin had a vineyard and stone winery. My dad started making the wine there. It didn't have a name; everything went out of there in bulk, in barrels. My dad would drive down the mountain with horse and buggy, pick up men and bring them up for several days to work. It was too far to go back and forth every day, so my mother would have to cook for the whole crew. She soon got tired of feeding all these old Italians, so she and Dad started looking for property of their own.

They finally found twelve acres on Fulton Road and bought it in 1915 or 1916. When my dad bought it, there was Carignane, Barbera, Petite Sirah, Napa Gamay, Grenache, Sauvignon Vert, and Green Hungarian. I still have the same twelve acres, ten of them in vines. I have eight acres of Cabernet and two acres of Petite Sirah.

During Prohibition, he tended vines. A few wineries were making wine for the church, and you had to tend the vines whether or not you made wine.

In 1934 or 1935, he bought the Laurent Winery [now Markham Winery] and started making wine there—all sold in bulk. He would buy the grapes for next to nothing because there weren't many wineries then, and he would send the wine back to New York in barrels.

In 1937, a dozen growers came to my dad and wanted to form a co-op. They would make wine from the growers' grapes, and however little it sold for, it was better than leaving it on the vine. The St. Helena Co-op eventually grew to about one hundred members because everybody wanted a place to put their grapes. After the co-op made a contract with Gallo, it prospered.

Yes, there were a lot of Italians in the Valley then. They were the ones who tended the grapevines before the Mexicans arrived. After my dad died, the old Italians would still come help prune.

About ten of my mother's classmates from Italy emigrated here, settling in Oakland, Berkeley, and Richmond. At least twice a month they would come up and have a weekend in the valley. I remember people sleeping all over, and they would all bring things for a barbecue. Ravioli, gnocchi, roast chicken. On Sunday morning, I would wake up and there would be a goat hanging from one of the olive trees. My dad had built a big pit under one of the trees.

We had a big arbor with a Golden Chasselas grapevine, and they would set a table under it and cut up the goat. Then they would sit down to lunch and there would be wine all over the table and conversation in Italian. I never learned Italian because my parents spoke only English to the kids. "We're in America now, we speak English," my Dad said. He thought this was the good life here. He never went back to Italy again.

Michael Chiarello (below, left) shares a word with his friend and neighbor Ernie Navone.

Barbara

Eisele

Milt Eisele was an executive with Kaiser Aluminum in California until he and his wife, Barbara, decided to retire to wine country—although retirement isn't exactly what happened when the couple bought 139 acres (40 of them in vines) just southeast of Calistoga. Under their ownership from 1969 to 1989, the Eisele Vineyard produced some of the most coveted Cabernet Sauvignon grapes in the valley. Today, it's owned by Bart and Daphne Araujo (see page 232), who make their own wine on this famous property.

Milt passed away in 1996, and today Barbara lives in a ranch house in Rutherford with a patio and pool in the back and vineyards all around. Kumquats grow in pots around the pool, and agapanthus and roses bloom in her garden. An active, handsome woman with strong cheekbones and a warm smile, Barbara is the sister of Katie Trefethen, who started Trefethen Vineyards with her husband Gene.

Her kitchen is open and comfortable, with shelves of favorite cookbooks. What grabs my eye are three blue binders filled with recipes from the Napa Valley Cooking Class (1973–1992). I've always believed this school had a huge impact on the culinary sophistication in the valley, and I've wondered how it started.

It was actually the brainchild of Molly Chappellet (of Chappellet Winery). She had organized the classes as a fundraiser for a theater that we tried to keep going in the Valley, but then she asked if I would take over. My sister was just then building a little building next to her house, and she said, "I'm going to have this as an entertainment center. What do you need in the way of a kitchen? What do you want for the cooking class?"

So the Napa Valley Cooking Class found an early home in a cooking classroom at Trefethen, and the great women of wine country in the 1970s—Belle Rhodes (Bella Oaks Vineyard), Jamie Davies (Schramsberg), Martha May (Martha's Vineyard), June Maus, Katie Trefethen, Barbara Eisele, and others—began teaching themselves how to cook.

We had to. When we moved up here, we had to entertain, and because there weren't many restaurants, we had to do all our own cooking. So we had our classes on Monday and Tuesday mornings beginning in January and going for six weeks. Everybody loved coming because it was something to do after harvest and the holidays, and there wasn't anything else going on in the Valley at that time.

Often they invited big-name guest chefs to teach—including Jeremiah Tower, Ken Hom, Wolfgang Puck, and Barbara Tropp. Barbara Eisele has the recipe handouts from every class—twenty years' worth neatly organized in binders, with her notes in the margins.

When they didn't have guest chefs, they taught each other. Belle, who was already a good cook, taught most often and really put her heart into it. When she did a class on Middle Eastern cooking, she would hand out maps and an explanation of the ingredients and some background reading. It was an education, not just a diversion.

I could spend hours flipping through Barbara's notebooks, looking at the dishes they cooked back then. Seeing page after page and year after year of recipes, you sense how serious and organized they were about this business of learning to cook. Many of these women eventually became renowned cooks and hostesses.

Much later, in the early 1990s, the group invited me to teach. That's when I knew, after five years here, that I had really arrived. I remember that they had an antique school bell they would ring to get everyone's attention—and then, believe me, you had their attention. This group was serious, and the guest chefs got drilled.

Twenty years after they started, the original Napa Valley Cooking Class came to an end. It had fulfilled its purpose, and the regulars were ready to pass it on to the next generation. John and Janet Trefethen (see page 106) have kept classes going at their winery, but they are more oriented toward visitors.

I knew that Barbara and Milt had moved to the Valley because of Milt's love of wine, but I wondered what got him started. Wine appreciation wasn't that common in the 1950s and 1960s.

I guess it started when my sister Kate couldn't think of anything to give Milt for Christmas one year, so she gave him a mixed case of French wine. They really were very fine wines, but we didn't know anything about them. I remember that I served a Mouton (Château Mouton-Rothschild) with hamburgers, not knowing the difference.

But Milt really loved wine. He just took to it very fast, and so we started going to France and visiting the wineries. And he loved the vineyard people. So when he got ready to retire, he said, "I don't want to make wine that I have to sell, but I do like the farmers in France." We thought maybe we would retire to the country and grow wine grapes.

Milt and I looked for six years to find the perfect vineyard. We had seen our property (the future Eisele Vineyard) many years before but thought it was too far out of the center of things. André Tchelistcheff said you couldn't grow Cabernet grapes in Calistoga, the prevailing theory at the time. So it took us a long time to decide, but we made a good choice. We bought such a beautiful piece of property.

Years later Milt said, "You know what? I haven't really retired. I've just taken on a new job." But he loved every minute of it.

Barbara and Milt reserved a few grapes for their own private label. Following pages: Barbara (left) and sister Katie Trefethen enjoy an autumn lunch in Katie's garden.

Milt and Barbara didn't know much about farming when they started, and they didn't know many people in the Valley. But they did know Belle and Barney Rhodes, who introduced them around, and they knew Jack Davies from Schramsberg—a good person to know.

One day our tractor died and Milt said, "Lord, I've got to rent a tractor. I don't know where to go." So he called Jack and he said, "Where do I go to rent a tractor?" And Jack said, "What the hell do you want to rent a tractor for? I'll send one over." And, you know, that never left us. That feeling of mutual friendship and helpfulness has always been in the Valley. And I think it still is, don't you? It's a wonderful characteristic of the Napa Valley. It sort of makes me teary thinking about it.

In the years before Barbara and Milt bought the property, the grapes had been sold to the local co-op. Nobody knew if the Eisele grapes would make great wine on their own because nobody had tried.

In 1971, the Eiseles took an overnight trip with the English wine writer Harry Waugh and several others. Harry wanted to see Ridge Vineyards in the Santa Cruz Mountains, so they stopped for a visit. When Paul Draper and Dave Bennion at Ridge mentioned that Ridge had never made wine from Napa Valley grapes, Milt said, "Why don't you try?"

The 1971 Ridge Vineyards Cabernet Sauvignon "Eisele Vineyard" was wonderful wine, which proved to Milt that his grapes deserved a better fate than the co-op. In 1972 and 1973, he sold them to Robert Mondavi. In 1974, he sold them to a Napa Valley vintner who made the wine but went bankrupt before paying for the grapes. The brand-new Conn Creek Winery bought the unfinished wine "practically off the steps of the county courthouse," according to Barbara, and bottled it with a mention of Eisele Vineyard on the back.

It won all kinds of prizes, but that was the only year Conn Creek used our grapes because they had their own grapes and their own plans. So in 1975, when Darrell Corti (a wine merchant and Napa Valley advocate) was here one day, Milt said, "What'll I do with my grapes this year?" And Darrell said, "Well, you know there's a new outfit that just started up. The owner is a builder from Colorado named Joe Phelps. Why don't you call him?"

Joseph Phelps Vineyards bought the Eisele fruit from 1975 until 1991 and (except for two years, when the grapes went into Phelps's top-of-the-line Insignia), bottled it separately as "Eisele Vineyard" Cabernet Sauvignon, a wine that helped make both the winery's and the vineyard's reputations. But Joe also loved Rhône wines and he soon talked Milt into planting Syrah for him. So arguably Joe Phelps and Milt Eisele were the first "Rhône Rangers." Sadly, they were before their time. Consumers confused Syrah with Petite Sirah, which had never had a strong following. Phelps couldn't sell the wine, so not long after asking Milt to plant Syrah, Joe was volunteering to help him bud it over. (For an interesting postscript about the Eisele Syrah that got away, see page 237).

Despite his success in the business world, Milt was more than a gentleman farmer. He was hands on.

We did the frost patrol, Milt and I, which meant getting up in the middle of the night. We would telephone for the frost report, then Milt would go out in his El Camino that had a sensor on it, so he could tell the temperature outside the car. He'd ride out into the vineyard, then he'd come back and say, "I think we'd better light."

Milt was very proud of the fact that we didn't use smudge pots (vineyard heaters that generate considerable smoke). We were one of the first vineyards in the valley to use a cleaner version—spot heaters. They were connected to a fuel tank, and diesel fuel was forced through the lines.

We were lighting the heaters and we were lighting "bricks" that burned and glowed and made heat. You just threw them on the ground, one at each vine, and lit them up. Then we'd drive around and see what everybody else was doing. Once you got up, you never went back to bed.

You should have heard me one night. It had rained, I think, but then it was clear and cold and we had to go light. I was wet and I was cold and I was mad. We had a walkie-talkie, so Milt would be at one end of the field and I would be at the other. And I had a few expletives for him. I said, "You know, I could be at Rossmoor playing bridge!" (Rossmoor is a local retirement community.) Now the thought of being at Rossmoor playing bridge…I've never played bridge in my life. But I was just mad enough.

One year, there were fourteen consecutive days of frost. Nobody got any sleep. People's eyes were absolutely red and they were burning tires because they had run out of things to burn. You could barely see to drive. The smoke was awful.

But then people switched to spot heaters, and they were a beautiful sight all lit up, just lovely. You knew that, beyond a rise, you could look down-valley and up-valley and see all the lights sparkling at night.

If Andé Tchelistcheff thought it was too warm to grow fine red grapes on this property, for once he was mistaken. As the Eiseles discovered, their forty-acre Calistoga parcel, nestled up against the Valley's eastern hills, had its own unique microclimate. On hot afternoons, when the rest of Calistoga was sizzling, a cool breeze from the Pacific Ocean would float over Calistoga and drop onto their vineyard.

Over the years, Eisele Vineyard became so famous that I figured many people must have asked for cuttings from it. Now, some people will readily give cuttings; others are more protective. When I first moved here, people talked about "P.M. clones," the ones that you take in the dark of night.

When I asked Barbara if anyone got cuttings from Eisele Vineyard, the only person she knew about was John Shafer of Shafer Vineyards. Lucky guy.

It was a funny story, too. One day John was talking to Johnny Pena, who managed our vineyard (and several others), and John said, "I need some Cabernet cuttings for my vineyard." Johnny said, "I'll get you some," and he proceeded to cut them from ours. He didn't tell Milt. Well, Milt was startled when he heard about it, but we laughed about it later, because John is a dear friend.

When I first moved here, people talked about "P.M. clones," the ones you took in the dark of night.

I wanted to know what Barbara thought made Eisele Vineyard Cabernet unique. What was its taste signature? And did she think the style changed when the grapes passed from Phelps to the new owners, Bart and Daphne Araujo?

It was just a rich, full-bodied wine, really an exciting wine to drink. It wasn't a soft wine. We were very proud of the fact that it was one hundred percent Cabernet. Yes, the Araujos have changed the style, as all Cabernets have changed in the last years. They've become much more elegant, somewhat softer in a good way. They're doing more blending, you know, to soften it a little. It's a more refined way of making wine, I think.

By 1989, Barbara and Milt had decided it was time to retire from grape-growing. Contrary to what many may think, they did not sell to the Araujos. They sold to a businessman from Chicago who was determined to buy a prestigious vineyard. But about a year after buying Eisele Vineyard, he had a financial reversal and was forced to sell the property. That's when the Araujos bought it. The real estate agents were so pleased at getting to sell the property twice in one year that they took the Eiseles out for a very nice dinner.

The Eiseles stayed in their house on the property for a few years, while the Araujos got organized. In 1992, Barbara and Milt moved to a house surrounded by vineyards in the Rutherford Bench.

Milt loved the Valley very much. We both did, and I do still. Coming from the high-powered corporate world, the wonderful sense of friendship here appealed to us. Not that he wasn't happy at Kaiser, because he was. But the Valley was the frosting on the cake. He thought he was going to retire and do nothing. Instead, this whole new world opened up.

I wanted to know what Barbara thought made Eisele Vineyard Cabernet unique. What was its taste signature?

Ripe Cabernet
Sauvignon grapes
contain the
promise of delicious
wine to come.

Picnic Time

Wine tasting is obviously the number-one visitor activity in the Napa Valley, but picnicking is probably in second place. Even for those of us who live here, picnicking is a year-round activity, thanks to beautiful weather, great specialty food stores, and a guaranteed stream of out-of-town friends who want to picnic in wine country.

I don't think a picnic is something you should have to think about and plan days in advance. My favorite outdoor meals are improvised. I like to grab a blanket, some napkins, wine glasses, and a corkscrew, and leave the menu to chance, depending on what tempts me and my kids or my guests at the store. Here are a few of my preferred gather-and-go spots:

Cantinetta at Tra Vigne for focaccia, a chunk of Parmesan cheese, and assorted biscotti.

Gordon's Cafe and Wine Bar for great sandwiches and box lunches to go.

Napa Valley Olive Oil Company for aged salami and thick breadsticks.

Oakville Grocery for spicy hummus, wedges of Gorgonzola-mascarpone torta, excellent olives, caperberries, pâtés, and made-to-order sandwiches.

Dean & DeLuca for incredible Scottish smoked salmon, the valley's best cheese selection, Serrano ham, prosciutto, and other charcuterie, fresh fruit from the farmers' market, and an almost comprehensive selection of California wine.

Sunshine Foods, St. Helena's family-run supermarket, for frittata, deli salads, juices and sodas, fresh bread, olives, and good cheeses.

A lot of the wineries have picnic tables, of course—some of which have to be reserved ahead. Pine Ridge Winery, Chateau Montelena, and La Famiglia di Robert Mondavi have particularly nice spots for eating outdoors. And I've had some great picnics at the summer concerts on the lawn at the Robert Mondavi Winery.

But the truth is, I don't usually picnic at wineries. I'll take my girls to Bothe State Park in Calistoga for a hike and a picnic. Or we'll go mushroom hunting at Las Posadas, a park behind Pacific-Union College in Angwin, then find a place to have our packed lunch outdoors; or we'll drive to Conn Dam at Lake Hennessey and look for a spot to throw out a blanket.

But my favorite picnics take place on clear, cold winter nights, when I invite friends to stop by and then build a large fire outside near my vineyard. While it is burning down to a mound of warming coals, I go inside to prepare a pot of *cioppino*. I'll warm a crusty loaf of bread and open a bottle or two of Napa Valley's finest. Then everyone grabs something and I lead them to the fire with oohs and aahs all the way.

Picnicking is a year-round activity in Napa Valley, even for those who live here. A couple savors some of the local product at Joseph Phelps Vineyards (top). Among the valley's most sought-after picnic sites is the gazebo at Chateau Montelena (bottom).

Growing Grapes Organically

Organic grape production is on the rise in Napa Valley, as vintners and growers seek ways to preserve and enhance their land. John Williams of Frog's Leap Winery is an acknowledged pioneer in this area. Today, the two hundred acres that provide the winery's grapes are all certified organic. "It seems ludicrous now, but when we started the winery in 1981, I didn't really relate winemaking to agriculture," says John. "Grapes were something that showed up that I performed my magic on. It wasn't until we purchased our first vineyard in 1987 that I was confronted with growing grapes. The property looked healthy, but I wanted the best for our vineyard. So I called one of the companies here in the valley that measures the soil, and, of course, there were many disastrous things, as it turned out. The vineyard was high in zinc and low in boron and had too much calcium and the magnesium was off the charts or too low—I can't remember. And by a stroke of good fortune, the gentleman who measured it sold all the things to make it better. So, as I remember, we got two of everything. It was really expensive and I expected the vineyard to be very appreciative and show an immediate response. But, in fact, the second year it had just as many things out of balance.

"About this time, I heard that Fetzer Winery in Hopland was growing grapes organically, and I was enough of an old hippie to be interested. Well, Fetzer followed the directions of a consultant named Amigo Bob, who was your worst nightmare if you're worried about hippies. He has extremely long hair and wears tie-dyed shirts and leather shorts and Birkenstocks three hundred and sixty-five days a year. But we sat there and listened to him and it was the most amazing three hours of enlightenment I think I've ever had—really talking for the first time about soil microbiology and the interdependence of plants and the biodiversity of the habitat, and the fact that a healthy soil produces a healthy plant, and that a healthy plant, just like a healthy person, resists diseases and doesn't need all the additives and pesticides that modern agriculture provides."

Now, every winter, Frog's Leap growers plant a variety of cover crops—mostly legumes—to improve the nutritional content of the soil. In the spring, when the cover crop is chest high, it's plowed under. In the short term, the cover crop keeps weeds down, prevents soil erosion and provides a habitat for beneficial insects; in the long term, the extra organic matter improves moisture retention, so that the vineyards can be dry-farmed, without irrigation. John is convinced that dry-farming improves the concentration and flavor of the grapes.

"And there's one more advantage, if you believe, like I do, that what you really want is a wine that expresses where it comes from. So much of modern farming is the addition of water and fertilizer. I call it the 'Coke and candy bar diet.' Those vines have a very limited root zone, and it seems to me that they would have more difficulty expressing what the soil is like. Our roots work harder and go deeper, which we believe, although we've not quantified it, adds up to a wine with a broader flavor profile.

"People say, 'Aren't you putting yourself at risk?' or 'Aren't you getting less of a crop?' or 'Doesn't it cost more?' If any of those things were true, I wouldn't do it. This vineyard here is twenty-seven years old. The university's studying it and what they discovered is that we have more phylloxera than conventionally farmed vineyards that are dying, but we have so many more microorganisms and fungi working our soil. The researchers now think there's a certain fungus that actually repairs the roots that the phylloxera eat. Our vineyard was dying of phylloxera when I bought it. It's not dying now."

John and Janet

Trefethen

In 1968, Gene Trefethen pieced together seven different ranches to get the six hundred acres that became Trefethen Vineyards. The land was a jumble of hayfields and orchards—mostly prunes, walnuts, and peaches. The grapes on the property were inferior varieties, but somehow Gene knew this Napa property had potential for greatness.

Today, his son John and John's wife, Janet, run Trefethen Vineyards, making their wine in the historic wooden winery on the property that dates from 1886. They're incredibly active people who travel constantly to promote their wine. In spare time, which must be rare, Janet rides cutting horses competitively (cutting horses are trained to separate a calf from the herd—say, for branding). John is a motorcycle buff and pilot who flies his own plane to visit markets. Often he'll take fellow vintners with him on what is known around here as Trefethen Air.

I knew Gene Trefethen had been a high-powered corporate executive, but I didn't know what brought him to Napa.

John: He set up mandatory retirement at Kaiser Industries, where he was CEO, and so when he reached that age, he retired. And like many of us, he was nowhere near ready to retire, so this was his retirement project. But there's a longer history, in that Dad spent a lot of time farming when he was growing up. I was raised partly on a ranch— we had had a walnut orchard as a family retreat since I was just a little guy.

So there's been a long history in the family of agriculture and love of the soil. Dad stepped away from it during his business career, but I think he wanted to come back to it.

Janet: On the other hand, he really was a builder. I mean, this was a man who helped build the Liberty Ships during World War II. He helped build the San Francisco–Oakland Bay Bridge. He helped build the Hoover Dam, and he came to Napa and he continued to build. In the first photographs you see of this place, there are tractors ripping out the peach and prune trees, and they're building the reservoirs. We had our own mini Hoover Dam in one of our reservoirs.

So Gene Trefethen wanted to get back to the land, but why wine grapes? There were hardly any wineries in Napa Valley in those days, so who would buy grapes?

John: In 1967, and probably in 1966, he was looking in Napa Valley to purchase land to plant grapes. A lot of grapes, not a few grapes. And he had had constant proof at his own table that Americans don't drink wine—but he saw beyond that. Dad was a visionary in a lot of areas that had nothing to do with his business career—in education and art and health care.

We were all introduced to wine by my mother. She started with a little Mateus Rosé, and then Mateus Rosé became German Riesling, and then the Riesling became Burgundy and Bordeaux. She traveled a lot, and if you travel to Europe long enough, you learn certain things. And she was a good cook and hostess. But I remember her introducing guests to wine and people not knowing what to do with it. They'd have their gin and tonic or Scotch and soda at the table, and they wouldn't know what to do with the wine glass.

So I think when dad retired, the question was: Are we going to get into the cattle business? the hay business? the rice business? And the answer was, let's at least do grapes. Obviously the property they selected had an old winery on it, but their initial interest was to raise grapes.

When we were planning what to plant and selling grapes to other winemakers and we brought up the subject of getting the winery going again, Dad's comment to me was something like, "You know, it takes a lifetime to make wine, so if someone's going to do it, it's you."

So John started making wine in small lots—home winemaking, really—guided by textbooks and, later, by Tom Ferrell, then the winemaker at Inglenook. He enrolled in Stanford Business School and developed a business plan for a fictitious winery. By fall of 1973, he had the old winery on the Napa property in working order and he was ready for the Trefethen Vineyards' inaugural crush. Just before harvest, he married Janet Spooner, who has been an active partner in the winery ever since. Their first vintage offered plenty of on-the-job learning.

John: California wineries had gotten into having everything temperature-controlled, especially for Pinot Noir. But in Europe, red wine was fermented much warmer than we were doing it. This was an idea I wanted to try. I had one tank of Pinot Noir, so I got the wine, added the yeast and got the fermentation going. It was a warm fermentation, then it was a hot fermentation, and I went home and went to bed.

About 2 A.M., I woke up and couldn't go back to sleep. I was unsure about this tank and unsure about making wine. I went back to the cellar and heard water pouring out of somewhere. There were no lights—we didn't have anything. We had a ladder tied up to the tank and a flashlight. I got the flashlight out and there was an opening in the top of this fermenting tank. And the pomace and red wine and juice were just shooting out of this hole about three feet in the air. It was like a volcano. The entire fermenting process that would normally take two to three weeks was over in a night.

But you know what was interesting? The previous Pinot Noirs we had made were okay, but they didn't have that real richness and character and dark color. No problem here. This wine had all the color and character you could imagine—along with a burnt sensation.

From the start, Trefethen established a name for its Chardonnay and Cabernet Sauvignon—the premium varieties of Napa Valley. But I really admire how they've hung in there with Riesling when so few other Napa Valley wineries have. Most wineries have replaced Riesling with grapes that have higher market value.

John: Riesling is so underrated in the United States. But we've had a loyal following for it and we like Riesling, so we still grow it—although it's a small planting by comparison to everything else. But it's a hard decision to replant Riesling, which sells for half of anything else I could grow.

Janet: It's probably the best bottle of wine that you can put on the table in a restaurant when a group orders a variety of appetizers. It goes with more starters than any other wine I know. And it's the very best wine to prepare dinner with. You're sitting there on a nice warm summer evening, you pour yourself a glass and drop a piece of ice in it—sacrilege—and it brings on creativity in the kitchen.

John: We sell about a quarter of our Riesling, sometimes a third, in Asia. I've been going over there for years and the question always is: Which wine are we going to have with this food? If there's some spice in the food and it's early in the evening, the best thing to start with is Riesling. And then your mouth is warmed up and you can move on to the red wines.

Like everybody else, they've changed their vineyard practices over the years, aiming for lower yields with greater intensity. It's expensive to reduce yield, but they believe it enhances quality.

Janet: We dropped half of our Merlot crop on the ground this year. It just breaks your heart. But it has to do with producing the very finest grapes we can. The crew goes down the rows and inspects every cluster, and if the cluster isn't equally ripe—because frequently you'll have some green and some rosy-colored berries amongst the really ripe ones—off it goes onto the ground.

When Trefethen began making wine in 1973, there were something like forty-five wineries in Napa Valley. Now there are more than two hundred. Marketing wine becomes as much of a challenge as making it. In the early days, when Trefrethen made less wine, the winery had a waiting list for it, and Janet kept a bound volume to record the calls so she could treat people fairly.

John: Today we have to reach out to the world market and continue to develop Napa's and Trefethen's reputation. We've always been in Asia. Now we're opening India and going back to the Philippines; we did Vietnam and Cambodia this year, and China last year. We're already in Hong Kong and Japan and Singapore and Malaysia. Wine has become part of the global market, and the Internet is part of it. Travel is part of it. The ability to bring a glass of Napa Valley wine to Singapore and talk about it is just one of the most fulfilling experiences. It also keeps us on our toes as winemakers—because in California, you're the preferred product, but internationally you're in absolutely equal competition with the rest of the wine world.

At home, John and Janet are leading the charge for an Oak Knoll District appellation. Like the Rutherford or Mount Veeder or Stags Leap appellations, it would recognize that there's something unique about that viticultural region—that wines from there have a distinct, identifiable character.

Janet: Napa Valley was being divvied up in terms of regions, and we felt maybe we ought to be proactive and define the Oak Knoll District before the ATF (Bureau of Alcohol, Tobacco, and Firearms) did it for us. The area has its own unique characteristics and we would like it recognized.

If you were to look at an appellation map of the Napa Valley, most of the valley floor is laid out now. But there is a hole, one big piece of the puzzle is missing. You've got St. Helena and Rutherford and Oakville, then you jump all the way down to Carneros. To the east is Stags Leap and to the west is Mount Veeder, but there's this big puzzle piece missing in the middle toward the southern end. Wouldn't it clarify things for the consumer if all the pieces of the puzzle were there?

So Janet got the people in Oak Knoll and Yountville together to talk about petitioning for two new appellations. They did the research to prove that the soil, climate, and wine styles are distinctive. They decided where to draw the line between them. Now Yountville has been approved, but they are still

Wooden wineries such
as Trefethen (top)
are rare in the Valley.
Built in 1886, it was
originally named Eshcol.

Janet Trefethen and daughter Hailey ride cutting horses through the vineyard with John Trefethen on his favorite mount.

waiting for the nod on the Oak Knoll District. The concept is that if consumers see those words on a Chardonnay or Cabernet label, they will have a clue to the wine's quality and character.

Janet: We have always believed Trefethen wines are at their best at the table. They are not usually the wines winning the tastings because they aren't the more powerful, big, muscular wines that stand out when you're tasting a lot of wines. The Oak Knoll District is a little bit cooler, and I think the structure, the backbone of the wine is different because of the coolness that gives better acid. Cabernets from here are maybe a little more feminine in style than they are up-valley. I've always said our wines won't knock your socks off, they'll slip them off. And that's what we're after.

John: I think we Californians still tend to plant Cabernet in areas that are too warm for it. I think you'll be seeing more and more Cabernet from Oak Knoll because there's a lot of it planted, and it has all of the attributes that Janet is talking about. It's a cooler climate so the grapes can stay on the vine longer. Everything indicates that Oak Knoll District Cabernet is going to be very intense.

My fondest memories of Trefethen will always include the Napa Valley Cooking Class (see page 92), where I had the honor of teaching some of the grandes dames of the Valley. For twenty years, Trefethen provided the setting for this annual private cooking school, organized and attended predominantly by local women in the wine business.

In 1993, Trefethen Vineyards took over running the program. The original group of students was growing tired—and, by then, many of them were quite accomplished cooks. For several years, Trefethen continued the school, promoting the classes to a wider audience. The students, many of them Valley visitors, would enjoy a tasting of ingredients—perhaps three different types of tomatoes—followed by a demonstration class and dinner al fresco.

Nothing remains the same, and today the cooking program's future is uncertain—in part because the valley is so full of good restaurants now, and visitors want to make time for all of them. But John and Janet deserve credit for raising the Valley's culinary sophistication by hosting the program for so long.

I've always said our wines won't knock your socks off, they'll slip them off.

Pasta Central

At the end of a side street that borders Tra Vigne, there's a modest white building that looks like a barn. It has a screen door, a shady side yard with picnic tables, and a row of orange trees that always seem to be loaded with fruit. Since 1931, people from near and far have bought their olive oil and other Italian provisions here at the Napa Valley Olive Oil Company.

I've known about this place since I was a kid in Turlock. My family would stop here every spring and fall when we went to Napa Valley to hunt for mushrooms, and my mother would stock up on olive oil and pasta. If it was cling peach season in Turlock, we'd trade peaches for salami and cheese.

Now, thirty years later, the Particelli family still runs the store, and it still looks the same, with salami hanging from the ceiling and big, open burlap bags of dried beans on the floor. They still don't have a cash register; they add by hand and toss the money inside a rolltop desk. I feel like I'm traveling backward in time when I go there.

I was so excited when Tra Vigne opened right down the street from the store. I've probably had fifty meals in their private back room, and they come to my restaurant for all their kids' baptisms and first communions. Since my mother died, Ferruccia, the Particelli matriarch, has called me on my birthday, at Christmas, at Easter, on my saint's day—all the times my mother would have called.

Today, Ferruccia's son, Ray Particelli, runs the store in equal partnership with his sister Leonora and his uncle Policarpo Lucchesi. If you walk in at noontime, you may see—and smell—an Italian lunch underway in the small back room. When Ferruccia cooks, it's typically Italian: pasta first, followed by pork or rabbit or duck with vegetables, followed by salad and cheese. They drink homemade wine—in most years, a blend of Cabernet Sauvignon and Zinfandel grapes scavenged from friends. Someone keeps an eye on the screen door and gets up when a customer comes in.

Ray says that the biggest difference between "then" and "now" is that customers don't buy as much as they used to. In the old days, big Italian families like mine would buy $200 or $300 worth of provisions—a lot of money in those days. Families from Fresno or San Jose or rural towns where there wasn't such a store would buy pasta in ten-pound boxes, cheese by the wheel, olive oil by the gallon.

Today the store sees many more customers, but shoppers don't buy as much per visit. Cooks don't have to stock up on imported tomato paste or Sicilian anchovies because they can get such things at the supermarket. But I still love coming in here. For me, it's a link to Napa Valley's Italian heritage. Lots of vintners are loyal customers here: the Mondavis (both Robert and Peter and their children), Chuck Wagner of Caymus, and Justin Meyer of Silver Oak. "We've been here long enough," says Ray, "that everybody has stumbled through the door at one time or another."

117

growth

y 1970, the wine revolution in Napa Valley had taken off like a runaway train. Prunes, walnuts, and pastureland were rapidly giving way to fine wine grapes. Wine historian Charles Sullivan reports that Napa lost seven thousand acres of prunes and one thousand acres of walnuts between 1960 and 1973, while wine grape acreage doubled.

In 1968, San Francisco banker Dan Duckhorn came up to the valley to oversee a new grapevine nursery financed by his boss, Charlie Crocker. The nursery made bench grafts—rootstock grafted to fruit-bearing wood, known as the scion—for the burgeoning fine wine industry. And the nursery business was booming, as newcomers ripped up the old Prohibition-era vineyards, replacing Petite Sirah and Alicante Bouschet with classic fine-wine varietals like Cabernet Sauvignon and Pinot Noir.

The growing allure of Napa Valley in the 1970s and early 1980s propelled a number of people into life-changing decisions. Bored with being a Los Angeles real-estate lawyer, Jim Barrett bought a white elephant called Chateau Montelena. Warren Winiarski left a teaching post at the University of Chicago to take a cellar worker's job at Souverain (now Rutherford Hill). John Shafer quit his job as a book publishing executive and moved his family to Napa Valley to buy a vineyard. Joe Phelps, a successful Colorado building contractor, caught the fever, too, and bought a huge cattle ranch in St. Helena with his eye on planting vines. Although Braniff pilot Koerner Rombauer and his wife, Joan, didn't move to Napa Valley for wine, within four years of their arrival in 1972 they were winery partners.

By all accounts, the 1976 Paris Tasting—in which Warren Winiarski's 1973 Stag's Leap Wine Cellars Cabernet Sauvignon and Jim Barrett's 1973 Chateau Montelena Chardonnay bested the top French wines—confirmed Napa Valley's legitimacy as a fine wine region. Naturally, that victory lured even more entrepreneurs who had visions of making world-class wine. Several of them hired Tony Soter, a young consulting winemaker with a reputation for magnificent Cabernet Sauvignons—and a growing obsession with Pinot Noir.

The 1970s and early 1980s were a period of dynamic growth and change in Napa Valley, an era we can relive through the stories of those who were part of it.

James and Bo

Barrett

For sheer consistency—the ability to make top-of-the-charts wine every year—it would be hard to beat Chateau Montelena. Its Napa Valley Cabernet Sauvignon is an industry benchmark. Even other winemakers consider this Cabernet an icon and say they try to make wine like Bo Barrett.

Jim Barrett, his son Bo, and daughter-in-law Heidi Peterson Barrett are a world-class wine family. In thirty years, Jim and Bo have not wavered in their desire to create a first-growth estate. As a fan, I've been relieved to watch the smooth transition from father to son—although, as you'll read, it almost didn't happen.

Jim has a wry sense of humor; don't take him too seriously.

Jim: I was a lawyer, the head of a twenty-six-man law firm in Los Angeles, helping destroy a significant portion of the United States by building shopping centers. But I just got tired of big deals and being a big shot. In 1968, I said, "I've got a case of industrial-strength burn out. I don't care if I'm selling frozen chocolate bananas, I've got to do something else."

One of my partners knew I liked wine, so one day he said, "Let's go up and look at the Napa Valley." And it's a weekend to just go play, you know? So we came up here and had a wonderful weekend and I started looking around the Valley. And one fine day, I saw this place and it was just full of ghosts and spiders and I fell in love with it. Being an incurable romantic, I said, "Hey, this may be it. This looks like a wonderful place to commit financial suicide."

I mean, what did I know whether this was going to be a world-class vineyard or not? All those things came to light later. I have a guardian angel, Leonardo, who takes care of me.

The Barretts are only the second family to operate the winery, which dates from 1882. The founder, Alfred Tubbs, was a contemporary of Leland Stanford, who once considered putting his university in Calistoga. The Barretts have a letter Stanford sent to Tubbs, asking to come take a look at the property for his institution of higher learning.

When the Barretts bought the property in 1972, the winery hadn't been operated for years. To hedge his bets, Jim kept up his law practice, piloting his plane up to the Valley from L.A. a few days each week.

Page 123: The lake at Chateau Montelena lures owners Bo (left) and Jim Barrett. The façade of the old stone winery (opposite) is imported cut stone.

Jim: We interviewed three or four winemakers and decided on Mike Grgich. He had the best qualifications, having worked under Tchelistcheff and Mondavi. Then we set parameters. If you want to make world-class wine, you look at the first-growth Bordeaux: They're mostly small, low-yielding vineyards, family-owned, limited production, consistent quality, consistent style. Those are some of the standards I thought we should try to set here.

Looking back, I think that was very ambitious. When you plant Cabernet, it's eight years later, or seven if you're lucky, that you're going to have money coming in. And I thought, we're going to go belly-up if we wait for that. So we had Grgich running around trying to find the best grapes he could. It wasn't until 1978 that we were able to put "estate Cabernet" on the label.

The property Jim bought had included vineyards, they just weren't very good. Like many vineyards that survived Prohibition, they included lots of poor-quality but thick-skinned grape varieties that could survive shipment to the east coast.

Jim: They were trash grapes like Carignane, Alicante Bouschet, Sauvignon Vert, and Palomino. The best grape we had was some Petite Sirah. It was a temptation to keep it in, but nope, we were going to stick to our criteria. We pulled it out so we could plant Cabernet.

Bo: The grapes were sold to the co-op. In those days, you didn't make a lot of money growing anything, even Cabernet. You'd get seventy-five dollars a ton and it cost you thirty dollars to pick them. The vineyards were all head-pruned (see page 89) and had a lot of disease. To say they were run down . . .

Jim: . . . would be saying something nice about them.

Right away they began to replant, ripping out the inferior varieties in favor of Cabernet Sauvignon. Of course they had to choose a rootstock, too, and although everyone else was choosing AxR-1, a high-yielding rootstock recommended by the university, they chose St. George. This was a fortunate decision—Leonardo again—because AxR-1 proved not to be phylloxera resistant, and almost every Napa Valley vineyard planted on it has had to be replanted, at great expense.

Bo: I graduated from high school in 1972 and started working in the vineyard. I'd work long enough to buy my season ski pass and get rent money. And when I was out of money, I'd come back. I thought for sure I was going to be a lawyer, but winemaking just suited my demeanor. You don't have to wear a suit. You work with a team of great

people. It's about equipment and science and art, and I like all of those. And it's close to the land. So I gravitated to it for a number of reasons, but also because it would have been really dumb not to take advantage of the opportunity.

Bo transferred from the University of Utah to Fresno State, where he could study enology. He made this decision before the famous 1976 Paris Tasting (see page 157), but he must have felt he made the right career choice when the French judges placed Montelena's 1973 Chardonnay first, over several of France's top white Burgundies. Jim got the news while he was in Bordeaux, on a wine tour with other Napa Valley vintners.

Jim: We were at Château Lascombe having lunch in their great room, with waiters scurrying all over the place. Joanne (the tour organizer) taps me on the shoulder and says, "Jim, there's a telephone call for you." I said, "Very funny, Joanne." I was still in the law practice at that time and I had told my law partners not to call me unless something extreme happened, and I meant extreme. I'm walking out to the telephone thinking, "My God, something's happened to one of the kids"—Bo is one of five—but being an incurable optimist, I said, "Nah, it's not one of the kids, it's one of my law partners."

I pick up the phone and a voice says, "This is George Taber from *Time* magazine. Do you know you just won the Paris Tasting?" Well, I knew if I said the wrong thing they would kick us all out of France, and they probably wouldn't let me back into the Napa Valley. So I said, "Well, not bad for a kid from the sticks." He said, "How did that happen?"

I'm thinking, we're in France, better do this right, so I said, "Well, we're building on the shoulders of giants. We've learned from them." And on and on . . . pretty soon he's snoring because he's looking for a war, California versus France, and he wasn't getting it.

Bo: We were working in the cellar, just a regular day, when Grgich comes out of his office and starts dancing around, doing a little Croatian jig. He's throwing his beret in the air. So, of course, we all stop working and think Mike's lost his marbles. But pretty soon he tells us what happened and we're all hopping around, too.

At that point, we had a huge opportunity to capitalize commercially on this great success, but the decision was made to stay the course and stick with Cabernet as our primary focus. We could easily have turned around and become a Chardonnay house. We could have sold Chardonnay by the container-load.

I don't think we realized for probably two years that it had been a catalytic moment for California—the refugee lawyer from L.A. whose wine goes to France and wins big, so that everybody says, "Hey, I want to do that, too." The California wine industry probably jumped twenty years ahead in that moment.

Jim: You can't buy that kind of publicity because it had to do with credibility. It wasn't just us. It was the whole Napa Valley. The Napa Valley took off after that, big time. And I could finally say to my law partners, "She's all yours, fellas. Adiós."

But nothing is all peaches and cream. Somebody came along with two bags of gold and, guess what, we didn't have a winemaker anymore. Mike decided to go work somewhere else, and God bless him. But everybody thought, "What's going to happen to Montelena when the famous winemaker leaves?"

The Barretts found a great replacement in Jerry Luper, who had made some impressive wines at Freemark Abbey.

Jim: Leonardo again. I really fell in love with Luper. We called him Super Luper, which he hated, but he was like a brother-slash-son to me. Then in 1981 he came in and he had tears in his eyes and it's the two bags of gold again. So, before Jerry left, I said, "Who shall I get as winemaker?" And he said, "Are you sitting down? Your son. He's the best qualified."

Bo had just taken a winemaker's job down in Paso Robles, and I didn't call him right away. I was thinking, what if he gets a big head? What if he makes bad wine? I'm going through all these what-ifs. And I thought, if he does, I'll sell the damn winery because I'm not going to let anything interfere with my family. So I called Bo and said, "Hey, red alert! red alert! One of the finest wineries in the Napa Valley needs a winemaker and you should be it." And he said, "I'll think about it."

I was thinking, what if he gets a big head? What if he makes bad wine?

Bo: That was only eleven months after he said, "You'll never be the winemaker here until you get more experience."

Jim: Yeah, he had come in to my office when Jerry Luper was still here as winemaker and said, "Well, I'm ready," and I said, "Ready for what?" And he said, "To be the winemaker." And I said, "Where are you getting this winemaker job?" He says, "Well, here, of course." And I said, "I don't think so. I'm not into nepotism." And he said, "Well, I'm not going to stick around here then." And I said, "I don't blame you. I wouldn't either."

Bo: So I thought about the offer for a few days. I asked for the same respect and authority he had given to Mike and Jerry, and he said okay, so I'm still here.

GROWTH

The Cabernet Sauvignon
vineyards at Chateau
Montelena have proven
themselves year after year,
delivering consistently
concentrated grapes.

It rained heavily during the harvest in 1982, Bo's first vintage as Chateau Montelena's winemaker. Jim says his son was practically in tears one day, wondering, why me? My first crush—why me? What a way to start—especially when you know all eyes are on you.

Bo: A lot of people were saying, "Well, there goes Montelena now that sonny boy's in there."

Jim: But the point is, we had Grgich from 1972 to 1976, and Luper from 1976 to 1982, and Bo's been the winemaker since. And we've had vertical tastings (comparing a series of vintages) and the wine never changed in style, in spite of having three very different winemakers over that period. A lot of that has to do with the vineyard.

And the vineyard itself is a constant learning experience. At first we started picking at the back of the property and picked continuously until we got to the front, and then we'd throw a pig in the ground and have a party. Then we started to realize we have a volcanic area, an alluvial area, and a loam area, and they make different kinds of grapes. And guess what? They get ripe at different times. So we started picking individual lots, and now we pick seven different areas at different times to achieve maximum physiological maturity. Big, big quality improvement in the fruit.

We don't baby our vines now; we baby our soil, and the vines get healthier.

A lot of Napa Valley wineries have made these kinds of refinements over the years. It's really remarkable how much has been learned in only one generation about growing better grapes and improving the wines. Bo says it comes down to ever-greater precision.

Bo: We have gentler de-stemming and pressing, which allows you to make the wines bigger but without any harshness. With the Cabernet, I'd say the primary focus has been to get rid of bitter tannins, in part by better pump-over methodology. (Wine is repeatedly pumped over while it's fermenting to extract more flavor and tannin from the "cap"—the skins and seeds that float to the top.) In the old days, we pumped everything over the same way. Now we have six or eight different techniques. It's all about tannin management so you can have really huge, extracted, concentrated wines that don't demand aging but enjoy all the benefits.

We've been farming the vineyard naturally since 1979. But we never really analyzed our soil, so we're looking at a little more precision there. Because the vines are old, we don't ever push them. If you take a big crop, you pay for it for years. It's kind of like a good horse or an old piece of equipment. You don't ask it for 100 percent anymore.

But I would say we don't baby our vines now; we baby our soil, and then the vines get healthier. What we actually have is this piece of ground. Everything else is replaceable, including me.

Jim has resisted a lot of offers to expand the business over the years, in part because he didn't want his son to have to travel. Bo's wife, Heidi Peterson Barrett, is a highly regarded winemaking consultant, and they have two children. Bo says he was angry at the time when his dad would shoot down deals, but he now realizes how wise Jim was. Staying small—at about thirty-eight thousand cases—has been great for his family.

Jim: It's not going to get any bigger and it's not for sale. We get romanced to sell all the time; it's been going on for fifteen years. The answer is always: not for sale. If I get *X* dollars, what am I going to do with it? Buy a yacht in Cannes? Buy some gold chains to put around my neck, get a pot belly, and chase young girls? I don't think so. You don't sell your good health, your hunting dog, or your way of life.

Chateau Montelena has been making great Cabernet Sauvignon now for more than twenty years. Some critics says it's California's most consistently great Cabernet winery. How do you top that? How do you stay challenged when you're already at the peak of your game?

Bo: The best metaphor for that is baseball: You're only as good as your last hit. There's always somebody out there wanting to take our spot, so we're very competitive. And just when you think you've seen it all, you get a year that's completely different. And your team changes. A lot of our great winemaking staff moves on, so I get a whole new bunch of guys to train, like Mike and Jerry trained me, and I get their energy and ideas and enthusiasm. As long as you have an open mind and listen to your new guys, you can always learn something.

Bo Barrett discusses a task with longtime vineyard worker Lupe Suniga.

Garen and Shari

Staglin

On a hill overlooking Rutherford is a magnificent vine-covered, tile-roofed villa that looks like it was transported directly from Tuscany. Garen and Shari Staglin's art-filled estate was made for entertaining, featuring breathtaking views, broad loggias, a pool, a bocce ball court, and extensive landscaped grounds and gardens.

Garen's father was from Calabria, as was mine. Like me, Garen grew up in California in a home with Old World ways, including wine on the table every night. Shari was raised mostly in South Dakota in a family with agricultural roots. She says she didn't know wine existed until she met Garen (on a blind date at UCLA). Later Garen attended Stanford Business School and became a venture capitalist—a highly successful one. But in the life they have built in the Valley, Garen and Shari give much more than they take.

Garen: Before we were married, we used to come up here and literally sit over at the Oakville Grocery and look back over here and say, "This is one of the greatest places on the planet. We have to figure out how to make it our home, not just a place we visit on the weekends or once a month."

In 1985, after years of searching, they bought a historic property on the Rutherford Bench. The ranch had belonged to the family that owned Beaulieu Vineyard, and Cabernet Sauvignon grapes from the property had gone into the famous BV Georges de Latour Private Reserve. The parcel was a jewel in Napa Valley's crown and the Staglins jumped on it.

Garen: We didn't start out saying we wanted to buy this piece of land. We said we wanted to buy the best vineyard possible and we would not be satisfied with just any place. Shari used to come up and spend three or four days a

week just driving around looking at spots. We did put in an offer on a place on the Rutherford Cross Road, but we didn't chase it and our heart wasn't in it and we didn't get that one. Then we found another property on Pritchard Hill, but we lost to someone who outbid us by a very small margin. We then basically said, "Okay, now we're in zero-compromise mode. We are buying property on the Rutherford Bench, no questions asked. Let's find it." Well, that's like saying you want the Mona Lisa in your house as a personal copy. It's difficult to do.

Luckily, their neighbor recalled a conversation with Walter Sullivan, the husband of Georges de Latour's granddaughter, who still owned some of the original BV property and was open to selling some of it. Many meetings later, the Staglins made an offer.

Everybody was telling me this was a very bad decision, to spend this much money when we'd never been in the wine business before.

Garen: Everybody was telling me this was a very bad decision, to spend this amount of money buying sixty-two acres when we'd never been in the wine business before. Fortunately, property values were at a low point of about twenty thousand dollars an acre, but it was still a big commitment. This was fulfilling a dream and that's about as emotional as it gets. But if you don't focus on rate of return but instead focus on your passion, you will achieve a higher rate of return than you ever thought possible—in emotional satisfaction, and it turns out that the numbers work better that way, too. Because people sense your passion and that creates loyalty.

The *Wall Street Journal* did an article about the wine business and the two people interviewed were myself and the CFO at Gallo. And they asked how you decide how much to spend, and I said I don't even think about it. If it's the right thing to do for quality, that's what we do, and by doing so, you'll take care of the rate of return. Gallo's answer was far more calculated around the cost of capital and market size and all those other things. That's not what we're doing here.

It didn't take long for Garen and Shari to make their mark in the Valley, not only for their wine but also for their philanthropy. The Staglins open their house constantly for charity benefits, and they give generously themselves.

Shari: It's just a natural for us because that's who we are. We knew it was a hospitality industry, and we designed our home so that we could entertain. We like to use our hospitality for charity, with wine as an enhancer for that. It brings people together and makes them even happier they're involved with whatever the cause is.

Garen: Money was not how we started in life. We've been fortunate to be successful in a variety of things, but I think that creates the opportunity, if not the obligation, for us to do good things in causes we're passionate about. We can take our business skills and our energy and focus on challenges we think are important. The high-profile arts—the opera, the symphony, the art museums—we're involved in those, but those are much easier causes for people to give to. Endangered children, terminally ill kids, mental health, cancer research—we tend to focus on causes that aren't as easy to get everybody involved in, and we use our environment to create a catalyst for generosity.

As for people who are in the wine business and then have their private life and don't mix the two, that's not who we are. The wine business is our life, and so it's natural for us to share our home, our wines, and our hos-

pitality as part of it. The wine is Staglin Family. We are Staglin Family. This house is Staglin Family, so it would be completely unnatural for us to send you down the road to enjoy our wine in some sterile environment.

Their giving is so persistent that they inspire others to give, too. Garen and Shari chair the $50 million fundraising campaign for Copia: The American Center for Wine, Food, and the Arts. They advise other nonprofit groups on how to stage benefits. They even helped their daughter's high school beef up its annual fundraiser, boosting profits from $20,000 to $100,000.

Every summer they have a huge benefit at their home called Music for Mental Health. All the cult wineries in the Valley (Harlan, Screaming Eagle, you name it) have donated wine to this gala, because it's hard to say no to Garen and Shari. The Staglins also host a conference at their home so that researchers can tell donors how their money is being spent and what progress is being made. They have worked hard to raise the profile of this sensitive issue.

Shari: The Napa Valley Wine Auction never used to fund anything related to mental health and now it funds many different programs, so I'd like to think that there's some connection to our work. It's just a matter of people understanding what mental illness is all about, that it's a chemical disorder of the brain, just as diabetes is a chemical disorder. I think the more that people like us talk about it and make it public, the easier it is for everybody else to understand it's nothing to be ashamed of.

When I look at what they have built here, I keep thinking about that Italian expression that says you plant olives for your grandchildren. An estate like this is meant to stay in a family, but children in America rarely continue what their parents have started. The Staglins have a grown son and daughter, Brandon and Shannon, and I was glad to hear that Shannon plans to join them in the business. I wondered if Garen and Shari planned and hoped for that.

Garen: The Antinori family has been in the wine business in Italy for four hundred years, the Frescobaldis for seven hundred. Some of the great Bordeaux estates have similar lineages. We feel like we're blessed to own this property and we're custodians of it while we're here, and hopefully we can pass it on to a generation that will take the same care of it and nurture it and make the best possible wine that they can from it. And without imposing that on our daughter Shannon, I think she has felt that sense of pride and opportunity and wants to be involved.

Shari: We've always told our kids, you should do whatever your heart wants you to do. Follow your dream. This was our dream. You don't have to do it. You kids can hire somebody to run it if you don't want to be involved with it. So I guess "relief" isn't really the right word when Shannon decided she wanted to do it. It was more of a joy. It was just a thrill to know that she felt that it was a good thing for her life, too.

I love the Staglin Sangiovese, which is not an easy varietal to make well in Napa Valley. They call it Stagliano Sangiovese—in honor of Garen's original family name. It has been a good ambassador for them, opening doors to Italy.

Garen: Because of the success of our Sangiovese, we've had [Angelo] Gaja's winemaker here. We've had [Piero] Antinori's winemaker here. We've had Badia a Coltibuono's winemaker here. We've gone there. The community of wine is a very open community and it's amazingly noncompetitive in that sense. People are willing to share with you their ideas and their skills because the "proprietariness" of what you do is really about the land, not about one technique or the other. Whatever we told the people from Badia a Coltibuono, their wine would never taste like ours, even if they made it exactly the same, and vice versa. So they've been willing to share a number of things about how to achieve optimal balance in the wines, how to get the grapes perfectly ripe, and how to keep all the structural elements that you want and keep the bad elements out.

Day to day, Shari runs the Staglin Family wine business. Garen still works in venture capital, in part to subsidize the Napa dream. I asked him why you don't see more venture capital coming into the wine business?

Garen: It doesn't work. Because you can't have the philosophy that I have, which is, whatever it costs we're going to do it. When your passion is about ultimate quality, you can't worry about ROI [return on investment]. So you've got oil and water. Venture is all about ROI, high risk, high return. This is about passion and dedication and patience. And that's the other end of the business spectrum.

When your passion is about
ultimate quality, you
can't worry about
return on investment.

Bocce Ball Before Dinner

Braised Rabbit Crostini

Angry Lobster *with* White Beans

Arugula *with* Whole Citrus Vinaigrette

Cheeses *with* Honeycomb and Walnut Toast

In my opinion, Garen and Shari Staglins' fabulous Tuscan-style villa wasn't truly complete until they built the bocce ball court behind it. One early autumn evening when both of their kids were home, we celebrated the debut of the bocce court with a hard-fought match, followed by dinner alfresco. On the menu: braised and shredded rabbit seasoned with fennel and juniper, moistened with broth and olive oil and served on crostini; one of my favorite lobster dishes, created by accident; a simple salad of young arugula with Whole Citrus Vinaigrette from The Tra Vigne Cookbook *(you could substitute a lemon juice—olive oil dressing); and an assortment of cheeses with honeycomb and toasted walnut bread.*

Of course we drank Staglin Family Vineyard wine: the Chardonnay with the rabbit and the lobster, and the Sangiovese with the cheeses.

The rabbit and the white beans can be prepared hours ahead, so the only last-minute work is cooking the lobster.

BRAISED RABBIT CROSTINI

I grew up in a part of California that produces rabbit commercially and we always raised rabbit at home, so in our house it was "the other white meat." It's subtle in flavor, very lean, and almost sweet; I try never to overwhelm its gentle taste. This recipe is from Italy's Piedmont region—the currants give it away. The Piedmontese borrowed the idea from the French, who often pair rabbit with prunes. If you're lucky enough to have access to wild fennel, use a handful of fennel fronds and seeds instead of storebought fennel seed.

1 whole rabbit, about 2½ pounds

½ cup diced onion

¼ cup diced celery

¼ cup diced carrot

4 cups chicken stock

1 cup dry white wine

3 sprigs Italian (flat-leaf) parsley, optional

10 juniper berries

1 bay leaf

1 tablespoon toasted fennel seed

1 teaspoon sea salt, preferably gray salt (see Note on
   page 26)

Freshly ground black pepper

⅓ cup currants or raisins plumped in warm water,
   then drained

3 tablespoons minced chives

2 tablespoons extra virgin olive oil

About 30 slices country bread, toasted

Preheat oven to 275° F. Place rabbit in a high-sided skillet just large enough to hold it. Add onion, celery, carrot, stock, wine, parsley, juniper, bay, fennel seed, salt, pepper, and 1 cup of water. Cover, bring to a simmer on top of the stove, then transfer to the oven and bake until rabbit is falling-off-the-bone tender, about 2 hours. Add more hot water as necessary during cooking to keep the rabbit barely covered. Let cool in broth.

Measure 1 cup of the rabbit broth into a small saucepan, simmer until reduced to ¼ cup, then let cool. Pull rabbit meat from the bones and shred by hand; watch carefully for small bones. Moisten meat with the reduced broth. Add raisins, chives, and oil, then season with salt and pepper. Spoon shredded meat over toasts to serve.

MAKES 30 CROSTINI

An array of cheeses
served with honeycomb
and walnut toast
provides a satisfying
finale to the meal.

I realize this isn't the world's easiest dish, but the results are worth the effort. I love the contrast of orange zest and herbs with the richness of lobster, but you could use crab or shrimp instead. You've probably heard of penne all'arrabbiata—*pasta in an "angry" sauce fired up with red pepper flakes. The spicy garnish on this lobster makes it "angry," too.*

The recipe came about partly by mistake when I left white beans in the pan too long. By the time I noticed them they were getting crispy, and I found I liked them that way.

Follow the lobster directions carefully to make sure you dispatch the creatures in a way that's swift and painless for them and safe for you.

For the beans:

1 cup dried white beans, preferably the largest available

2 sage leaves

1 clove garlic, peeled

2 teaspoons sea salt, preferably gray salt (see Note on page 26)

For the flour mix:

1 cup all-purpose flour

1½ teaspoons mild chili powder

½ teaspoon sea salt, preferably gray salt (see Note on page 26)

¼ teaspoon freshly ground pepper

1½ to 2 cups extra virgin olive oil

Four 1¼-pound live lobsters

2 tablespoons thinly sliced garlic

1 tablespoon thinly sliced serrano or jalapeño chili

1½ cups basil leaves

1 tablespoon julienned orange zest

Place the dried beans in a saucepan with cold water to cover by 2 inches. Bring to a boil. Cover, remove from the heat and let stand 1 hour, then drain. Add cold water to cover by 2 inches. Add the sage and garlic and bring to a simmer. Simmer gently, uncovered, for about 20 minutes, then add the salt. Continue simmering gently until beans are tender; timing will vary depending on age of beans. Cool in the cooking liquid, then refrigerate for up to 3 days.

Combine all ingredients for the flour mix and set aside.

Drain the beans well, then place in a strainer held over a bowl. Heat 1 cup olive oil in a 10-inch skillet over high heat. While oil is heating, sprinkle some of the flour mix over the beans and shake in the colander to coat the beans with the flour. Repeat, if necessary, with the flour that falls into the bowl. Add the beans to the hot oil and cook without stirring until they are browned and crisp on the bottom, 6 to 7 minutes. Turn with a spatula and brown on the other side, another 6 to 7 minutes. Transfer beans to paper towels to drain.

Preheat the oven to 450° F.

Prepare the lobsters: Working with one at a time, grab the lobster around the body shell where the body meets the tail and gently pinch with thumb and forefinger; the pressure will keep the lobster fairly still. Lay it on a cutting board, underside down and head facing you. The tail will want to curl, but press it flat. With the tip of a heavy knife, pierce the shell firmly where it meets the tail, piercing all the way through to your cutting surface, then roll your knife downward through the head to split the head lengthwise. Turn the lobster 180 degrees and split the tail. Rinse gently to remove the organs; don't wash vigorously or you'll wash away flavor. Remove the claws and crack the shells with the back of your knife to make them easier to eat.

Heat ⅓ cup oil in a 12-inch skillet over high heat. Add the lobster claws and cook about 2 minutes on each side. Transfer to a large sheet pan.

Sprinkle the lobster bodies with salt and pepper. Dredge the cut side in flour mix, patting off excess. Reheat the oil, adding more if necessary; when oil is hot, add half the lobster pieces, cut side down. Cook until lightly browned, about 1 minute, then turn and cook 1 minute on the other side. Transfer to the sheet pan with the claws. Repeat with remaining lobster, adding more oil as needed. Transfer to the sheet pan.

Put the lobster in the oven and roast until done, 6 to 8 minutes. Put the beans in a separate pan and reheat alongside the lobster.

While the lobster cooks, prepare the garnish: Add 2 tablespoons more oil to the pan used to sear the lobster.

When hot, add garlic and chilies and sauté until garlic begins to turn golden. Add basil leaves and stand back; they will spatter. Sauté until the leaves turn crisp. Add orange zest, then remove from heat.

Arrange the lobster pieces on a serving platter or individual plates and sprinkle with beans. Top with the garlic-chili-basil garnish and drizzle with any oil remaining in the pan.

SERVES 4

Napa Cheese for Napa Wine

Like many beautiful rural areas, Napa Valley lures people who want to escape the stresses of city life. Goat farmer Amy Wend is one of those urban refugees, a former San Francisco office worker who dreamed of living in the country and working with food.

In 1989, Amy started a small organic farm with friend Ted Connolly, a former San Francisco 49ers football player who had bought an eighty-acre property in the remote western hills above the town of Napa. They built terraces on the hillsides and began to grow salad greens and vegetables for farmers' markets and local restaurants. But it soon became clear that they would never break even. So the following year, they added goats and began to make cheese, and by 1992, they had abandoned the produce entirely.

Today, Skyhill Napa Valley Farms oversees seven hundred goats, including Emily, whose picture is on the label of the farm's yogurt and cheeses. Cheesemaker Heath Benson, who learned the craft from his father-in-law, produces small quantities of goat feta, goat fontina, fresh logs of chèvre—some flavored with chives and garlic, some with roasted peppers and olives—and whole-milk goat yogurt. Heath also uses the whey to make a twice-cooked cheese they call Ri-goat-ta, a creamy cheese with a pronounced nutty finish.

Napa Valley restaurants use Skyhill cheese—the flavored goat cheeses are delicious in ravioli, the goat fontina a nice match with pears—and several local markets carry them. Amy and Heath are also building a base of retail customers around the country. In fact their cheese business has grown beyond the capacity of the tiled cheesemaking room allotted to it, and they anticipate a move. They hope that a new, larger facility will allow them to make blue cheese and aged crottins—both of which involve molds that can "travel" and must be kept separate from the yogurt production.

The goats are smart and endearing, says Amy, and she enjoys producing a food she sees as wholesome. Her herd forges a link to Napa's early nineteenth-century past, when the Valley provided pasture for the cattle, sheep, and horses needed by the new Sonoma mission. It's been a long time since livestock grazed in the Napa hills in significant numbers, but it's nice to know that Skyhill is keeping the tradition alive.

Amy's herd forges a link to Napa's early-nineteenth-century past.

Warren

Winiarski

I don't know Warren and Barbara Winiarski well, although I've had the pleasure of cooking up at their house for important guests, like Italian winemaker Angelo Gaja and French chef Roger Vergé. The Winiarskis are serious, well-educated people who don't care about being in society columns or basking in the spotlight. I think of them as part of the rock-solid foundation of the Napa Valley. Barbara has been active in land-use issues in the valley on the conservation side, and Warren is a philosopher-winemaker. He has a mind that questions and wants to understand everything, and he gives each decision deep thought.

Each year I'm eager to see what Stag's Leap Wine Cellars donates to the Napa Valley Wine Auction. The Winiarskis always come up with something meaningful. One year they pledged to match the money that their wine raised with a donation to the restoration of the Star-Spangled Banner, the flag that inspired our national anthem.

I know that the family name means "son of a vintner," but were there vintners in the Winiarski family tree?

There were. You know, during Prohibition, you were permitted to make two hundred gallons of wine per household for family use and my father did make wine. I remember it bubbling, bubbling, bubbling—putting my ear against the little barrel in the cellar. I even put my finger in there and tasted it. I remember he used raisins and grapes, but where the grapes came from I don't remember.

So homemade wine was on the family table in Chicago on special occasions, but Warren didn't really encounter wine as an everyday beverage until he went to Italy as a student.

Wine was part of my experience there, and the experience stayed as a memory. Much later, when a friend of ours brought over a bottle of New York wine, I had an epiphany. It was hybrid grape wine, and we had it at our table in Chicago, and the world changed. All the pleasure of wine in Italy came back in a big rush that afternoon.

I mean, how do you explain it? There was suddenly a light, you know, an illumination. Something showed itself. It wasn't a very good wine, but it revealed some inner qualities to me that went back, I'm sure, to Italy. Those memories weren't really there consciously, but that afternoon, they all came back.

Warren was teaching in the liberal arts program at the University of Chicago at the time, but his epiphany pushed him into action. He began reading about wine, buying wine, and tasting wine with a passion. At the same time, he and Barbara began to question their life in Chicago. Was the city really a good place to raise their growing family?

It was the sixties, you know. There was some chaos and unwinding of the social and political fabric taking place. And we thought there might be some alternatives—a way of living together and raising our family and doing something we all could love. We were thinking that some kind of farming endeavor would have a unity and cohesiveness that we could share.

I looked at apple-growing in the Rio Grande Valley. I brought some grapes back to Chicago and made wine. And I liked the sequential thinking of winemaking—each part of the process took more thinking and caring and skill.

So, in 1964, they packed up their children and possessions and moved to California. Warren had written a few letters beforehand, and he had a reply from Lee Stewart at Souverain Cellars in Rutherford, inviting him to come to work. I found this surprising given Warren's lack of science background or wine experience, but he says it was a different industry then. There weren't many enology or viticulture graduates, so some employers expected to do on-the-job training. Basically, Stewart also needed somebody to wash pots.

But Warren watched and analyzed and learned, and Stewart was a stickler for detail. He taught Warren the importance of cleanliness and attention to the fine points of winemaking. For instance, he insisted on putting the bung, the barrel closure, in the barrel the same way each time so the grain of the bung would line up with the grain in the barrel staves.

Warren spent two years at Souverain, then two years with the Robert Mondavi Winery, which was just getting off the ground. In fact, he was the acting winemaker for the first harvest because Michael Mondavi, Bob's son and the winemaker in name, was called up for the National Guard. That first vintage was, in a word, chaotic, reports Warren—a completely different experience from Souverain. "Robert Mondavi had no taste for details, but he did have a sweeping vision," says Warren.

Soon after the harvest,
autumn weather turns
Napa's vineyards into
shimmering rows of
burnt orange and gold.

At Stag's Leap Wine
Cellars, a worker clears
a vineyard for replanting
with new rootstocks,
clones, and trellises.

155

So I had two years of small winery experience with fantastic grounding in all the minutiae, all the small things that make a huge difference, and then two years of the opposite approach—winemaking on a larger scale, with big brush strokes. The grounding was good, but the vision was good, too.

Before he joined Mondavi, he and Barbara had bought fifteen acres high on Howell Mountain. Warren thinks they might have been the first to plant Cabernet Sauvignon there. In any case, the venture was doomed to difficulty. They battled deer and cutworms, and they didn't have enough water to get young vines started. Ninety percent of their grafts didn't take the first year. The little wine they made from the property was terrific, but the land wasn't economical to farm.

In the meantime, I'd tasted wine made from Nathan Fay's fruit, and that was another epiphany. I had been going around the valley tasting wines, so I was developing a kind of geography of what Cabernet was like at different elevations, in different locations. And the day I tasted Nathan's homemade 1968 Cabernet—well, in my mind, it expressed the perfection of that varietal. So when we found out that an adjoining parcel—then in prunes, cherries, and apples—was for sale, we put together a partnership.

Fay's property was in the Stags Leap area of Napa, against the eastern foothills. He had been selling the grapes to Charles Krug, but the homemade wine he made from his own grapes in 1968 is

legendary. Other winemakers were influenced by it, too. Warren and Barbara assembled a partnership with friends and friends of friends, and bought the property next to Fay's in 1970. (Later, when Fay retired, they bought his property, too.) They figured that building a winery was a distant dream, but fate intervened when Warren fell in love with the beautiful house at the top of the hill above his property.

Building a winery was a distant dream until Warren fell in love with the house on the hill.

David Backus [the home's owner] had suffered a stroke a few years earlier, and he talked with an impediment. Words didn't come out smoothly. I said, "Your wife said the house is for sale. What are you asking for it?" "Thirty-seven five." Well, my heart started to race. Thirty-seven five! I practically ran back to Angwin and told Barbara, "We can do this! Thirty-seven five! We can do this!"

But when David and I sat down with his wife, what he had said was "one thirty-seven five." So then we couldn't do it—unless we put together a partnership and the house became part of the winery, which is what happened. We put another partnership together to buy the house, which would become sort of the château for winery entertaining and business.

Warren planted Cabernet Sauvignon on the property in 1970. Amazingly, his first wine from the vineyard—the 1973 vintage, made from three-year-old vines—won the prestigious Paris Tasting in 1976. *Time* magazine reported the results, telling the world that French judges had put a California wine first, over some top-ranked French competitors. The story catapulted the new winery to stardom, but Warren says he and Barbara didn't immediately realize the impact their victory would have. What made it an even bigger story was that the reporter for *Time* spoke French.

He heard all the little comments the judges were making to each other. They were making mistakes in identifying the wines. For example, they said, "This wine soars; that wine has no grace. French wine, California wine."

But they had it wrong, and the reporter said so. The embarrassed French judges later argued that the French wines were at a disadvantage because they don't show as well as the Californians when they're young. But when the tasting was repeated ten years later in New York, a California wine (the Clos du Val) again came out on top. Clearly, the top California Cabernets do age as well as the top Bordeaux. In fact, some wine writers believe we're drinking California Cabs too young.

I could agree with that, but I could also disagree with it. It depends how you like your wine. Some people prefer the robust fruit, and you lose that with age. Michael Broadbent [the wine writer] said, "Wine's always losing, and it's always gaining." Between the robust, forward quality of a young wine and the subtleties and seamless quality of an aged wine—who's to say where the balance point should be?

I think Warren's wines age particularly well. When they're young and compressed, you taste them as two or three distinct layers. When they're older, they open up like an accordion, with no gaps in between. That's the art of it, although he gives more credit to the vineyard than to his own skills. From the dramatic windows of his house, you can see the variation in soils on his property. At one end, the soils derive from volcanic rock. At the other end, they're mostly up-valley sediments overlaid by alluvial deposits.

So we have fire here and water there, and we're trying to put them together. That's why the property is divided into so many pieces. Everything in between the pure fire soils and the pure water soils has a different composition, so while the grape variety is the same, the resulting wine is different in every block. They're harvested separately and kept separate throughout fermentation and aging. Only later are they put together to balance fire and water. The water soils give you softness, roundness, suppleness—just like water. And the spirited, intense, concentrated quality comes from the volcanic soils.

We don't practice agriculture anymore. We practice horticulture, meaning our vineyard is a garden.

Warren may be a vintner now but he's still a teacher at heart. He's always researching, learning, asking questions. In 1989, he went to Pakistan to search for the primordial vine—the original wild vine that would resemble the vine that Noah planted. He wanted to bring cuttings back to Napa, propagate vines, and make wine that might taste like the wine Noah made. He did indeed bring back seeds and cuttings, which had to go through a long quarantine. Now, with his own time so limited, he's trying to find an interested student to take the project to the next step.

The whole adventure reminds me of an experience I had when I was at cooking school in New York. We had been taught about Carême, the father of classic French cooking, and I got it in my head that I wanted to make Carême's recipe for Sauce Espagnole. Well, it was this outrageous old recipe that involved four calves, two goats, one sheep, and so forth, but I raised the money at school and I made it—in a smaller batch, of course. It cost $92 to make a liter. And I got in trouble for it. The chef said I was wasting my time and the resources of the school. But I said, "Chef Metz, it's very simple. For once in my life, I want to taste what Carême tasted."

Warren has that drive to understand things from the bottom up. Understanding every detail of the vineyard, and believing that every detail is important, is part of his nature.

We don't practice agriculture anymore—agriculture, from the word "agri," meaning field. In agriculture, you treat all the plants as a field. Every ear of corn is treated the same. We practice horticulture here—"hortus" meaning garden, meaning our vineyard is a garden. Each plant is treated separately, understood separately. The big improvements in quality will come from horticulture—counting leaves, cutting off leaves at the right moment, watching closely so you don't re-grow what you've just cut off. All this balancing between exposure of the fruit and sunburned leaves and leaf shading, so that you get perfect development of the grape skins. We're not changing the genotype, we're changing the way we treat it. And that's where the quality improvements will be.

The afternoon sun casts a warm glow on vines on the east side of the valley, site of Warren Winiarski's famed Stags Leap District vineyards.

GROWTH

Are They Ripe Yet?

Deciding when to pick the grapes in the fall is one of the most anxious moments for any winemaker. Pick too soon and your wine may taste thin, undeveloped, unripe. Pick too late and your wine may be overly alcoholic and raisiny—or, worse, a heavy rain could ruin the crop. "Once you've chosen your site, grape variety, and rootstock, and your physical vineyard exists, the next most important thing is the day you pick your grapes,"

says John Kongsgaard, winemaker for Arietta, Kongsgaard, and Luna Vineyards in Napa. "That becomes the single most compelling decision of the vintage."

Like many other winemakers, John has changed the way he determines when to harvest. As a young winemaker just out of graduate school at the University of California, Davis, he watched the numbers. He knew what average Brix (sugar level) he wanted his grapes to be, so if some were a little underripe, he'd pick some slightly overripe to make his average.

"It's a perfectly normal obsession for a young winemaker to try to equate the flavor of wine with some analysis of it," says Kongsgaard. As he became more sophisticated in his winemaking, he added some other targets, like a certain pH and acidity.

Then, in 1987, while he was the winemaker at Newton Vineyard, John had the chance to work with Michel Rolland, an international winemaking consultant from Bordeaux. Rollard changed John's thinking dramatically.

"What he taught me was so profound that when I talk about it, I feel like I'm describing a religious conversion," says John. "I almost can't remember how I used to think before Michel got ahold of me."

Michel encouraged John to set his target numbers aside and to simply taste the grapes for ripeness. If you know what to look for, you can recognize the flavors that indicate peak maturity. For the Bordeaux red varieties—Cabernet Sauvignon, Cabernet Franc, Merlot, Petit Verdot—the flavor changes from something akin to green vegetables to a taste more suggestive of red or black fruit.

"In other words, Michel said when it goes from something like salad to dessert, you've arrived," recalls John. "Certainly it has to do with pH and a lot of things, but it's very clear that there's a day or a couple of days when the grapes change from tasting aggressively tannic, you could say 'chalky' in tannin, when you really chew on the skins, to something more like dessert."

Another indicator is the seed: When it turns from green to brown, the flavor takes a turn for the better and you know the fruit is mature. At that point, the pulp no longer clings to the seed—another sign of ripeness. So these days, you're likely to see John walking the vineyards at harvest time, putting a sample grape in his mouth and another in a bag for the lab.

"You still want to have the science backing you up because you could occasionally be fooled," says John. "It could be a year where the flavor arrives early and you think the grapes taste marvelous, but the sugar's only 21 percent—too low to produce enough alcohol to balance the wine. So you have the lab look at pH, Brix, and acidity. But once I know we're in the acceptable range, I often don't even bring a sample back to the lab."

For growers accustomed to picking when the grapes hit a certain Brix, this new way of thinking has meant some adjustment. "When I started my lessons with Michel, if you approached a grower and said, 'Your vineyard's 24° Brix, but the seeds aren't brown yet and I'm not satisfied with the flavor,' they would come after you with a picking knife," says John. "But now I think the growers are sympathetic to this kind of thinking. And more and more winemakers are picking on flavor rather than just on the laboratory."

A Cook's Treasure from Unripe Grapes

Growing up in an Italian household with a resourceful cook for a mother, I've got a deep-seated aversion to waste. Most good cooks do: I think it's our respect for food that makes us look at ingredients about to be discarded and wonder, what could I make with that?

My friend Jim Neal, who is also a chef, has the same instinct. When he worked for a Napa Valley vineyard company one year and saw grapevines being thinned and the grapes left on the ground, he was bothered enough to hatch an idea.

Jim studied cooking with the great Madeleine Kamman, who introduced him to *verjus,* the tart, unfermented juice of underripe wine grapes. In earlier times, French cooks like Kamman's grandmother would use verjus in place of vinegar to flavor sauces or make salad dressings.

To get more intensity in their wines, winemakers will often thin their grape crops in late summer, so each vine has fewer grapes to ripen. Typically, in California, these underripe grapes are simply left on the ground but in some parts of France, they are turned into verjus (literally 'green juice') by being pressed into a sweet-tart juice.

Jim wanted to try making a California verjus using grapes from the late-summer thinnings. Since 1994, he has arranged with growers to get their thinnings; then he finds a winery willing to turn the grapes into verjus.

The process is not complicated; the hardest part is keeping the grape juice from fermenting. When the grapes arrive at the winery, they are about 10° Brix (a measure of their sugar content—ripe wine grapes are typically around 24° Brix). Immediately after they are crushed, the resulting "must" is pressed to separate juice from skins. Then the juice is allowed to settle for several days so any solid matter falls to the bottom. The clear juice is poured off and filtered, then pasteurized and packaged.

"It helps balance a lot of dishes," says Jim, "because it has the acid and the sugar. For example, when the tomatoes aren't perfectly sweet, I'll make a tomato salad and add verjus to it." It's also delicious sprinkled on berries or fruit salad, or made into a summer beverage with sparkling water and orange slices.

I use verjus to deglaze the pan when I'm cooking duck breasts. And it's fantastic in marinades because the sugar in it makes grilled foods caramelize.

Verjus has a much softer acidity than vinegar. Wine vinegar has acetic acid, which clashes with wine; verjus has none, which is why it works so well in dishes you want to pair with wine. If I'm preparing a dinner for wine lovers who are opening important bottles, I'll use verjus in the salad in place of vinegar.

I think it must have thrilled Jim when Madeleine Kamman tasted his verjus and told him it gave her chicken "the taste of my grandmother's sauces—a taste I never thought I could ever find again."

Tony

Soter

Tony Soter is one of the great gentlemen of the Napa Valley and one of its most respected winemakers, too. What's remarkable about Tony is that he knows as much about the vineyard as the cellar. I see him out in the vineyard all summer long, in hiking boots and shorts and a sun hat, keeping a close eye on his grapes.

Tony's winery, Etude, produces acclaimed Pinot Noir and Cabernet Sauvignon, as well as small amounts of two Alsatian-style white wines: Pinot Blanc and Pinot Gris. Until his recent retirement from consulting, Tony was a star on that circuit, too, helping set the wine style at Spottswoode, Araujo, Dalle Valle, Viader, and others. For a man with so many successes, he's incredibly humble. Making Pinot Noir keeps him that way, he says.

Wine wasn't a part of my childhood, although I did have an early connection with it and maybe it was more telling than I thought. I used to love to play in the basement of my grandma's big old house in Portland, Oregon. One day I ran in, said hi to grandma, then charged down the stairway and was immediately hit by this haunting aroma. I heard some noise, so I snuck around sort of stealthily. And I saw my grandfather and a crony of his making their homemade wine. The Greeks and Italians and Slavs in the area would all pitch in and buy a carload of grapes from California. Everybody would get a few boxes, and they would take them home and make their wine.

When I graduated from college with a degree in philosophy, I didn't really want to go to law school, but that was about the only thing I was qualified for. I didn't know what I was going to do exactly. I came up to Napa on a tour and decided to just stick around and see if I could learn more about wine—and I never really left. In the span of two years, I worked for five wineries.

He also went back to school, for graduate study in enology and viticulture at U.C. Davis. And by 1977, within two years of deciding to "learn more about wine," Tony was the winemaker at

Previous page:
Tony Soter and
daughter Olivia
take a pruning break.
Winter pruning directs
new growth and
helps control yield.

GROWTH

Chappellet Winery. He stayed there until 1980, then moved into wine consulting—which, in his case, wasn't a euphemism for being unemployed.

I guess I just had more energy than what was possible to use in any one situation. Consulting allowed me to be on a lot of different properties and see a lot of different wines made. I started as a sort of ambulance chaser. You know, if somebody had a problem wine, I'd try to help them figure it out. Later, the work evolved into really starting with a blank slate: a property with owners who had great ambitions and a long-term commitment.

I soon realized that the first thing to say to a potential client was, "The first meeting's on me," because it's really about wanting to know if we would care to work together. I'd also tell them I'd try to talk them out of it, which was a way of testing their commitment, because it always costs a lot more than people anticipate it will. But more important was their personal commitment to some ideals that I have, because I didn't want to be constrained by compromises.

Often I would say, "You know, it's going to take a few years for the vines to mature. We rarely make the best wine with the first grapes from a new vineyard. Even if they're mature vines, I don't know enough about your property until I put my hands on the material for the first time, so don't count on the first wine going to market. Since you don't get a second chance to make a first impression, you want to make sure your first wine is one you can get behind."

Tony is a perfectionist, which explains why he spends so much time in the vineyard. He's not content to sit back and take what a grower brings him; he wants to specify how the grapes are grown.

Twenty years ago, I thought all the magic happened in the winery. Just bring me the grapes. Eventually you realize that, just like in the kitchen, you're limited by the quality of your materials. The task becomes not just making a good wine, but making one with style and character, and that means looking at the vineyard. It's also a matter of learning the difference between the hand and the land. You know, we talk a lot about terroir, but it's really hard to see.

If you give three good winemakers the same vineyard to work with, you'll get wines that taste like they were made by three individuals, not wines that taste like they came from the same vineyard. We've been studying this in blind tastings for years, and we can't make sense out of all the Burgundy appellations except by matching up the winemakers, not the vineyards.

What's the lesson here? That terroir is just myth and hype? No, I think it's a real phenomenon, but the only way you see it is when the winemaker's hand is constant. So if the same winemaker makes wine from three vineyards, then you can appreciate those subtleties, but you come to see that what the winemaker does has significant potential to overpower the expression of terroir.

The cooking analogies are obvious. If you really want to show off the character of fish, you don't do much to it. Tony likes good food and follows the food world, so I can imagine how he got the idea to name his newest Pinot Noir 'Heirloom.' Everybody's talking about heirloom vegetables—the old varieties with great flavor that haven't been "improved" for the commercial market.

There's an inherent conflict of interest in paying growers by the ton.

The Pinot story parallels the rediscovery of heirloom vegetables. Heirloom is a wine that's really an homage to the rediscovery of vines that might otherwise go the way of oblivion because of strong pressures for homogenization and standardization.

The reason we have certain kinds of tomatoes is not because they taste good, but because they ship better than others. The same pressures occur in grapevine selections. An example is a couple of Pinot Noir clones that are chronically low-producing. They inherently make clusters that are about one-quarter the size of a normal cluster and with a lot of what we call "shot berries" that never increase in size. These clones produce maybe a ton to the acre where others would do four, five, six tons to the acre.

I had access to about two acres of one of these heirlooms a few years ago. The farmer was really sorry he planted it, but I made it more worth his while by paying him an exhorbitant price for the grapes.

But from his point of view, every year was another dismal crop of very small tonnage, so he finally just took the tractor and pulled it out. He planted Chardonnay that would produce six tons to the acre and make him a bunch more money. Luckily we had taken some cuttings from this vineyard, so we still have this genetic material.

Well, there are a number of these heirloom or "suitcase" clones that don't come to us through approved channels, through the university. A lot of them would have never made it through the university because they express some kind of defect, whether it's a small crop or a disease of some sort. So the university wouldn't propagate them.

Instead, they come from individuals who have visited famous vineyards in Europe and taken cuttings and sewn them into their jackets or put them in their suitcases and brought them here—smuggled them, in effect. And then passed them along from one generation to the next, like you pass down family heirlooms.

A lot of them make interesting wine, and we're willing to deal with the fact that they have super-low crops or that they have some disease that makes for delayed ripening or a shorter lifespan—maybe twenty years instead of forty. Our bottom line is, the wine is exceptional, and that's reason to save them. But a researcher's criteria would be, "Well, if they're not really productive, then the farmer isn't going to make enough of a living, because he gets paid by the ton. So they're not suitable clones." That's why at Etude we pay for grapes by the acre now, not by the ton.

Historically wineries have always paid growers by the ton, just as shoppers purchase grapes by the pound. But there's an inherent conflict of interest in that system because large crops can diminish wine quality. For example, a vine may produce more grapes than will ripen, especially if the summer is cool. In that case, the winemaker may want to reduce the size of the crop—often over the grower's objections—so that what remains on the vine will get ripe.

The logic of paying by the acre is that the winery that seeks to have low tonnage and more concentrated fruit and, hence, more concentrated wine, takes the extra cost upon itself. If we pay by the acre, the grower's incentive is no longer to grow more tons. If we reduce the crop, our costs go up, but it doesn't take money out of the grower's pocket. He's guaranteed a per-acre price that's equivalent to a handsome per-ton price.

I admire Tony for choosing to make Pinot Gris and Pinot Blanc, white wines that are unfamiliar to many. It gets tiresome to drink the same varieties all the time. That's partly why I'm keeping the old-vine Petite Sirah and Zinfandel that were planted around my house instead of replanting to Cabernet Sauvignon. But that's a hard decision to make if you're bottom line–driven.

Other varieties could be grown in Napa, but would they pay the bills? I mean, there's always the struggle between what's well adapted to a site and climate, and what the marketplace pressures are. The fact that Zinfandel is rarely grown in Napa anymore is a crime because there were some great old Zin vineyards here. But they don't pay the bills the way Cabernet does. You can grow Zinfandel and sell it for twenty-five dollars a bottle or grow Cabernet and sell it for fifty dollars.

Not that, when it comes to business, I take my own best advice. Twenty years ago, I was telling clients that they didn't want to be in the Pinot Noir business because, quite frankly, there was very little market for it. We hadn't figured out how to make them consistently, and certainly we couldn't sell them for nearly as much as you could sell Cabernet for. But for me, it was a personal quest that turned into a business.

Pinot Noir is the best teacher of technique. It's so unforgiving and temperamental, and it's also transparent. It allows you to see whether you've handled it well. If the balance is off in Pinot Noir, it's painfully off, where you might not even notice a little imbalance in a more robust grape like Syrah or Cabernet.

So if Pinot Noir is such a good teacher, what have we learned?

That, in California, virtually every year it needs to be crop-thinned. It's inherently a very fruitful variety. There are a few of these "heirloom clones" that are chronically low-producers, but most Pinot Noir selections are really bountiful. That's probably one of the reasons why it's such an ancient variety. I've seen clusters growing right out of the trunks, and I've never seen that in any other variety. Cabernet is pretty self-regulating at a good quality level, but Pinot is not very forgiving of a big crop. With the exception of the heirlooms, I don't know of a clone that doesn't need some crop adjustment or some catering to its idiosyncrasies.

Dorothy Tchelistcheff (see page 57) told me that her husband, André, only made two Pinot Noirs he was really proud of in his long career at Beaulieu Vineyard. I wondered if Tony also felt he didn't "nail it" very often.

Pinot Noir is extremely humbling. Every year we allow for about 20 percent of the Pinot Noir to not make the grade, whereas with Cabernet, it can be as little as 5 percent. And in some years, a third of the vintage doesn't make our standard. [These wines are sold in the bulk market, before bottling.] Being rigorous in your selection is one of the ways you protect the integrity of your label. Even the most gifted growers or winemakers don't bat a thousand every year.

The way to distinguish talent and rigor, I think, would be to look at how consistent a winery is in the off years. And sometimes that's not a matter of doing a better job, but of being unwilling to compromise. I walked away from an entire vintage of Cabernet in 1988, one of the worst years in two decades. My business was just starting and it seemed like a monumental loss, but I still think it was the right thing to do.

Pinot Noir is the best teacher of technique. It's so unforgiving and temperamental.

Tony's clients must have been sorry to see him go. In the consulting world, he was unusual in that he didn't have a winning "formula." He wanted each winery he worked for to have its own signature. I applaud that because I'm bothered by the homogenization I see as more wineries try to make wine to please a handful of critics.

Chardonnay's a perfect example. I mean, you're hard-pressed to find one that tastes different from another. They're sort of interchangeable. There's not really any courage of style there.

One of the challenges for me in handling five or six estates was how to make each of them sing individually. You have to have the handling subservient to some sense of style, and that's a delicate phenomenon. It would have been possible to make Araujo and Spottswoode taste more alike than apart if I attempted to, but that was certainly not the ambition. The ambition was to see if we couldn't express really distinctive styles for each, so that meant different fermentation regimens, different barrel regimens and a lot of subtle variations in technique, but the clues always came from how the grapes tasted in the field.

Now his focus is entirely on his own projects: building Etude and establishing a presence in Oregon. Tony and his wife, Michelle, bought some property there recently and plan to make Oregon Pinot Noir and sparkling wine under a new label: Soter.

Oregon was affordable and it's also our roots. I was born there and my wife was raised there. And I love the taste of Oregon Pinot Noir. I think of it as a retirement project. We're building a little place to live, planting the vines, making the first wines. I've never had an opportunity to make sparkling wine before, and I'd like to explore it because I'm disappointed with a lot of the typical domestic sparkling wine and a lot of French wine, too.

Ours is going to be a sparkling wine that's grown first and made second. I think the great mythology about sparkling wine is that it all happens in the cellar. But I hope ours will demonstrate that a more satisfying sparkling wine is one that actually tastes like it was made from ripe grapes, not from grapes that are excruciatingly acidic.

It's a little technical trick to get a good, mature taste in the grapes at a sugar level that still allows you to do the second fermentation in the bottle. Because the more mature your grapes, the harder it is to get the second fermentation to finish. If people pick at 18° sugar, that gives them a generous fudge factor to have the fermentation finish. If you pick at 21° or 22°, you have very little room to tread, but you have vastly more flavor.

Now I see why Tony called his winery Etude (French for "study"). He's a perpetual student, never satisfied that he's got it all figured out. When he gets close to the answer (as anyone would say he is with Pinot Noir and Cabernet Sauvignon), he takes on another challenge, like sparkling wine.

It's probably fair to say that I've been led more by my own curiosity about the craft than by the fastest way to make a buck in the wine business. It's all about perfecting the craft. What I loved about André Tchelistcheff was that, at the age of ninety, he still had that twinkle in his eye for a great wine, and he still had the ambition. I've just always hoped that I could grow that old and still maintain that passion for great wine.

GROWTH

What's Yeast Got to Do With It?

Just as bread needs yeast to rise, wine grapes need yeast to ferment. Not long ago, most Napa Valley winemakers inoculated their crushed grapes with cultured dry yeast isolated from wine regions around the world. Supply houses offer dozens of yeasts from Burgundy, Bordeaux, California, and South America; all the winemaker has to do is rehydrate the yeast in warm water, then stir it into the tank to launch the fermentation. But in

recent years, some winemakers have decided not to inoculate the must (the skins, seeds, and juice) and to let the fermentation proceed with only the yeasts naturally present.

"Wherever there are grapes and wine, there are yeasts," says Jack Stuart, general manager and winemaker at Silverado Vineyards. "They are present in the atmosphere and on the surfaces of equipment and walls in the winery."

Most of the time, these indigenous yeasts (also called "native" yeasts) can turn grape juice into wine with no help from cultured yeast. And in the opinion of some winemakers, the results are better.

David Ramey, winemaker at Rudd Vineyards and Winery and proprietor of Ramey Wine Cellars, has been a fan of indigenous yeast fermentations since the early 1990s. His early experiments were so encouraging that he quickly adopted the technique.

"In every case, the wine made with indigenous yeast was more complex aromatically," says David. "The texture was more delicate, yet fuller and rounder at the same time. That may sound like a contradiction but, in fact, that's what we often look for in wine—something soft on the palate, but at the same time, powerful, rich, and voluptuous."

The oak was better integrated in Chardonnays fermented with native yeasts, says David. So was the buttery quality that comes from malolactic fermentation. "There was just a more seamless, harmonious character," says the winemaker.

So why don't all winemakers dump their purchased yeast and go native?

"We haven't been able to determine that uninoculated fermentations are really any better or worse," says Jack, who has experimented with them at Silverado. "The advantage to inoculating is that you know what you've got. You've got a pure, isolated wine

yeast during the active part of the fermentation. The problem with uninoculated fermentations is, if you get the wrong yeast growing and making it difficult for a healthy yeast to do the fermentation, you can have a number of problems such as off odors, weird flavors, or stuck [incomplete] fermentation."

David acknowledges that wines fermented with native yeasts sometimes fail to complete fermentation. In those cases, he steps in with a cultured yeast to get the job done. But even then, he thinks the wines benefit from the typically slow native yeast fermentation.

"White wines especially can go mostly dry, then the last little bit of fermentation can take three or four weeks, or even a couple of months," says David. "The wine stays cloudy all that time, whereas when you inoculate, the fermentation goes rapidly and the wine falls bright quickly. But down the road, my sense is that it's less complex and textured."

Jack Stuart remains unconvinced.

"Louis Pasteur showed that spoilage of wine occurs when fermentation does not proceed healthfully," says Jack. "When you get a red wine that does not go through fermentation and you have significant sugar left in it, it tastes like something between Lambrusco and boysenberry syrup. It's not something you can sell.

"Uninoculated fermentation is risky business and some people seem willing to take that risk and think there's a benefit. To us, the benefit hasn't been demonstrated. We think any flavor or aroma differences that can be attributed to yeast strains probably don't last very long. Or if they do, they're less important than clonal selection, site, type of oak used, and so on. We try to remain open-minded, but we don't think yeast, per se, amounts to all that much in the finished wine."

Joseph

Phelps

Joseph Phelps's father was a farmer turned insurance salesman who started a small building and remodeling business later in life. After college and the Navy, Joe joined his father in the business, and the company quickly grew.

Early on, Joe developed a taste for wine—inspired in part by a college roommate whose family had a wine cellar. In 1966, he opened a company office in Northern California, which did a lot of work on BART, the San Francisco Bay Area's future mass transit system. Then his banker asked him to bid on the construction of a new St. Helena winery to be named Souverain Cellars (now Rutherford Hill). Joe's company built Souverain, and one thing led to another. By 1973, he was in the wine business himself, establishing Joseph Phelps Vineyards in St. Helena.

This used to be a purebred polled Hereford cattle ranch, the Connolly Ranch. There was not a grape on six hundred acres here, but there was a lot of beautiful terrain. I felt this was one of the last large open spaces in Napa Valley, and I had an affection for it. So I became acquainted with Mr. Connolly, who was terminally ill with bone cancer and had to auction his herd off in 1972, and I began to talk with him, and finally in early 1973, he decided he would sell it to me. He was a very good businessman. It wasn't cheap.

Joe took possession of the property in the spring of 1973, and by the fall of 1974 he was crushing grapes in his new winery. (It helps to be your own building contractor.) For his winemaker, he hired Walter Schug, who had been working for Gallo in Napa and Sonoma.

We planted Cabernet, Zinfandel, Sauvignon Blanc, and some Chardonnay. When we finished planting, we had about twenty acres uncommitted. I had always loved Hermitage and Côte Rotie and the wines of the Rhône Valley, so I asked Walter to try to obtain some cuttings for Syrah. Not Petite Sirah, but the original French Syrah. He talked

This was one of the last large open spaces in Napa Valley, and I had an affection for it.

to Professor Olmo [Harold Olmo from U.C. Davis], and Olmo convinced him that we could find Syrah right across the river at Christian Brothers.

Olmo had brought Syrah into the university's experiment station at Oakville in 1939 to try to get people interested in it. He was unsuccessful because Syrah was relatively shy-bearing compared to Petite Sirah and Zinfandel. So it just fell by the wayside. By 1946, he had convinced the Christian Brothers to move the Syrah from the experiment station to their Wheeler Ranch and to keep ten acres alive for him. They did, but they put it into Christian Brothers Burgundy and never made a Syrah from it.

In 1973, we got budwood from the Wheeler Ranch and planted our own, and we made a 1974 Syrah. It was pretty well ahead of its time. Now Syrah is one of the big three.

Our experience with Syrah is generally the opposite of the Australian experience with the grape, which is called Shiraz there. They do warm-climate Syrah and it makes wonderful wine. We keep moving the vineyards south [where it's cooler], and we find that the closer we get to the bay, the better the results. Some of the best Syrah we make now comes from Monterey County.

Our experience with Syrah is generally the opposite of the Australian experience.

In those early days, everybody knew and helped everybody else. Joe Heitz crushed Phelps's Pinot Noir in 1973 because Phelps's winery wasn't ready. Another important friend was Ivan Shoch, one of Robert Mondavi's early investors. Through Shoch, Joe was able to lease the Backus family ranch from 1977 until he bought it in 1996. It's south of the Oakville Crossroad on the Silverado Trail, just below Dalla Valle and across the street from Jean Phillips's Screaming Eagle—a pretty exclusive neighborhood. Phelps's Backus Vineyard Cabernet Sauvignon has been a standout from the start.

Even better known are the vineyard-designated Cabernets that Phelps made from the Eisele Vineyard from 1975 until 1991 (with the exception of two vintages, when the fruit didn't measure up). Bart and Daphne Araujo (see page 232) own this vineyard now, but the wines helped make Joe's reputation. I couldn't imagine why he didn't buy the property when the Eiseles were ready to sell.

Lack of foresight. We felt we already had quite a bit of Cabernet land. Now we're looking for more. We just didn't appreciate the value as much as we should have.

In Joe's defense, the deal really didn't make sense for him then. The asking price for the Eisele Vineyard reflected its value as a possible winery site, but Joe didn't need another winery. He already had two on his property—one for red wines and one for whites.

So he passed on Eisele, but it would be hard to accuse Joe of lacking foresight. His launch of Insignia in 1974 was pathbreaking. Here was a high-priced red wine without a varietal name on it. Was it a Cabernet? Was it a Merlot? What was it? Without intending to, he had launched the concept of "meritage" wine—a high-end blended red wine with a proprietary name.

*From the start, Joe
befriended top chefs
like Alice Waters and
Jeremiah Tower.*

I had a fixation against using the term 'Reserve.' We looked for two years for another name, and this one just happened to come to me while shaving. Now there are Insignias being made in Chile and Argentina and Australia. But it was a very fortunate brainstorm.

Our concept changed a bit as we went along. Originally Insignia was intended to be the best red wine we had, whether it was Merlot or Cabernet, but within two years, we had changed to a Bordeaux blend: Cabernet Sauvignon, Merlot, Cabernet Franc. Every vintage is slightly different. A typical Insignia of the 1990s has been probably 75 to 80 percent Cabernet Sauvignon, with Merlot and Petit Verdot and less or no Cabernet Franc now.

Joe's rolling six-hundred-acre spread is one of the most sensitively landscaped and maintained in the valley. And he has taken pains to secure its future. Not long ago, he granted a conservation easement on 450 acres of the property to the Napa County Land Trust.

I would never want to see it change much, and that's one way to make sure it won't. It's a preservation easement, which means the property can never be subdivided and no houses can be added. We can use the land for agriculture and winemaking, but everything else is in preservation. About one hundred and fifty acres can't even be farmed. They're called "forever wild." I would encourage others to look into this. It's a good direction to take.

Where the Phelps property meets the Silverado Trail, there's a beautiful little green schoolhouse I've always wondered about. Joe says it was built in the 1860s and was a functioning county school until the end of World War II. He's actually talked to people who attended school there. He restored the inside and used it as a guest house for people in the wine trade. It was quite in demand, but now it's reserved for friends and family.

Joe is a terrific cook and food lover—and great fun to cook for. From the start, he befriended top chefs like Alice Waters and Jeremiah Tower and brought them to the winery for special events. He also bought and revitalized the Oakville Grocery in Oakville (there are now several locations), making it one of the leading specialty food stores in the country. Joe says he bought the business for his children, but I think he bought it so he would have a local place to buy great cheese, bread, and olive oil.

He has a reputation for treating all his employees like family, and people rarely leave Phelps. His vineyard manager, Bulmaro Montes, has been there since day one, in 1973; his executive assistant, Evelyne Deis, since 1975, his winemaker, Craig Williams, since 1976, winery president Tom Shelton, since 1992. Employees own 49 percent of the stock in the various winery companies. And from those who do leave, you never hear a sour word.

I don't think there's anything more important in operating a business than having the support and participation of employees in decisionmaking and in the execution of responsibilities. They need to feel that they can call their own shots.

With leadership like that, it's not surprising that Joseph Phelps Vineyards has grown way beyond Joe's initial idea. He imagined it as a twenty-thousand-case winery. Now he's talking about building another winery in Sonoma County and topping out at 145,000 cases.

We don't have a mission statement, but if we did, it would probably have to do with innovation. We're never too timid about trying something new and different, and I encourage that in everybody who works here. Now I'm being encouraged to be the same way by Tom and Craig. I'm too old-fashioned to suit everybody here.

Joe Phelps granted the Napa County Land Trust a conservation easement on 450 acres of his property to protect it from future development.

A Little Summer Night Music

One thing I've always liked about Napa Valley is how it manages to blend the pleasures of small-town life with some of the cultural features of a city. Many of the people who live here have also lived in cultural centers like New York and San Francisco, and they have no intention of settling in a place, no matter how beautiful, where there's no art or music. So they bring art and music here.

Music in the Vineyards, a summer concert series, was started in 1995 and has blossomed over the years. The executive director, Gail Adams, says she didn't know if anybody would show up the first year. Now almost every program sells out.

Today, the series consists of ten chamber music performances in Napa Valley in August, in beautiful vineyard or winery settings. Maybe the location will be the Joseph Phelps Vineyards barrel room—it seats only sixty—and the performance a Beethoven recital-with-lecture by a prominent pianist. Maybe you'll hear Handel and Britten in the caves at Clos Pegase, or Dvorak and Mendelssohn at the RMS Brandy Distillery. Sometimes, the locations themselves become a big part of the draw, as when the Novak family agreed to host a concert on the lawn at Spottswoode, their lovely old home in St. Helena.

Wherever your tickets take you, the audience will be small, as it was meant to be for chamber music, and the performers will be artists of national caliber. The programs and the musicians are chosen by Michael Adams (Gail's son) and his wife, Daria Adams, who are themselves professional musicians in Minnesota. Gail lives in Sonoma County, and it was while visiting her that Michael and Daria got the idea for a music festival in neighboring Napa. "There's no better place on earth for great music to join great food and great wine," says Michael.

What I love about these musical evenings is that they are learning experiences. Michael or one of the other musicians always introduces the music and tells you a little about its structure or clues you in on something to listen for. The other great thing about Music in the Vineyards is that wine is served at intermission—delicious Napa Valley wine, at no further cost.

And if you're in the valley in the spring, don't miss Kitchens in the Vineyards. That's the annual fundraiser for the music series, and it's as popular as the concerts. On one Saturday in late April or early May, you can buy a ticket for a self-guided tour of a half-dozen private Napa Valley kitchens selected for their great design and style. I was flattered to have my own home kitchen on the tour recently, and I know people find it inspiring to get a glimpse of others' design ideas.

Koerner and Joan

Rombauer

I'm grateful to count Koerner and Joan Rombauer in my circle of vintner friends. I don't know how many Christmases my family has spent at their home, with Koerner playing Santa for my three daughters. Joan is a delicate-featured woman with a gentle, sweet nature, while Koerner is a man of large appetites. He loves flying planes and collecting old cars, and he adores gutsy food like anchovies and short ribs.

Koerner and Joan grew up in the same small farming town in Southern California. They went to the same high school, a few years apart, but they didn't meet until Koerner came home after college. Then they married and began to adjust their lives around his career. Koerner had been to Air Force flight school and was flying on weekends for the California Air Guard when Braniff Airlines offered him a commercial pilot's job.

Koerner: That was in 1965. We had two little kids and had just finished building a new house in Escondido [near San Diego]. Then Braniff hired me, so I left. I told Joan, "Sell the house and I'll meet you in Texas."

Joan: That's a true statement. He had found a house outside of Dallas, a little country estate. But there was nobody else out there. It was Lonelyville.

They lived there for two years, until Braniff transferred Koerner to Travis Air Force base near San Francisco to fly troops to Vietnam under government contract; then, after another brief stint in Dallas, he was moved back to San Francisco in 1972 and began flying DC-8s to South America. That's when Koerner and Joan began looking for a home in the Napa Valley.

Koerner: We were looking for a rural setting where our children could grow up, and St. Helena had that—and still does, in my opinion. It's the kind of area where you can keep track of your children. It's a setting we both grew up

in and we wanted our kids to have the same. So we moved here for the kids' schooling originally. We weren't really interested in wine.

The Valley was a completely different place in 1972. There were only about forty wineries, few restaurants, and fewer tourists. Finding a suitable family home in this land of prune and walnut orchards was a challenge.

Joan: We rented a house on Highway 29 for a year. Every Monday, I would go to the realtors—there were only two at the time, I believe—and I'd ask them if they had anything new. And they would say, "Well, no. But if you find something, let us know and we'll be glad to show you through." And we did find something.

They found a house with a barn and some Zinfandel vines on a hill just north of St. Helena. The kids had room for 4-H projects but were still close to town. Today, they're still in the same house but they've been joined by a winery: Rombauer Vineyards.

In 1976, Koerner and Joan were at a 4-H potluck dinner when an acquaintance began talking about a new winery venture that needed another partner. So, four years after they moved to the Valley with little or no interest in wine, Koerner and Joan became active partners in the new Conn Creek Winery. Joan worked in the office and Koerner helped in the cellar during his time off from Braniff.

Koerner: In 1979, Conn Creek built a new winery building [it's now Villa Mt. Eden], and my job was to order all the new equipment. So I got to know all the suppliers, and when we got ready to build our own winery, we knew what we wanted. We cut our teeth at Conn Creek. We learned the business from the ground up.

In 1982, they sold their interest in Conn Creek and began building their own winery next to their home. Koerner and his winemaker, Bob Levy (who's now at Harlan Estate), were the general contractors because money was tight.

Koerner: Justin Meyer [the former owner of Silver Oak Wine Cellars] always said there's only one way to go into the wine business and that's broke. Because then you've *got* to make it work. You can't waste money, let's put it that way. You analyze everything you buy. Is this really going to help us make better wine? If it did, we'd buy it. If it didn't, we wouldn't.

The winery had extra capacity from the start, and the Rombauers soon began to make that pay. They offered custom crushing to other vintners who might not have a winery, or who might have exceeded their capacity, an arrangement that's still common in the industry, and still done at Rombauer today.

Say you want to launch your own brand and you have enough money to buy grapes and barrels, but not enough to build your own facility. Or maybe you're not willing to invest in a building until you know your brand stands a chance. You can pay a winery like Rombauer to process your grapes accord-

ing to your specifications. Neyers was made at Rombauer for years, until Bruce and Barbara Neyers bought their own building. So were Tony Soter's Etude wines (see page 164) and Cathy Corison's wines (see page 225). My own wine—Chiarello Family Vineyards—is also made at Rombauer.

Income from custom crushing helped Rombauer survive the early years. Koerner continued to fly for Braniff while he and Joan worked to build their brand. In the meantime, Joan went to work for Warren Winiarski at Stag's Leap Wine Cellars (see page 150) and learned the sales part of the business.

In 1988, Koerner developed an infection that went undiagnosed for six months. It eventually attacked his heart and he fought for his life for weeks. He finally got back on his feet, although he couldn't return to Braniff. But the experience had a silver lining.

Joan: After that, Koerner stayed at the winery. And if you look at the records, that's when our popularity started—when Koerner started working with the blends.

Koerner: It's not a hobby business. You have to be there. You have to pay attention, and the staff has to have guidance.

About the time Koerner left commercial aviation, the Rombauers had a stroke of luck. They were offered some Chardonnay grapes in Carneros that allowed Koerner to make the style of wine he had come to love: rich, creamy, fully malolactic Chardonnay, like Kistler in Sonoma County. The public loved it, too. Since then, Rombauer's Carneros Chardonnays have been critical winners and a popular success.

Koerner: It's horrible in a way because we get a lot of flak from our distributors. "Why don't you make more?" Well, the issue is not making more. The issue is getting grapes to make this kind of wine, so we don't change the taste or the feel. It's about consistency—like at Tra Vigne. You may make subtle changes but you don't make huge changes because you know your customers are coming back for a reason. They like what they had before.

The Rombauer Chardonnay is very particular. I would almost say the flavor is addictive. Probably 60 percent of the white wine I drink at home is Rombauer Chardonnay. It's what I want at the end of a monster day, when I've worked eighteen hours and I just crave a giant glass of wine.

The Rombauers also make Zinfandel from the grapes on their property—grapes that they used to sell to Beringer for White Zinfandel before they realized their potential. They also make Merlot and Cabernet Sauvignon, increasingly from their own grapes, and a Bordeaux-style blend called Le Meilleur du Chai, meaning the winery's best. They got that idea from Christian Moueix, the owner of Dominus Estate, whose family owns Château Pétrus in Bordeaux.

Christian was a custom-crush client at Rombauer for years (until Dominus built its own winery) and he and the Rombauers became friends. When Koerner and Joan visited France years ago, they stayed with Christian and his wife at their house in the countryside. One night, when everyone was too tired to go out for dinner, they sat around the Moueix kitchen in their bathrobes and ate scrambled eggs with Pétrus.

The camaraderie the Rombauers share with fellow vintners extends to winemaking, too.

Koerner: We don't want any bad wines coming out of the Napa Valley, period. We want everybody to be a four- or five-star. Our winemaker is part of a local winemaker group that gets together once a month, and if somebody has a problem wine, they bring it. The other guys taste it. And they'll say, "Well, I had this problem last year. Here's what you do." So we're continually elevating the quality of the product here in the Valley.

The Rombauers' two children are both active in the winery. Their son K.R. is the national sales director, and daughter Sheana works in public relations. Koerner and Joan knew better than to push, but naturally they're pleased that their kids seem eager to carry on what they started.

As I figure it, that makes the fourth generation of Rombauers in the food and wine business in America. Koerner's great-aunt was Irma Rombauer, who wrote the *Joy of Cooking* in 1931. Ethan Becker, Irma's grandson, occasionally comes to the winery for events and book signings, and guess what cookbook is sold in the tasting room?

Koerner, who pilots his own Citation jet, might say life so far has been an interesting ride—from the citrus ranches of Southern California to Napa Valley via Grapevine, Texas. Both he and Joan are genuinely modest about their success, as if they still can't quite believe what's happened.

Koerner: You know, it's the American dream. You rub a bunch of credit cards and a couple of nickels together and you end up with a project like we have. It's pretty amazing, and it can still happen here for anyone.

A Counter Dinner of Koerner's Favorites

> FRITTO MISTO *with* TWO-MUSTARD SAUCE
> MINESTRA DELL'ORTO
> WINE-BRAISED SHORT RIBS *with* CREAMY POLENTA
> ROMBAUER JAM CAKE

When I designed my home kitchen, I knew I wanted a counter for casual meals, where guests could eat and still watch the action at the stove. I even had the upholstered stools made extra wide for comfort. People can dive in to help if they want, or just observe.

After years of cooking for large groups, I love entertaining almost one-on-one, when I can plan a meal precisely around my friends' tastes. I had a great time when Koerner and Joan Rombauer came for dinner, and there was no question of what to make.

Koerner loves short ribs, so I knew those would be the centerpiece, served with Rombauer Zinfandel. To start, we had fritto misto, which I thought would be fun to cook together and would go well with their Chardonnay. Then I wanted to share a dish my mother used to make: the minestra, or all-green vegetable soup, from the fall garden. (In her southern Italian dialect, it was menisha.) For dessert, I turned to the Joy of Cooking and found a recipe for a moist, old-fashioned jam cake.

Fritto Misto *with* Two-Mustard Sauce

This rice coating is the best crispy coating I have ever tasted. Not only is it great on fried fish and vegetables and even fried chicken, but I also dust it on fish fillets before sautéing.

This recipe makes extra rice coating, but if you're getting your blender dirty, you may as well make a lot. The mixture freezes well in an airtight container, and it's handy to have around for any kind of deep-frying. I rarely use table salt, but it's the best choice in the rice coating because it stays evenly distributed.

A mandoline or V-slicer will help you slice the lemon and onion thinly.

For the sauce:

⅓ **cup honey mustard**

⅓ **cup Dijon mustard**

¼ **cup Champagne vinegar**

2 **teaspoons black or yellow mustard seed, toasted**

1 **teaspoon minced shallots**

Sea salt, preferably gray salt (see Note on page 26)

For the batter:

1 **cup uncooked Arborio rice**

1 **cup semolina**

3 **cups all-purpose flour**

2 **tablespoons salt**

1 **teaspoon freshly ground pepper**

1 **pound cleaned calamari (not giant squid)**

1 **medium fennel bulb, sliced lengthwise ⅛-inch thick**

1 **medium onion, very thinly sliced**

1 **lemon, very thinly sliced (discard ends)**

Buttermilk for moistening

Peanut or canola oil for deep-frying

Make the sauce: Whisk together mustards, vinegar, mustard seed, shallots, and salt to taste.

Make the rice coating: Grind the rice in a blender until very fine. In a bowl, stir together the ground rice, semolina, flour, salt, and pepper.

Slit calamari bodies open so they lie flat. Place calamari (bodies and tentacles), fennel, onion, and lemon in separate bowls. Toss each with enough buttermilk to moisten them.

Heat several inches of oil to 375° F in a deep fryer or wide, deep pot.

While oil heats, drain the calamari, then place some of it in a strainer over a large bowl. Sprinkle generously with rice coating and shake; repeat until the calamari is well coated. Fry until golden-brown and crisp, then transfer to a tray lined with paper towels. Season immediately with salt. Transfer to a low oven to keep warm. Repeat with remaining calamari, then drain, coat, and fry the fennel, onion, and lemon slices in the same way, working in batches and transferring them to the low oven as they are done. Do not crowd the fryer.

Put a generous pool of mustard sauce on each plate, then top with an assortment of fried squid, fennel, onion, and lemon.

SERVES 4

When I was growing up, my mom would make a soup like this in late summer and fall, when the close-to-bolting greens in the garden were getting too coarse and pungent for anything else. Let your own garden or market determine what greens you use, but a variety will produce the best flavor. At my house, we would have this substantial soup for supper, with bread, extra virgin olive oil, and a wedge of pecorino cheese for dessert.

⅔ cup dried cannellini beans

2 ounces prosciutto, in one piece

½ medium onion, peeled

1 small rib celery, halved

1 small carrot, peeled and halved

Sea salt, preferably gray salt (see Note on page 26)

Freshly ground pepper

3 tablespoons extra virgin olive oil, plus more for drizzling

½ bulb fennel, diced

1 cup chopped onion

1½ teaspoons minced garlic

2 quarts roughly hand-torn and lightly packed greens, such as chard, collards, mustard, spinach, and cabbage

⅓ cup tomato *passato* (fresh tomato passed through a food mill) or canned crushed tomatoes

1½ cups peeled and diced russet potato

1 cup diced zucchini

½ cup diced green beans

½ teaspoon toasted and ground fennel seed, plus ¼ teaspoon if not using fennel fronds

2 whole small jalapeño chilies

¼ cup minced fennel fronds, if available

3 cups bread cubes from day-old bread

Cover dried beans with cold water. Bring to a boil, cover, remove from heat and let stand 1 hour, then drain. Return beans to a large pot with 2 quarts water, prosciutto, onion half, celery, and carrot. Simmer gently, uncovered, until beans are tender, about 1½ hours. Cool in broth. Remove prosciutto, onion, celery, and carrot; dice prosciutto and set aside.

In a large pot, heat 1½ tablespoons olive oil, then add diced fennel, chopped onion, garlic, and a pinch of salt. Cook slowly until vegetables are softened but not browned, about 15 minutes. Add greens and toss with tongs until they wilt evenly; adjust heat to keep vegetables from burning. Add beans and their broth, tomato, potatoes, zucchini, green beans, fennel seed, and whole chilies. Simmer gently for 30 minutes. Stir in prosciutto and fennel fronds, if using, then season with salt and pepper. Transfer chilies to a small bowl and discard stems. Mash with a fork, adding a little broth and potato from the pot to make a thick purée.

Preheat oven to 325° F. Toss bread cubes with remaining 1½ tablespoons olive oil. Season with salt and pepper. Bake until crisp and golden, 15 to 20 minutes. Divide bread among 6 warm soup bowls. Ladle soup over bread, then drizzle with olive oil. Pass the chili condiment on the side.

MAKES 2 QUARTS (6 SERVINGS)

WINE-BRAISED SHORT RIBS

I was looking for a way to cook short ribs until perfectly tender without having the meat fall apart. As I discovered after much experimentation, brining is the answer; it firms the meat enough to keep it on the bone and adds flavor, too.

We weren't sure we could get away with serving short ribs at Tra Vigne. Some of the partners thought the dish might be too rustic, but customers like Koerner Rombauer have made them a hit. He ordered them the first week they were on the menu, and now he's disappointed when they're not.

For the brine:

2 quarts water

2 cups brown sugar

2 cups kosher salt

2 tablespoons juniper berries

3 bay leaves

4 cross-cut short ribs, about 1 pound each

Olive oil

2 cups coarsely chopped onion

1 cup coarsely chopped carrot

1 cup coarsely chopped celery

1 cup red wine

1 quart chicken stock

Make the brine: Bring all ingredients to a boil in a saucepan, stirring to dissolve sugar. Cool completely. Cover short ribs with brine and refrigerate 3 hours.

Preheat oven to 325° F. Remove short ribs from brine and pat dry. Heat a large high-sided sauté pan over moderately high heat until hot. Add a film of olive oil. When oil begins to smoke, brown short ribs on all sides. (They brown quickly because of the sugar in the brine.) When richly browned, place in a dish that can go from stovetop to oven.

Add onion, carrot, and celery to sauté pan and cook over moderately high heat until vegetables are well caramelized. Transfer vegetables to dish with short ribs. Add red wine to sauté pan and simmer until reduced by half, scraping up any stuck-on bits with a wooden spoon. Add stock, bring to a boil and pour over short ribs. Bring short ribs to a boil on top of the stove, then cover and bake until fork-tender, about 3 hours.

SERVES 4

Rombauer Jam Cake

We all fell in love with this taste of the past and quickly added it to our recipe files. You will, too. Adapted from Joy of Cooking *by Irma S. Rombauer and Marion Rombauer Becker (The Bobbs-Merrill Company, 1976).*

1½ cups sifted all-purpose flour

1 teaspoon baking powder

½ teaspoon baking soda

½ teaspoon ground cloves

1 teaspoon cinnamon

1 teaspoon nutmeg

6 tablespoons butter or shortening

1 cup packed brown sugar

2 eggs

3 tablespoons sour cream

1 cup raspberry or blackberry jam

½ cup chopped toasted walnuts

For the quick brown-sugar icing:

1½ cups brown sugar

5 tablespoons heavy cream

2 teaspoons butter

⅛ teaspoon salt

½ teaspoon vanilla

Preheat oven to 350° F. Butter a 7-inch tube pan or Bundt pan. Sift together flour, baking powder, baking soda, cloves, cinnamon, and nutmeg.

Cream butter and brown sugar until light. Beat in eggs, one at a time. Beat in sour cream. Stir the flour mixture into the butter mixture until barely blended. Stir in jam and nuts. Pour into buttered pan. Bake until done, about 30 minutes. When cool, invert the cake onto a platter and ice with quick brown-sugar icing.

Make the icing: Combine brown sugar, cream, butter, and salt and cook slowly to the boiling point. Remove from heat. Cool slightly, then add vanilla. Beat the icing until it can be spread.

MAKES ONE 7-INCH CAKE

GROWTH

Defining a Barrel Regime

Many people think of wine as containing only grapes and yeast, but most winemakers consider barrels an ingredient, too. In the world of fine wine, barrels are an important component of flavor, so the best winemakers are continually evaluating which barrels to use. Early winemakers may have used oak barrels for storage because the wood was ubiquitous and inexpensive. But over time, consumers have come to like the taste that oak imparts. Today, winemakers can choose among hundreds of different coopers (barrelmakers) using oak from France, America, Yugoslavia, Russia, and elsewhere. The inside of the barrel may be lightly or heavily charred by the cooper to impart a toasty flavor to the wine. The strips of oak, or staves, that make up the barrel may be thick or thin. And the hand of the cooper makes a difference, too. To complicate matters, wineries may want some of their barrels new, some used.

Deciding which barrels to buy and how long to keep a wine in barrel is a large part of the winemaker's art.

"I would say integration is the number-one goal—to get the characters that come from fruit, yeast, and barrel to be so well-knit, somebody can't pull the wine apart," says Ashley Heisey, the former winemaker at Far Niente and now a consultant.

The barrel decision is ongoing in Far Niente's cellar. New coopers are constantly being tried and different barrel regimes assessed. At any one time, the winemaker may have both the Far Niente Chardonnay and the Cabernet Sauvignon in barrels from eight different coopers—half of them core suppliers, and half of them on trial.

"Some people believe that you just find your favorites and use them one hundred percent," says Heisey, "but I think it's like coffee. It's better to blend. Then the wine's more complex and harder for somebody else to reproduce."

Typically Far Niente Chardonnay is aged half in new barrels, half in year-old. "I didn't want the Chardonnay to be too oaky," Heisey says. "I hope the person tasting it is noting its complexity and isn't saying, 'Ahh . . . oak.'"

Fermenting the Chardonnay in oak barrels—rather than fermenting it in stainless steel tanks, then transferring it to barrels to age—also enhances the wine, says Heisey. Both Far Niente's Chardonnay and Dolce, its dessert wine, are barrel-fermented. "Both wines have better oak integration for being barrel-fermented," she says. "You have the characteristics from the oak woven into the characteristics from the fruit and the lees [the spent yeast that falls to the bottom of the barrel]. It's to your advantage to get all these together as soon as possible."

Red grapes are crushed and the juice ferments with the bulky skins, so barrel fermentation isn't possible. But because red wines have more flavor and body than whites, they can take more new-oak aging, says Heisey. Depending on the strength and concentration of the vintage, Far Niente's Cabernet Sauvignon may go into 70 to 90 percent new barrels. Used barrels are sold to other wine producers who prefer a more neutral taste, a way of recuperating a small part of a new barrel's cost (about $600 apiece).

Barrels aren't just a flavoring agent; they also help the wine age by allowing a very slow oxidation. But being porous, they also allow wine to evaporate—at the rate of 1 to 2 percent a year or more, a portion known as "the angel's share." Cellar workers have to replace the lost wine periodically because wine in a partially filled barrel may spoil. At Far Niente and other fine wineries, winemakers reserve some of their best wine for this "topping-up" process so they're constantly elevating the quality in the barrel.

Architectural Gems

A handful of Napa Valley wineries occupy landmark nineteenth-century buildings that recall the earliest days of winemaking in the Valley. Beringer, Trefethen, Spottswoode, Schramsberg, Chateau Montelena, Markham, Niebaum-Coppola and Regusci are among those that continue to use historic premises. They're inspiring to visit because they remind us that Napa's renown as a wine region is longstanding.

Equally fascinating, however, are the striking contemporary structures built by the wine entrepreneurs of the late twentieth century. Although Napa Valley has its share of faux châteaux, it also has some magnificent examples of visionary modern architecture—buildings that function not only as efficient production facilities but, in some cases, as hospitality centers as well.

The Opus One winery (opposite, middle) in Oakville was completed in 1991. The joint venture of Robert Mondavi and the Baroness Philippine de Rothschild of Château Mouton-Rothschild in France, the winery was designed by architect Scott Johnson to blend elements of Old World and New. Surrounded by a grassy berm and barely visible from the road, the building seems to emerge from the earth like a giant mushroom. Incorporating redwood, stainless steel and cream-colored limestone, it marries classic architectural ideas of colonnades and courtyards with a low, open profile that embraces the Northern California light and landscape.

As passionate collectors of both modern art and wine-related artifacts from every age, Clos Pegase owners Jan and Mitsuko Shrem wanted a winery building that suggested a merging of wine and art. A discussion with the director of the San Francisco Museum of Modern Art led to the idea of a design competition, announced in mid-1984. The winner, chosen from ninety-six entries, was architect Michael Graves.

Graves' design for Clos Pegase (opposite, top) was completed in 1987 and surprised the Valley with its bold shapes and colors. Many admired it immediately as a dramatic departure from conventional winery architecture; others have only slowly come to realize how well its ancient Mediterranean themes work in the Napa Valley landscape and how well-suited the building is to a public display of art. The sculpture garden, with works by Richard Serra, Mark di Suvero, and others, is alone worth a visit to this Calistoga winery.

Although Dominus (opposite, bottom) is not open to the public, you can admire its subtle and highly original design from Highway 29 in Yountville. Owner Christian Moueix, whose family also owns Château Pétrus in Bordeaux, chose Swiss architects Herzog and de Meuron to build Dominus.

"We didn't want to build a French château or a Tuscan villa," says Cherise Moueix, Christian's wife. "We wanted the architects to respond to the landscape. When they asked Christian how he wanted the building to look, he said, 'I'd like it to be invisible. I want the winery to be about the grapes, not about the building.'"

To that end, the architects came up with the novel idea of a structure that would resemble a low rock wall, or natural rock outcropping. After an engineer said the architects' plan was not only sound but cost-effective, the Moueixes approved the use of steel baskets filled with unmortared rock—typically used as retaining walls on steep embankments—to create the winery walls. Air and light filter through these gabions, and two pass-throughs provide access and lovely views of the Mayacamas range beyond. "It was a little leap of faith," says Cherise, "but it's gratifying to have it work."

Dan and Margaret

Duckhorn

Dan and Margaret Duckhorn and I have had some fun times together cooking duck dinners at the winery for their guests. Dan is a hunting and fishing buddy and a dispenser of business advice who always keeps a fatherly eye on what I'm up to.

Margaret is one of the great ladies of Napa Valley—steady, level-headed, and a respected voice on all the political and social issues that swirl around wine. She is one of only two women ever to head the Napa Valley Vintners Association since it was founded nearly sixty years ago.

As a young couple, Dan and Margaret had little interest in wine. Margaret was a public health nurse, Dan a venture capitalist. But in the late 1960s, Dan's boss invested in a small grapevine nursery in Napa Valley, and Dan was sent up from San Francisco to run the business. Their timing was great: The nursery got in on the ground floor of the vineyard expansion in the Valley, providing an estimated 1½ million bench grafts, the fruiting vine grafted on to rootstock. The company also began managing some of these new vineyards because so many owners were absentee.

With the nursery business thriving, Dan and Margaret and their three young children moved to the Valley in 1973. They began buying wine and trying to become more critical tasters. But only two years later, the tide turned. Bordeaux prices collapsed, dragging Napa Valley prices down, too. The tax laws changed, eliminating vineyards as tax shelters. New planting slowed way down, and Dan's boss decided to pull the plug on the business.

By then, the Duckhorns were too taken with Napa Valley to consider moving back to the Bay Area. So they called some friends and put some money together to purchase the nursery property (ten acres for $50,000) and start a winery. They retrofitted the grafting shed to store oak barrels, and they bought three stainless steel fermentation tanks and put them under an oak tree. They also hired an unknown winemaker named Tom Rinaldi.

Tom had come recommended, but the Duckhorns were a little taken aback when a long-haired fel-

A few specimens from Dan Duckhorn's large and growing decoy collection.

low with a beard rode up on his motorcycle. This was a winemaker? But they couldn't afford to be choosy, so Tom joined the team and stayed at Duckhorn for more than twenty years.

In 1978, they made their first wines: a Merlot from grapes purchased from the Three Palms vineyard and a Cabernet Sauvignon blended from Stag's Leap and Howell Mountain grapes. Margaret continued nursing, serving as the sole nurse for the northern Napa Valley schools. Dan took some consulting work until the wines could provide some income.

Merlot was practically an unheard-of varietal then, but Dan was smitten by it. He and Ric Forman, then the winemaker at Sterling Vineyards, had gone to France together in 1977 and drunk a lot of Merlot.

Dan: I just liked the grape, and Ric was enamored of it. In business, there's a lot of luck involved and relying on your own intuition. If you have a sense that something is good, other people generally do, too. Some of the Cabernets that were being made then were trying to slap you in the face, they were so bold and tannic. We were young drinkers, and we liked Merlot because it tasted great.

Margaret: Back then, when you bought grapes, there were "sugar points." The grower got a little bonus if the grapes had more sugar, so growers were always trying to push the sugars higher. So you got these huge wines that were thick and tannic and chewy.

Dan: The wineries wanted intensity; the grower wanted the crop harvested. The longer the grapes stayed on the vine, the lower the tonnage and the greater the risk, right? So the winery, in order to encourage the grower to leave the grapes out there to get the intense wines, would offer bonus points. The grower got the base price for grapes at 22° Brix [percent sugar], another 10 percent at 23°, and another 15 percent for 24° Brix. The growers decided when to pick. You waited at the winery and they delivered the grapes.

Margaret: That's one of the things we walked away from. All our contracts were structured so that we made recommendations about when to pick and we hauled the fruit. It wasn't based on sugar and there was no bonus for sugar, but we paid a high price. We've done it the same way ever since.

The Duckhorns were charting new territory with a varietal Merlot—it wasn't like Americans had been clamoring for it. Back then, only sophisticated wine drinkers knew that Merlot was the dominant variety in the French region of Pomerol and in the prestigious Château Pétrus. How do you sell a wine that nobody knows?

In fact, says Dan, enough people knew about Pétrus to make the Duckhorn Merlot an immediate hit. It had no competition, and the press wrote about it because it was new and different. Restaurateurs liked the wine because it didn't have to be aged, which costs them money, and diners liked it because it was so approachable. It didn't turn your palate inside out like young Cabernets can.

Margaret: I think what solidified us as a Merlot producer was our second vintage, which was not exactly the greatest vintage in the world. When we got ready to harvest our 1979 Cabernet, we had a deluge. I have pictures of us harvesting and we're dripping wet. What little Cabernet we harvested that was worth anything we ended up blending with the Merlot. Instead of eight hundred cases of Cabernet and eight hundred cases of Three Palms Merlot, which was our first vintage, we now had seventeen hundred cases of one wine, a Merlot. And I think that solidified us in people's minds as making Merlot. Besides, we had this funny name. If you remember, they came out with *The Preppie Handbook* and ducks were the theme. And here we had this name, Duckhorn, and an association with only Merlot. It really helped us establish ourselves.

They said, "Why not just call it Duckhorn? It's a weird name and it might work."

Dan: One of our shareholders at the time was a graphic designer. We had this long list of names for the winery, but he came back with this design of a label with a duck on it. And he said, "Why don't you just call it Duckhorn? It's kind of a weird name and it might work." We were hesitant because we didn't have the majority of the money in the company, but everybody sat around in our living room and said, "Why not?" It's the same exact label we have today, except the duck has been redrawn by a contemporary artist.

So the Duckhorn wine had a strong debut, but Dan and Margaret were just getting warmed up. They used their Christmas card list to create a mail-order base, because if friends and family won't buy your wine, who will? They called up restaurants Dan had patronized during his business travels. And they began traveling around the country to pour their wine for consumers, a time-consuming and expensive effort they have never stopped.

Margaret: The whole winemaker dinner concept became a marketing strategy that was perfect for most of the smaller wineries. People loved the opportunity to go to a restaurant and taste some wines they'd heard about. That's how we got into Sauvignon Blanc—because when we were doing winemaker dinners, we didn't have a white wine, and we were tired of using somebody else's.

A sweeping view of Pope Valley from Duckhorn's Candlestick Ridge vineyard on Howell Mountain.

In those early years, Duckhorn Vineyards couldn't afford to own vineyards. Dan and Margaret bought all their grapes, which had some advantages. Buying from a lot of sources gave them flexibility and spread their risk, but it also meant lack of control.

Margaret: One of the reasons we were successful in the early years with our contracted grapes was because of Dan's experience with planting so many of the vineyards. He knew where the good grapes were grown.

But over the years, we lost some of those great vineyards. The owners either died and left their vineyards to somebody else, or they decided to make their own wines. You've got to control your own destiny. This is a finite valley as far as the amount of fruit we can produce.

You get to be in your fifties and you start thinking Pinot Noir because it's just gorgeous wine to drink.

Now they're making a push to become an estate winery—a winery that owns the vineyards its wines are made from. They've bought several properties around the Valley and are looking for more.

They've also decided to grow the business laterally. Instead of making more Duckhorn wine, they are launching new brands. One of these is Goldeneye, an Anderson Valley Pinot Noir, first released in the spring of 2000.

Given how well the Duckhorns have done with Bordeaux varieties, I was surprised that they wanted to take on this difficult Burgundy grape. Making Pinot Noir is notoriously humbling, but they're tackling it head on. They bought 140 acres in the Anderson Valley so they wouldn't repeat their earlier mistake of not owning the fruit.

Margaret: Dan wanted to die with a bottle of Pinot in his hands.

Dan: You get to be in your fifties and you start thinking Pinot Noir because it's just beautiful, just gorgeous wine to drink. It's very difficult to make, as was Merlot in the early days. It's a very temperamental grape. There aren't many people making it well—only a handful, as a matter of fact. Relative to Cabernet, there are few cult Pinot Noir wineries. And there's a revolution going on today in Pinot Noir, so we jumped in.

Dan has always had strong business intuition. I remember when he looked me in the eye and told me not to get into the flavored oil business, that nobody would buy it. Well, that was nine hundred thousand cases of oil ago.

In addition to Duckhorn and Goldeneye, Dan and Margaret have also launched Paraduxx, a Zinfandel-Cabernet blend; Decoy, a less expensive red table wine, which is where they use grapes from young vineyards; and King Eider, a magnificent dry vermouth. This last has not been the runaway hit they had hoped. They had thought that Americans were ready for a civilized aperitif—fine vermouth served over ice with a twist of orange peel.

Dan: I thought we could sell vermouth everywhere. It could be the flavored oil of the business. You wouldn't be restricted to hoity-toity restaurants. You could have it in the bar of some nice village or neighborhood restaurant. You could have it at the country club or at the golf club—even all those golf clubs that don't sell Duckhorn Merlot. You could be everywhere! But it didn't do it.

Not that they've given up. They'll keep talking about vermouth, trying to build an audience just as they did for Merlot in 1980. The wine business is nonstop marketing, but they wouldn't want to be doing anything else.

Margaret: There is no other business, no other product, that can bring so many different parts of one's life together, whether it's travel and going to good restaurants, sitting down with family and friends, or bringing a memory from the past to the present. You know, it's all inside that bottle. The vintages remind you of certain things that happened in those years. Good things, bad things, it's all in the bottle. In addition, we live in a gorgeous place, a beautiful valley.

You're never enjoying wine in a bad situation.

Dan: And you're never enjoying wine in a bad situation. You're with friends or at home cooking. And to take the point one step further, not only are our customers our friends, but I think that carries through to our fellow wineries. Would Microsoft ever have Apple over for a social dinner? Hell, no. They're mortal enemies. These guys are all fighting each other because tomorrow they're technologically obsolete if they don't go forward. We don't have to worry about technological obsolescence. So we're competitors of the most friendly nature.

Fortunately today the business is very healthy, which has not always been the case. Our forefathers who pioneered Napa Valley, we owe them everything. They did it. We came along at the right time, but Louis Martini and Robert Mondavi struggled for years.

It does bother me that there's a backlash against wineries in Napa and Sonoma counties—mostly for environmental reasons. Wineries are accused of causing erosion on hillsides; usurping scarce water; promoting monoculture, which can make it harder to combat pests and diseases; and luring too many tourists in polluting cars.

Some who moved here for the peace and quiet of the country complain when wineries run their noisy wind machines at night for frost protection. Some worry about what will happen if the glassy-winged sharpshooter invades Napa Valley, as it has Southern California. This insect, which has no completely effective natural controls, transmits a deadly vine disease. Would vintners push for aerial spraying?

Like the Duckhorns, most vintners believe they've been good environmental citizens, supporting ordinances for erosion control, embracing sustainable—and in some cases organic—agriculture, and using water wisely. The Duckhorns also donate to wetland conservation efforts.

Margaret: I'm just nuts over some of this environmental stuff. I think that we've tried to be good stewards of the land here. We've been very restrictive with what we do in our vineyards, and to get criticism that we're taking water from people and fouling streams and fouling the air . . . . If wineries weren't here, this would all be paved. What are people thinking?

She's right about that. Without the wineries, Napa Valley would probably be just another San Francisco suburb. Instead, it's home to people like the Duckhorns, who have taken the Napa Valley message of quality around the world. They now have sixty investor families, up from the five they started with, but they manage a much bigger company than they first envisioned, too.

Margaret: We have five brands now, and the equipment and vineyards needed to get those started take a certain investment. So we're building a bigger company. And, yes, we now have a small part of a much larger company. Who knows which way is better? We'll only find that out in the end, won't we?

Pottery that Makes the Table

Not long after Tra Vigne opened, a couple came in for a meal and left behind some beautiful pottery as a gift. It didn't take me long to return the visit. After several trips to Jeff and Sally Manfredi's Calistoga Pottery, a few miles north of Tra Vigne, I asked if they would consider producing some tableware for me.

Our first project together was a pasta bowl glazed with ash made from old uprooted Zinfandel vines. I loved the idea that the vines were living again on those bowls, and, of course, I hoped my customers would be inspired to drink some old-vine Zinfandel with their pasta.

When I decided I wanted to have some special bowls just for risotto, I went to see the Manfredis again. We considered a number of designs, then settled on a gently sloped bowl in rust-red with an aquamarine ring near the rim. By now we must have served at least a hundred thousand risotti in those bowls!

The Manfredis are a local treasure. They have been making pottery together for more than twenty years—Jeff throws the pots, Sally glazes them. In the tradition of potters throughout the country, they use regional clay—in their case, from California's Mother Lode. It takes about eighteen hours to fire the pieces, then another fifty hours to cool the kiln down. Open it too soon and you will hear the pop-pop-pop of cracking pottery.

I love the straightforward, rustic simplicity of their designs. These are pieces to use, not to display. They made the salt and pepper cellars we use at Tra Vigne, as well as the sugar-and-creamer sets.

"We make functional pieces. We don't make art," says Jeff, who used to be a sous-chef in San Francisco.

Nevertheless, there is great natural beauty in their plates, bowls, and platters; their honey and mustard pots; their olive jars and mugs. They make a vinegar mothering pot with a screened lid that allows you to make vinegar at home on a kitchen countertop; all you need is a culture, or vinegar "mother," and the accumulated remains from those nights when you don't finish your wine.

Being right on the highway and so close to Calistoga, the famous spa town, Sally and Jeff see their share of visitors. "Because of the spas, people come to Calistoga religiously," says Jeff. "We've met people who've been coming here for fifty years. We're now making dinnerware for the second generations of some families."

John and Doug

Shafer

The Shafers bought their hillside property in the Stags Leap District in 1972, before there was an official "Stags Leap District" or even any real confirmation that the area could produce great red wine. Today Shafer Hillside Select is one of California's most sought-after Cabernet Sauvignons, Shafer Merlot is a perennial bestseller, and Shafer Firebreak is counted among California's few successes with the difficult Sangiovese grape. I don't know John Shafer well, but his son Doug, who now runs the winery, eats at Tra Vigne often. Everybody on the staff adores him and his quick sense of humor.

Like many Napa Valley vintners, John had a successful career before he came here.

John: I worked for a textbook publisher in Chicago called Scott Foresman and Company, which was famous for producing the Dick, Jane, and Sally reading books. I worked in sales and marketing, promotion, market research, long-range planning, mergers and acquisitions, that kind of stuff. I was there twenty-three years.

Doug: I remember being in grade school and seeing my dad in the principal's office and thinking, "Oh, no. Is it me or one of my brothers?" And he was there to introduce the new math program.

John: But I'd always had an interest in agriculture, and I wanted to work for myself. So I basically applied to my personal life some of the things that I'd done for the corporation. I researched the budding California wine business and read a lot of books, and I made up my mind that I wanted to get involved.

I got this property because one of the things that stuck in my mind is "hillside vineyards," that the odds for good quality would improve with hillside exposure. Grapes had been grown on this property back in the 1890s and they were replanted in 1922—mostly Zinfandel and Golden Chasselas. So the vineyard was fifty years old when we bought it, and the grapes were going to the Napa Valley Co-op. They went into Gallo's Hearty Burgundy, and Gallo's Hearty Burgundy was a wonderful wine.

Doug was seventeen when the family moved to Napa Valley from suburban Chicago. Napa back then must have seemed like a cow town to these city folks. No restaurants, no shops, no night life. But there was too much to do in the vineyard to think about what they had left behind.

Doug: I grew up seeing my dad go back and forth to work on the train in a three-piece suit. Here I'd come home from high school in the afternoon and Dad would be on the tractor with jeans and a straw hat and a big grin on his face. On the weekends, with my little brother, he'd have us pulling rocks out of the vineyard, digging ditches. I can remember there was one fencepost that we never could get to stay straight because we were a bunch of city boys. We didn't even know how to put a fencepost in right.

John: The initial plan was to get in the wine business, but I didn't know anything about winemaking or grape growing, so I decided I'd do it in stages. We took seven years to redo the vineyards and extend them. In 1977, our first crop went to Spring Mountain. Then in 1978, we decided to do our own wine. We made a thousand cases—crushed it at Markham, fermented it at Round Hill, then borrowed Joe Phelps's flatbed truck and brought forty barrels back. I had no equipment, so this was non-intervention winemaking.

I couldn't get it to start malolactic [the second fermentation, which converts malic acid to lactic acid, making the wine taste softer and smoother], so I took all the electric blankets off the beds to warm the wine. We called it the electric blanket vintage, and it was and is a great wine. It won the Vintners Club Taste-off in San Francisco.

The wine debuted at a tasting for wine writers and the trade at the Silverado Country Club, and about one out of three people said, "How much Merlot did you put in here?" And I said, "We didn't put any." One restaurateur came back a half-hour later and said, "Look, if you tell me how much Merlot you've got in that Cabernet, I swear I won't tell anybody. I know you don't want others to know." He didn't believe me. The reason that's significant is that he was identifying what we now refer to as the Stags Leap District Cabernet character. It's softness, subtleness, soft tannins, velvety texture. Most of the wineries in the Stags Leap District use little or no Merlot because they don't have to.

After high school, Doug headed off to the University of California at Davis to study viticulture, but he didn't return to the winery after college. Instead he moved to Arizona and taught junior high school for a couple of years, then decided he wanted to come back to the Valley.

Doug: I remember it was over Christmas break. I said, "Dad, I think I'm going to come back in the wine business." And he said, "Great. I don't have a job for you." So I ended up working in the cellar at Lakespring [a Napa Valley winery that has since closed].

By 1983, however, John Shafer needed a new winemaker. Doug had spent three years at Lakespring by then, but he still didn't feel ready to take the reins. Nevertheless, John decided to offer the job to Doug, with backup consultant help. Otherwise, John figured, there might not be a place for Doug when he was ready. The learning curve was pretty steep, but Doug and John and Elias Fernandez— the young Davis graduate hired as a "cellar rat" in 1984—learned together.

Today, Elias is the winemaker and Doug manages the business, with John as chairman. That transition from one generation to the next (which several of the Valley's wine families are facing) seems to have been fairly painless at Shafer. John says that he and Doug not only see most things the same way, they can almost read each other's thoughts.

John: One day I went in and said, "Doug, there are a couple of things I want to talk to you about," and he said, "Just a minute," while he wrote something. Then he said, "Okay, go ahead, what are they?" He'd written them down. He knew exactly what I was going to say.

Doug: I mean, for the three of us, it's been a neat team effort. Early mornings, late nights. Do we pick or not pick? Is it going to rain or is it not? I remember the first crush when our fancy press broke down and we were going to have to be up all night, and Dad comes out and he's got pillows and blankets. Elias and I slept on the floor of the cellar, taking shifts.

One change that Doug has guided is the move toward sustainable agricultural practices—methods of growing grapes naturally, with few or no chemical inputs.

Doug: John Williams of Frog's Leap [see page 105] turned me on to all this, so I agreed to meet with his consultant, Amigo Bob. [Bob Cantisano is an agricultural consultant who promotes organic methods.] The reason I liked Amigo Bob is that he never shoved it down my throat. Also, realistically, I thought there was going to come a day where some of the things we were using would be outlawed.

Our main tool is cover crops—the vetches, oats, clovers, and legumes that add nitrogen to the soil. We use a lot of grape pomace in the fall as a soil amendment, and then the cover crop grows in winter and it's a great habitat for the good bugs. And we mow that cover crop two or three times and mulch it down and it's great for the soil. During the winter, it's good erosion control. We used to lose a lot of soil. Now when the water runs off, it's clear, it's not dirt.

The problem with the cover crop is that you get a lot of gophers, moles, and meadow mice. But after I read an article about predators, we put in hawk perches and barn owl boxes and now we have hawks and owls that eat gophers. There's lots of dive-bombing. Now people are calling and saying, "How do you build those owl boxes?"

When we had clover out here one year, I called the local bee guy and he brought his boxes. I hear the honey bees are endangered, so we're helping save the bees. It's kind of fun, and it goes on and on.

I don't think you save money this way, but I do think you're growing a stronger vine and a stronger habitat overall. And I think you get better-balanced fruit.

Every serious winery is always experimenting, looking for that competitive edge. Because there aren't many ingredients in wine, winemakers obsess about things like which oak barrels to buy for aging (see page 199)—whether the oak should be French or American and from which forest, whether it should be lightly or heavily toasted (barrels are toasted on the inside), and which cooper (barrelmaker) to use. If the cooper doesn't age the oak properly first, the barrel can leave a "green" taste in the wine.

Doug: When I was just starting out here, I used one or two coopers and pretty much a basic toast. Elias, when he took over the winemaking, just went crazy. He'd buy barrels from ten or eleven different coopers and with each cooper, there might be two or three different types of oak and four or five different toast levels. I'd see a spreadsheet on what he had in the cellar and it was a zoo! I'd say, "Can't you make it easier?"

He'll set up a barrel experiment with the same Chardonnay in thirty different barrels, and we go through and taste as it ages. It's fascinating. And every couple of years, we invite the coopers in for a blind tasting. Just seven or eight people, seven or eight different glasses, each with wine from a different barrel. So when one guy says, "Well, this tastes pretty 'green'," and the bag comes off and it's his barrel, he knows he's not going to get the order this year. Life's brutal.

In 1981, John's home was threatened by a wildfire, but the quick-thinking Shafers and their neighbors lit backfires, which saved their homes. The Shafers later planted Sangiovese on the scorched knoll and named the vineyard 'Firebreak.' It's one of my favorite Shafer wines, a Sangiovese–Cabernet Sauvignon blend that's just right with my Italian-influenced cooking. Sangiovese can behave like an unruly teenager in the vineyard, producing a huge crop, but Elias seems to know how to tame it.

John: The idea for Sangiovese goes back to the mid-1980s, when I wanted to do a proprietary red wine but I didn't want a Bordeaux blend like Phelps's Insignia or Opus One. One night I had dinner at an Italian restaurant in San Francisco with one of our brokers, and she said, "Have you ever had Antinori's Tignanello?" [a trendsetting Italian wine that blends Sangiovese—the main grape in Chianti—and Cabernet Sauvignon]. And I had not. So we ordered it and I was intrigued by it and wanted to learn more. So for a week I went tasting all over Tuscany and that made up my mind. I came home and said to Doug, "We finally have our red proprietary wine." And Doug said, "Sangio-what?"

Doug: I didn't know anything about it. The stuff grows like a weed. Big mambo clusters. The first vintage, we had eight hundred gallons and it looked like Kool-Aid. No color. And it had tannins that would knock you out and acid that would take the enamel off your teeth. Dad would come out and say, "How's my Sangiovese?" and I'd say, "Well, it's a little funky right now." Elias and I are thinking, "What are we going to do with this?"

We did have a style in mind and, that year, to get to that style, it took 40 percent Cabernet. But over the last few years, we have gotten better at growing it and making it work. We've gotten better at acid and tannin management and not aging it too long in wood, to the point where we're really quite proud of it now. It's a nice wine, a really pretty wine—usually 80 percent Sangiovese and 20 percent Cabernet. The Cabernet gives it some color and actually softens the tannins a bit. It's probably the wine that I drink the most at home.

The demand for Shafer wine is huge, and the winery has grown over the years to try to meet it. But clearly Doug wouldn't want to grow at the expense of quality. How do you decide how big to be?

Doug: The answer to that is fruit source. Grape supply. The eventual size of the winery will be directly related to our ability to secure top-quality grapes, year in and year out. I can't go to my Chicago distributor and say, I have to cut you down to three hundred cases of Merlot this year. They helped build the brand.

Owl boxes (opposite, bottom right) help keep gophers and other vineyard pests under control by providing a home for the predators.

We own close to two hundred acres now in the Napa Valley and we've made an effort to get there, just to ensure supply. I've probably lost three of my good growers in the last couple of years. They sell their places to dot-commers who just want to have a house in the valley. The buyers gets five acres of grapes they don't care about, and they sell them to somebody else or make their own wine, and I lose my source. We need to have fruit in our own control.

Now that Doug is making most of the day-to-day winery decisions, John has more time for community involvement. His favorite project these days is Napa Valley's Clinic Olé. He spent twelve years on the clinic's board of directors and is still an active adviser.

John: Clinic Olé started in 1973 in a little room in Rutherford, an outpatient clinic that was putting Band-Aids on field workers. In the second year of the Wine Auction, in 1983, a few people persuaded the auction committee to include Clinic Olé as a beneficiary. The clinic moved to a trailer with a couple of rooms, then about five years ago it moved down to Napa. My big goal was to develop a stronger awareness in the community for Clinic Olé, particularly among the vintners. Sixty percent of the patients are winery and field workers and their families, but the winery owners didn't know about it. Due to our fundraising, it now has a budget of over $1.5 million. We treat twenty thousand patients a year. But the quarters are all chopped up and we're paying a lot of rent, so I decided we needed a permanent place.

We came up with the idea of combining several health-oriented nonprofits under one roof, and I went to the Auction board with a proposal. We got $3 million from the vintners, but it's going to cost $7 million so we're fundraising. We're going to build a 24,000-square-foot building—half of it for Clinic Olé, with twenty patient rooms. Care is on a sliding scale, but they often give free care. Anybody can go there. I'm thinking of going there myself. The clinic gives very good care.

A spring bud break
(opposite) launches the
vine's growing season.
Each bud becomes
a cane that supports
two grape clusters.

GROWTH

Making the Blend

Some months after their wines have finished fermentation, winemakers must decide how to blend them to create the best possible final result. Even wines from a single vineyard—like Duckhorn Vineyards' Three Palms Merlot—are typically blended from several different "lots" that were fermented separately. Perhaps the winemaker harvested the vineyard in several stages. Or perhaps some of the wine was aged in French oak, some in American oak. Or in the case of Bordeaux-style red wine, the winemaker may be blending several varieties, such as Cabernet Sauvignon, Cabernet Franc, Merlot, and Petit Verdot.

Cathy Corison of Corison Winery faces the challenge every year of blending wines from five different vineyards into one seamless bottling: the Corison Cabernet Sauvignon. Such a wine may not have the cachet of a single-vineyard bottling, but it has other advantages, says the winemaker.

"I think you can make a far more complex wine by blending," says Corison. "All these vineyards are within a couple of miles of each other, all in the same soil series, but every one of them brings something different to the blend."

By the summer after the harvest, the individual wines have evolved enough that Corison can assess them and do a blending trial. The sooner she makes her final blend the better, so the wines have time to knit together.

She starts by making a one-hundred-milliliter sample based on proportions that, if scaled up, would use all the wines she has available that year.

"You'd love to have everything make the blend, of course," says Corison, "so you start there and then you say, 'Well, if I take this out, does it make the wine better?' And that's how I often wind up with something I can't use. I sell that wine in bulk [typically to a broker who sells it to another winery], and it almost always goes into wines that are even more expensive than my own. There's nothing wrong with the wine usually. It just doesn't fit in the blend."

Although the final decision rests on her palate alone, Corison says she tastes with others she trusts, always tastes blind, and always repeats her trials, typically over several days.

"What I'm trying to do is make wines that are number one, elegant; number two, complex. I want them to be aromatic; the best vintages have a floral perfume. And I want them to be structured for aging but be approachable. So there are a lot of seeming contradictions there—approachable but complex, soft but full—but those are all the things that are on my mind when I sit down to blend.

"It's a sequential process, too," she says. "Often there'll be a wine that I don't know for sure belongs in the blend, so I'll leave it out. But three or four months later, I'll retry it in the blend, and I'll often do that right up to the end."

When you make as little wine as Corison does—about twenty-five hundred cases—it hurts to sell any of it to the bulk market. But it's an easier decision when your name is on the bottle. "Blending isn't magic," says Corison. "You have to start with great wines to make great wines."

Carpets of Gold

If you live in Napa Valley year-round, you know that every season has its beauty. Some visitors like to come in summer when the vines are lush; others want to be here at harvest time, when grape gondolas trundle up and down Highway 29 and you can smell grape juice in the air. Still others prefer the off-season, when restaurant reservations are easier to get and the traffic is bearable.

My favorite season here is early spring. The energy in the Valley is pretty high right then. Everybody has had a rest, and people are excited to be farming again. It feels like the Valley is coming back to life after dormancy, just like the vines. When you talk to the growers and winemakers, you can hear the optimism in their voices. This year, maybe, the sun, rain, and stars will all fall into place and produce an incredible vintage.

About ninety days after the first autumn rains, the wild mustard starts to bloom between the vine rows. By February, the valley is a carpet of gold, with thick, stubby black vines poking through. A few people—

myself included—can't resist gathering some of that wild mustard for the table. In fact, I've been picking it since I was old enough to walk.

I remember my mother boiling the mustard leaves in salted water, then cooking them with olive oil and garlic. She'd put a splash of vinegar on the greens and put them in the fridge, and we'd eat them as a side dish all week. When young, the leaves are tender and not too peppery, and you don't even have to boil them. I sauté them in olive oil with garlic, or mix them with eggs for a frittata.

That's my way of making art from the mustard. Others paint the fields of gold, or photograph them. To the artist's eye, wild mustard season is one of the Valley's most beautiful moments, and fortunately it lasts for weeks.

Until recent times, only a handful of the Valley's visitors came in February and March. Restaurants, bed-and-breakfasts and hotels struggled to fill their empty beds and seats. Finally, some Yountville mer-

chants developed the idea of a Mustard Festival that would lure visitors to the Valley during these slow months to witness the beauty.

Today, the annual Napa Valley Mustard Festival is a two-month-long celebration that involves the whole Valley. Throughout February and March, mustard-related events are scheduled almost every weekend, with tastings, cook-offs, a mustard competition, a serious photography competition (images of mustard, of course), and exhibitions of mustard-themed art. Restaurants serve mustard-laced dishes and festival organizers commission a commemorative mustard each year.

The success of this idea has astonished everyone. The opening and closing events of the festival are always sold out, and restaurants and hotels are filled with visitors. I think people enjoy experiencing wine country when it's less hot, hectic, and harried than it is at harvest. And it pleases me to know that more people are seeing that magnificent carpet of gold.

Renewal

*E*very industry needs new players and fresh thinkers to stay vital, and Napa Valley is fortunate to have them. The late 1980s and 1990s brought dozens of new wineries to the Valley, including several extremely small producers whose wines have gone straight to the top of the charts. In fact, you could argue that the 1990s was the era of the ultra-premium boutique winery, whose owners sought out the best available land, engaged the most prestigious winery and vineyard consultants, and generally spared no expense to produce tiny quantities of very expensive wine.

Garen and Shari Staglin and Bart and Daphne Araujo epitomize this painstaking philosophy—that no detail is too small and no compromise allowed when you're trying to make some of the world's finest wine. It's no coincidence that two of the top wineries established in the nineties have the word "estate" in their name—Araujo and Harlan—meaning that the winery grows its own grapes. Controlling the grapes is just another way that a winery controls its destiny. If any single trend dominated the nineties in Napa Valley, it was probably the shift toward winery ownership of vineyards.

Napa continues to draw adventurers, risk-takers, people who seek challenges. People like Lyndsey Harrison, a former flight attendant who learned to make wine when she and her husband Michael bought a home with a vineyard. People like Larry Turley, a former emergency room doctor who loves resuscitating old vines and has created a cult around old-vine Zinfandel and Petite Sirah, or Bill Harlan—pilot, surfer, gambler, sailor, a man who always lived for the moment until he decided to build the California equivalent of a first-growth estate.

Today, renewal in Napa Valley is coming from within, too—from second-generation vintners and growers who are building on what their parents achieved. At Charles Krug, Mondavi sons Peter, Jr., and Marc are taking that venerable winery to new heights. Son Hugh Davies is in place at Schramsberg, Doug Shafer at Shafer Vineyards. Jim Barbour, whose parents farmed grapes in Napa Valley in the 1960s, now oversees some of the Valley's top vineyards. With any luck, Napa will continue to lure the visionaries and original voices who lead the way to the top.

Bart and Daphne

Araujo

To my eye, Araujo Estate is one of the most picturesque properties in the Valley. The buildings aren't grand or grandiose. There's no reproduction French château, no dramatic architectural statement. Instead, there's something purely Californian about what Bart and Daphne Araujo have built at the northeast end of the Valley: A new redwood winery that snuggles up against the hillside and echoes the lines of the adjacent century-old barn; a long drive lined with olive trees and stone walls; a well-tended but relaxed vegetable garden with quince and peach trees and espaliered pears . . . buildings and a landscape in harmony.

What has impressed me about the Araujos (apart from their impeccable wines) is how quickly they have made their mark. In 1990, as newcomers here, they bought the prestigious Eisele Vineyard, thirty-five acres of mostly Cabernet Sauvignon that Milt Eisele planted. Joseph Phelps made Eisele Vineyard famous by putting its name on bottles of Phelps Cabernet Sauvignon for fifteen years.

By the end of the nineties, Araujo Estate "Eisele Vineyard" Cabernet was on everyone's list of "cult" wines—wines with small production, high ratings, and long waiting lists. The Araujos make only about twenty-five hundred cases of Cabernet, and about five hundred cases each of Syrah and Sauvignon Blanc—all from their own grapes and all identified on the label as Araujo Estate "Eisele Vineyard." They're so committed to controlling every aspect of production that they own their own bottling line—an extravagance for a winery their size. (Most small wineries use a mobile bottler, a company that brings the necessary equipment and workers to the winery at bottling time.)

Both of them left successful careers—Bart in home building and mortgage banking, Daphne in landscape architecture—to launch this risky winery venture, and I wanted to know why.

Bart: I had sold my former business in Southern California and I wanted to move back home. I had grown up in Burlingame [near San Francisco], which was the country in those days, so my vision of going home was to go back

to the country but still be close to San Francisco. And the only places with that potential were Napa and Sonoma. So our decision was really geographic. It didn't have to do with wine, at least at first.

We spent about four years looking for property. We finally found something that we liked about five miles south of here, and we were quite happy with it. But in the course of our search, in 1986 through 1989, we'd become aware that some of the treasured vineyard properties in the Napa Valley were, shall we say, underutilized. So we told our real estate agents to call us if any of the great historical properties ever became available. And they did—about two months later. I was figuring it might be ten years later.

The real estate agents Jean Phillips and Ren Harris (who have their own Napa Valley wineries—Screaming Eagle and Paradigm, respectively) brought the Araujos some interesting news: The famous Eisele Vineyard was for sale.

We told our agent to call us if any historical properties became available. And they did—about two months later.

Bart: Everyone felt that Joseph Phelps was going to acquire it, and since he'd had an exclusive relationship with the grapes since 1975, none of the locals wanted to upset the apple cart. But Joe, for whatever reason, chose not to acquire it. So we were Jean's second phone call. And we didn't let her make the third.

Acquiring Eisele wasn't just acquiring a vineyard. It was acquiring a piece of Napa Valley history. As far as we can verify, the property has been continuously in grapes since 1886, which is unusual here.

It also produced one of the first vineyard-designated Cabernets in California. The only two that pre-date it to my knowledge are Ridge Monte Bello and Heitz Martha's Vineyard. And that was in an era when vintners designated the vineyard because the wine was unique, not just to increase the price.

We fell in love with the idea of being stewards of this very special property. Our view is that we have a treasure, a little jewel, and it's our tremendous responsibility to preserve and improve it.

Daphne: Our intent was to have a vineyard. But before we even closed escrow, Bart realized that it was important to also make the wine, to control the whole process from beginning to end. So, effectively, we entered two businesses about which we knew very little.

If we wanted a winery, we had to act quickly. Milt Eisele had seen clearly that it was going to get harder to get a winery permit, not easier. He had obtained a permit for a small winery, but we had to act within a certain time. My recollection is that we closed escrow in May and had until the end of June to perfect the permit.

That's a huge decision to make quickly. Starting a winery means years of capital investment with no return. You need a winemaking staff, a sales and marketing staff, a winery building with hundreds of thousands of dollars in equipment for crushing, pressing, fermenting, and aging. Even a small winery is not a small investment.

The redwood winery
at Araujo Estate.

Daphne: The Eiseles had introduced us to a lot of people in the Valley, and they all said, "Whatever you do, don't start a winery." And I said, "Well, you know, we've pretty much decided we're going to do that." And they said, "Well, then, whatever you do, don't make your winery too big because we've seen so many people we care about come and start a winery, and it all seems so easy and fun, and then they're doubling and tripling the size, and it isn't fun anymore."

So we decided that it was appropriate to have a winery, but a small winery based fully on the estate. We would not buy grapes from others. We would just concentrate on what we grow here.

For the winery, Milt had designated this two-car corrugated-metal garage with about eight-foot ceilings. We thought it was fine, but what did we know? When we started interviewing winemakers, we would point out the garage and say, "Here's the winery," and they all looked at us like we were crazy. They said, "You can't make wine in there."

So the Araujos built a winery, a beautiful redwood barnlike winery that looks like it has always been there. They dug caves into the hillside to keep the wines cool during barrel aging. And they went looking for people who could help them aim for greatness. Of course, everyone wanted to get their hands on the Eisele fruit and they had their pick of consultants. In the end, they hired Tony Soter (see page 164) as consulting winemaker and David Abreu as viticulturist. Tony has since retired from consulting, but his protégé, Françoise Peschon, is the Araujos' winemaker now.

The Eisele vineyard had been a star for years, but in 1990, it was showing its age. In some ways, the Araujos realized, buying Eisele was like buying a vintage sports car: It might be a thrill to own, but it would need lots of work to bring it back to peak performance.

Daphne: We had a sense when we bought the vineyard that it was time to replant, and of course, that was one reason that Milt and Barbara decided to sell. At their ages, it wasn't a time to put yet more capital into the vineyard.

The vine spacing was pretty wide and the infrastructure—the vineyard trellising and irrigation—was old. Also, there were a lot of vines that had once been something else but had been budded over to Cabernet over the years. And one could argue that they weren't first-class vines because they had been budded over.

Bart: So we replanted the Eisele clone on phylloxera-resistant rootstocks with the increased vine densities that David and Tony felt were more appropriate. We added Cabernet Franc and Petit Verdot [varieties often blended with Cabernet Sauvignon], which had never been planted here before. We started an estate white wine program with Sauvignon Blanc, and then subsequently began to experiment with another noble red—Syrah.

Finding Syrah at Eisele Vineyard was a complete surprise. When the Araujos bought the property, they thought they were buying a Cabernet vineyard.

Bart: In 1991, just before harvest, Tony and I were walking through one of our older Cabernet blocks. I said, "Tony, what's wrong with that vine there? The Cabernet clusters don't look right." He looked at me and said, "That's Syrah. What's Syrah doing here in block six?"

I called Milt and said, "Milt, did you know you had Syrah in block six?" And he said, "Oh, did I forget to tell you?"

Joe Phelps had been so pleased with the Eisele Cabernet that when he started making Rhône varietals in the late 1970s, he wanted to do a vineyard-designated Syrah from Eisele. So he convinced Milt to plant seven-and-a-half acres out of thirty-five—a significant portion of the vineyard—to Syrah. When the Rhône program didn't really take off [Phelps would try again later with Rhône varietals and succeed], he encouraged Milt to bud the Syrah over to Cabernet.

For whatever reason, about a hundred of the vines hadn't taken the graft and were still Syrah. So we just harvested it separately and made the wine. And the wine was so extraordinary, it encouraged us to plant more Syrah.

I had to wonder if it didn't make the Araujos nervous to make so many changes to a proven vineyard. Didn't they worry about messing with success?

Daphne: I said something to Joe Phelps early on about replanting, about whether that didn't seem risky. And he just laughed. He said the quality is in the ground, and we needed to replant. It was time. And our timing was good because it really was the beginning of a whole revolution in the way things were planted, and people understood enough of AxR-1 not to plant it anymore. [AxR-1 was a widely planted rootstock that proved susceptible to phylloxera.] I don't think we talked to anyone who knew the vineyard who didn't feel it was the right thing to do. So that gave us confidence.

I had been thinking a lot about the Araujos' commitment to estate-grown fruit—making wine only from grapes you grow yourself. In some ways, it reminds me of my efforts as a chef to control my ingredients as much as possible. When I couldn't find mozzarella or prosciutto I liked for Tra Vigne, I made them myself. Whether you're a chef or a winemaker, you're only as good as your raw materials.

Vintners these days are more eager to own their own grapes so they can dictate how they're grown and harvested. And they're more attuned to the nuances of each site. When your wine comes from a single vineyard, you have a chance to "taste the place"—to understand what that particular patch of dirt can do.

Daphne: When Tony was our consulting winemaker, he would gather his clients together once a year or so for a tasting. Since we all had the same winemaker, what showed through very clearly in each wine was the voice of the soil: a distinctive character that cannot be copied or reproduced in any other location.

People who are knowledgeable in wine and taste a lot can always find this. Take Barney Rhodes, for example. He was always too modest to say so, but his wife, Belle, would say he was one of the great tasters of the world. You'd give him a bottle blind and he could tell you the producer, the vineyard, and the vintage.

It's that voice that makes having an estate so exciting. Everything we're doing here is trying to eliminate the external influences to make the voice more pure. We compost our own grape pomace and grow our own cover crops and till them into the soil so we're not importing so many amendments. At some point, it would be wonderful to have our own cows, so even the manure would come from the property. I think the more pure the voice becomes, the more interesting the wine can be, especially given that we have a multitude of different growing areas on our forty acres.

So what is the "voice" of an Araujo Cab? I wanted to hear the Araujos describe their wine in their own words.

Daphne: Well, it tends to be more black fruit than red, such as black currant, blackberry, black cherry. Then there's a wonderful mineral note because the soil's extremely rocky. And there are some very deep roasted tones: some roast coffee, roast tobacco, cigar box.

Bart: My descriptors are a little different than Daphne's, but primarily, it's not as fruit-driven as most Napa Cabernets, whether they're benchland or mountain Cabernets. I find red and black currant, black cherry, chocolate. There's always major chocolate in there. Cedar tones that develop over time into fabulous saddle leather or cigar box. And there are some underlying herbal tones that Beth Novak at Spottswoode claims come from our olive trees. It's a very distinct signature.

It couldn't have been easy for the Eiseles to give up a vineyard that had their name on it and that had so much history and reputation.

Daphne: They loved this property so much. I remember when we first met them, we were in escrow but still hadn't really seen the house. Jean said, "Let's go up and have a look," and it happened to be on Milt's eightieth birthday. I mean, what horrible timing. We didn't know it until we walked in the door, and there they were with their children to help Milt celebrate. Barbara is very disarming. We walked in the door and she looked at us and said, "So what are you going to do with us?"

After the sale, they stayed in the house for over two years. I could tell it was difficult to make the transition from owning the property to not owning it. Milt used to watch very carefully what we were doing in the vineyard, and he liked what he saw. So they decided that we were okay, and what we were doing with the vineyard was okay, and the fact that we were going to continue to call our property the Eisele Vineyard meant a lot to them, so I think that made them comfortable introducing us around.

The Araujos' mission statement makes their intentions clear. Here's part of it: "To develop and operate a world-class wine-growing estate. To produce organically grown fruit and with this fruit make a singular wine of the highest caliber and distinction [that expresses] the uniqueness of the precious resource that is Eisele."

Bart and Daphne told me about one vintage where a large block of Cabernet had to be picked on a very hot day, and the wine made from those grapes took a long time to come around. It represented about 25 percent of the harvest, so leaving it out of the final blend was almost out of the question. But when Tony and Françoise did the blending trials and the Araujos realized the blend would be better without the wine from that block, they didn't hesitate.

The more pure the voice of the soil, the more interesting the wine.

Daphne: We had a similar conversation with Françoise when we decided not to declare the 1997 Syrah. We felt that the vintage didn't live up to our requirements and that we shouldn't bottle the wine. It may be expensive if you look at the bottom line for that year, but in the long term, the only way to preserve the brand is to make the right decision every year. Because the moment people can't trust what's in the bottle with your name on it, that's really expensive.

Could this attitude be the difference between a good winery and a great one? I'm starting to think that management philosophy may be just as important as the source of your grapes.

Bart: We tell our people that we don't want any compromises—in any aspect of the business. Nor do we want to think that we can be 100 percent better than anyone. We want to try to be 1 percent better in a hundred different ways. If you think you can get 100 percent better than others, you start developing arrogance that can sidetrack you. Better to start thinking about what can be done 1 percent better.

The Araujos have experienced extraordinary success in such a short time. Is there anything more they could want from the valley, anything they would change?

Daphne: My background makes me sensitive to the land, and I've often thought that there aren't nearly enough people who speak for it. I think we have to be more careful than we have been about preserving a thing of real beauty that people have written about ever since they first saw it. It's our turn now. We don't have Jack Davies anymore. [Jack was an outspoken advocate for slow growth in the Napa Valley. See page 70.] It's a new generation, and who among us is standing up and saying, What is the proper scale of any development that does occur? Don't we want to be proud of how we leave the Valley for the next generation?

I think there are some special places in the world and, clearly, Napa Valley is one of them. I think we have to speak up for it and maybe give up some personal things for the community to survive as a beautiful and productive place.

Lunch in the Olive Grove

ASPARAGUS AND GRILLED POTATOES
with BEET-BASIL DRESSING

PEA PANZANELLA

GRILLED LAMB LOINS *with* NAPA CABERNET JUS

BING CHERRY COMPOTE *with* BASIL GELATO

For a chef, the busiest time in the Valley is the week of the Napa Valley Wine Auction—always the first weekend in June. Restaurants are even more jammed than usual, and wineries host events that draw on all the local culinary talents.

I've had the pleasure and honor of preparing auction-week lunches a couple of times for Bart and Daphne Araujo and their winery guests. On both occasions, I aimed for a menu that would really showcase their wines and other bounty from the estate.

One year, we started the lunch with Araujo Estate Sauvignon Blanc and a warm potato and asparagus salad with Araujo Estate olive oil. To accompany their elegant Cabernet Sauvignon, I roasted lamb loins on the stone grill in their olive grove and served them with a Cabernet jus and a spring pea panzanella. Dessert was inspired by Daphne's garden: gelato infused with June basil and surrounded by warm Bing cherries.

When I made this dish for the Araujos, I used their wonderful estate extra virgin olive oil on the potatoes. Because the potatoes cooked slowly, they really absorbed the oil flavor. Be sure to use the best olive oil you have, and note that you'll need a juicer to make beet juice. The beet dressing is unlike anything you have ever tasted.

4 medium russet potatoes,
    unpeeled, sliced ½-inch thick
Approximately 1½ cups extra virgin olive oil
12 sprigs of fresh thyme
8 garlic cloves, peeled
Sea salt, preferably gray salt (see Note on page 26)
Freshly ground black pepper

2 cups beet juice (from 6 large red beets)
1 tablespoon lemon juice, plus more
    for the asparagus
⅓ cup basil oil, or extra virgin olive oil
2 pounds jumbo asparagus, woody ends removed
Ricotta salata cheese
Edible flowers or herb blossoms for garnish, optional

Prepare a medium-hot charcoal fire and preheat oven to 325° F. When the coals are covered with gray ash, toss the potato slices with a little of the olive oil, then grill them about 5 minutes on each side to mark them. Put them in a baking pan large enough to hold them in a single layer. (You may need more than one.) Add enough olive oil to come one-third of the way up the sides of the potatoes. Scatter the thyme and garlic cloves over the potatoes, season with salt and pepper, and bake until tender, about 20 minutes. Let potatoes cool in the pan. You can bake them several hours ahead.

Simmer the beet juice in a saucepan until reduced to ½ cup. Watch carefully; the juice may want to boil up and overflow. Add the 1 tablespoon lemon juice and continue simmering until volume is reduced to ⅓ cup.

Strain into a bowl; when cool, whisk in basil oil. The dressing will not emulsify; it is meant to be "broken." Season with salt and pepper. Boil asparagus in a large quantity of salted water until just tender, about 3 minutes. Drain, shock in ice water, then pat dry. Dress the asparagus lightly with some of the herb oil that floats to the top of the dressing. Season with salt, pepper, and a squeeze of lemon juice.

Make a bed of potato slices in the center of each plate. Stack a bundle of asparagus on top of the potatoes. With a cheese plane or vegetable peeler, shave ricotta salata over each portion. Shake or whisk dressing, then spoon some over the cheese. Garnish with edible flowers or herb blossoms, if using.

SERVES 8

Sometimes I like to take a familiar dish that people understand and present it in a way they couldn't imagine. In most kitchens, panzanella is a summer bread salad with tomatoes, garlic, and basil. But why not rethink the bread salad idea for other seasons? This pea panzanella is a celebration of spring. Once you become familiar with this recipe, you can make seasonal variations of your own. The vitamin C in the dressing helps preserve its bright green color.

½ cup unsalted butter

3 tablespoons chopped garlic

6 tablespoons minced fresh basil

3 tablespoons minced fresh thyme

1 pound day-old country bread in ½-inch cubes (remove crust if hard)

Sea salt, preferably gray salt (see Note on page 26)

Freshly ground black pepper

⅓ cup freshly grated Parmesan cheese

⅓ cup freshly grated pecorino romano cheese

For the dressing:

1½ cups fresh or frozen peas

½ cup heavy cream

⅛ teaspoon powdered vitamin C (ascorbic acid)

½ cup chicken stock, plus more for moistening the salad

¼ cup extra virgin olive oil

⅔ cup thinly sliced scallion greens

1½ cups cooked peas

½ cup grated pecorino toscano cheese

3 tablespoons lemon juice

1 tablespoon grated lemon zest

6 cups spring greens lightly dressed with extra virgin olive oil, lemon juice, and salt

Preheat oven to 375° F. Turn on the convection fan if you have one.

Heat the butter in a skillet over moderate heat until it begins to brown. Add the chopped garlic and stir briefly to release its fragrance. Remove from the heat and add the minced basil and thyme. Stir to combine. Pour the butter mixture over the bread cubes in a bowl and toss briskly so butter coats the cubes evenly. Season with salt and pepper and stir in the two cheeses. Place the bread cubes on a baking sheet, scraping all the seasonings over them. Bake until lightly browned but still soft, about 12 minutes. Transfer to a bowl to cool along with any of the bits sticking to the baking sheet.

Make the dressing: If using fresh peas, blanch them for 30 seconds in boiling water, then shock in ice water. Drain. If using frozen peas, defrost according to package. In a stainless steel saucepan, simmer peas in cream until the cream is hot, then puree in a blender or food processor with the vitamin C. Cool the puree, then whisk together with chicken stock and olive oil. Season with salt and pepper.

In a large bowl, combine toasted bread cubes, scallions, peas, pecorino toscano, lemon juice, and lemon zest. Add the dressing and toss well, adding a little more broth if panzanella seems dry. Put the ring from a 10-inch springform pan upside down on a large plate. Fill with panzanella, pressing it into place. Let stand for 30 minutes to 1 hour, then remove the ring. Mound the dressed spring greens lightly on the panzanella.

SERVES 8

GRILLED LAMB LOINS *with* NAPA CABERNET JUS

It may seem extravagant to simmer two bottles of good wine and eight cups of stock down to two cups of sauce, but great ingredients yield great results. And if you're going to the expense of treating your guests to lamb loins, you want a sauce that shows it off. Ask your butcher to remove the silverskin, the fine membrane that covers each loin.

For the lamb stock:

4 pounds lamb bones, in 2- to 3-inch pieces
 (ask your butcher to cut them)
2 cups coarsely chopped onion
1 cup coarsely chopped carrot
1 cup coarsely chopped celery
4 sprigs fresh thyme
12 sprigs fresh parsley
1 teaspoon black peppercorns
1 teaspoon juniper berries
3 bay leaves

Make the lamb stock: Preheat oven to 375° F. Turn on convection fan, if you have one. In a roasting pan, roast the lamb bones, turning occasionally, for 1 hour, then add the chopped onion, carrots, and celery. Roast 20 minutes longer, stirring occasionally. Transfer bones and vegetables to a stockpot. Add thyme, parsley, peppercorns, juniper, bay leaves, and 1½ gallons of water. Bring to a simmer, skimming any foam. Adjust heat to maintain a bare simmer and cook for 8 hours. Strain.

For the jus:

3 tablespoons olive oil
½ pound lamb stew meat, fat trimmed, in 1-inch cubes
2 cups chopped onion
1 cup chopped celery
1 cup chopped carrot
6 sprigs fresh thyme
6-inch sprig fresh rosemary
1 bay leaf
2 bottles (750-ml. each) Napa Valley Cabernet Sauvignon
2 quarts hot lamb stock

3 pounds well-trimmed lamb loins
Extra virgin olive oil
2 tablespoons minced fresh thyme
Sea salt, preferably gray salt (see Note on page 26)
Freshly ground black pepper

Make the jus: Heat oil in a large pot over moderately high heat. Add lamb stew meat and brown well on all sides. Remove with a slotted spoon and set aside. Add onion, celery, and carrot and sauté until vegetables are well caramelized, about 15 minutes. Drain vegetables in a sieve, discard the fat, and return lamb and vegetables to pot along with thyme, rosemary, and bay leaf. Raise heat to high. Add the wine and simmer until reduced to 1 cup. Add the hot stock. Simmer, skimming occasionally, until the sauce is reduced to 2 cups. Season to taste with salt and pepper, then strain through a fine sieve and return to low heat to keep warm.

Prepare a medium charcoal fire. Rub lamb with olive oil, then season with thyme, salt, and pepper. When coals are covered with gray ash, grill lamb 2 to 3 minutes per side for medium-rare (about 120° F). Let rest for a few minutes before carving on the diagonal into ½-inch-thick slices. Divide the lamb among warm dinner plates and pass the sauce separately.

SERVES 8

BING CHERRY COMPOTE *with* BASIL GELATO

Basil in ice cream? Herbs in dessert may be a trend, but there's nothing new about it. I've had rosemary granita in Italy and seen recipes for medieval sweets that use savory herbs. Spring basil is always so delicately perfumed and fruity that it wasn't much of a leap to imagine it with fruit. This is a showstopper!

For the gelato:

8 loosely packed cups unblemished basil leaves

½ teaspoon sea salt, preferably gray salt (see Note on
  page 26)

⅛ teaspoon powdered vitamin C (ascorbic acid)

1 tablespoon sugar

1 quart vanilla ice cream, softened

To make the gelato: Blanch the basil leaves in boiling salted water for about 5 seconds, then place in an ice bath. Drain and wring the basil dry in a dish towel. Chop coarsely.

In a food processor, puree the basil with salt, powdered vitamin C, and just enough water to make a puree (about 6 tablespoons). You should have about 1½ cups basil puree. Transfer ½ cup puree to a small bowl and stir in 1 tablespoon sugar. Freeze the remaining puree for later use in pesto.

Place the ice cream in a bowl over ice. Quickly fold in the sweetened basil puree; you can fold it in completely or leave it streaky. Return ice cream to the freezer until serving time.

For the compote:

6 tablespoons unsalted butter

⅔ cup light brown sugar

1 bay leaf

¾ cup orange juice

2 tablespoons lemon juice

Pinch sea salt, preferably gray salt (see Note on page 26)

4 cups pitted Bing cherries

To make the compote: Melt butter in a sauté pan over high heat. When it begins to brown, stir in sugar and bay leaf. When sugar dissolves, stir in citrus juices and salt. Cook, whisking, until sauce is reduced to ½ cup. Add the fruit and cook just until cherries are warmed through.

Put a generous spoonful of compote in each of 8 dishes. Top with a scoop of the gelato.

SERVES 8

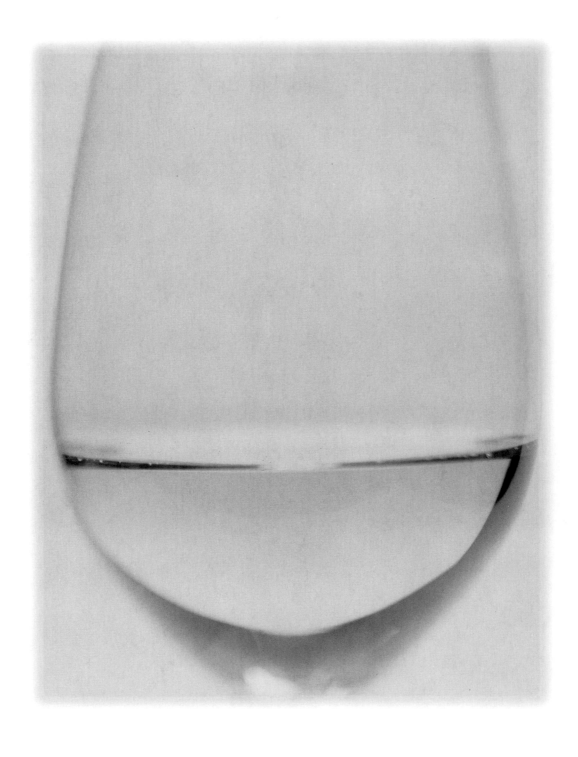

A Final Decision: To Fine or to Filter?

Just before their wine goes into the bottle, winemakers have one last chance to make a difference. That's when they decide whether to fine or filter the wine, choices that can have a noticeable impact on appearance, texture, aroma, and flavor. For Byron Kosuge, winemaker at Saintsbury, these decisions are among the most stressful ones he makes all year.

"It's a calculated risk any way you look at it," says Kosuge, who makes mostly Pinot Noir and Chardonnay. Fining and filtration take bad things out: excess tannin in red wines; yeasts and bacteria that could possibly cause spoilage; and solids that make the wine cloudy. But they also remove some desirable things, such as color, aroma, and flavor.

"The less you take out, the more that's left in the wine to enjoy," says Kosuge. "Especially with Pinot Noir, we spend so much time and energy in the vineyard and the cellar getting all the yummy flavor into the wine, it's kind of galling to do anything that takes some of that flavor back out again."

Consumers expect clear wine, especially clear white wine. If left in a barrel or tank long enough, white wines would gradually clear themselves as solids settled to the bottom. But most whites are bottled before gravity can do its job, so winemakers turn to fining agents such as egg whites, bentonite or casein (milk protein). These proteins grab on to charged molecules in the wine, then quickly settle out, leaving the wine clear. Chefs take advantage of the same reaction when they add egg whites to broth to make crystal-clear consommé.

"It's a time-honored technique," says Kosuge, "but it's a blunt instrument. It takes out things you don't want, but also things you do want."

Filtering is also "a double-edged sword," says Kosuge, with known risks and benefits. To filter, wine is passed through a medium, such as a filter pad with tiny pores, that traps the undesirables—spoilage yeasts like Brettanomyces, for example—while letting the rest of the wine pass. The problem is that the pads can trap flavor and aroma molecules, too.

"I have to decide where to draw the line," says Kosuge. "If you don't filter, you're leaving in yeast and bacteria that can change the character of the wine. Sometimes the change is for the better, and sometimes it's for the worse. Cabernets and some of the bigger red wines can stand up to a certain amount of filtration because they have a lot of 'stuff' in them. But Pinot Noir is pretty delicate. It doesn't have as much to spare."

At Saintsbury, Kosuge fines the Chardonnay so it will be clear in the glass. But he rarely filters either the Chardonnay or the Pinot Noir.

"If you believe, as I do, that nine times in ten, fining and filtration take more good out of the wine than bad, what do you do about the one time that it doesn't?" says Kosuge. "It only takes one failure to tarnish a reputation. Having said that, I will always come down on the side of greater risk for greater reward. Perhaps I am too much of a gambler, but I would rather let a wine be—for better or worse—than beat it into submission."

Masters of Mesclun

Napa Valley wine grapes are so valuable today that it hardly makes sense to grow anything else here. Fortunately, Peter Forni, Lynn Brown, and Barney Welsh don't care about maximizing return on investment. If they did, they wouldn't be growing salad greens on prime Zinfandel land. But I'm thrilled they are.

Many of the top Napa Valley restaurants serve Forni-Brown lettuces, herbs, arugula, or other greens, and many restaurant menus even identify them by name. In season, they also supply the Valley's professional cooks with vine-ripe tomatoes, squashes, beets of many colors, and hard-to-find produce like white carrots, white *fraises des bois,* and *cipolline* (Italian baby onions).

I like a lot of things about these three men, but one thing I particularly like is their custom approach. They plant what chefs request, and they don't pick anything until we're ready for it. They make a mesclun mix that's unique to Tra Vigne, and they grow my favorite Genovese basil because I asked for it. Lettuces harvested in the morning are in our kitchen by lunchtime looking as perky as freshly cut flowers. Welsh's daughter Genevieve, who makes a lot of the deliveries, jokes that when the lettuces arrive at the restaurant, they don't even know they're dead yet.

Lynn and Peter have no interest in building an empire, they just want to grow things. They say no a lot more than they say yes. On Friday afternoons, they quit early to play Ping-Pong and bocce ball; if I show up, they hand me a beer and I'd better not want to talk about arugula.

Barney is the salesman, the storyteller, the gregarious front man. In the late 1980s, Barney pulled up the old Zinfandel vines on his Calistoga property and cast his lot with Lynn and Peter. The three partners now farm five acres of lettuces, herbs, and greens behind Barney's house. They also farm tomatoes and root vegetables in Knight's Valley—renowned Cabernet country—on a parcel deeded to the Sonoma Land Trust. For some reason, the deceased man who donated the property to the trust specified that it couldn't be used for grapes. I wonder how he would have felt about forty varieties of tomatoes.

The Forni-Brown farm isn't open to the public, but Calistoga locals know they can call ahead to get some salad greens or heirloom tomatoes for a dinner party. For three weekends a year in spring, the partners do open the Calistoga farm for a plant sale—a hugely popular event that brings fans from afar. So many people had asked, "Where can I get what you grow?" that they decided to offer nursery starts for home gardens. If you are in the Valley around Easter, don't miss it.

Larry

Turley

I don't know any vintner whose personality comes though stronger in the glass than Larry Turley. Larry is a former emergency room doctor who makes huge, high-alcohol, richly extracted Zinfandels and monster Petite Sirahs. His passion is mountain-grown Zinfandel and Zinfandel from old vines. Robert Parker, the wine critic, raves about Turley wines and they're snapped up quickly, mostly by mailing-list customers. Larry's sister Helen Turley is a top wine consultant in the Valley. She helped him make the first couple of vintages of Turley Wine Cellars.

Larry is one of those people who's larger than life—the kind of guy who prunes a vine with a chain saw. He gave up motorcycles after seeing too many bikers in the ER, but he still pilots a private plane and thrives on risk. It doesn't surprise me that his wines, which I love, often go to extremes. When I looked for help in developing my old-vine Zin and Petite Sirah into wines that match my style of cooking and life, the good doctor was one of the people I turned to.

I grew up in Georgia with "demon alcohol," but when I went to medical school, my sister sent me Julia Child's first little paperback cookbook and I made leg of lamb cooked in Burgundy. Well, the only Burgundy in Georgia was Hearty Burgundy, so I drank about half of that while I was cooking. I was living in an old dorm and everybody came down, and I thought, this fine wine and cooking is really great! That's how I got an interest in it. And then I made beer all through medical school. I could make much better beer than anything commercially available, I thought.

In 1972, I rode to California on my motorcycle and got to Mondavi in time for the last tour of the day. I thought this was paradise. I interned at St. Mary's in San Francisco and then went to work in Santa Rosa, and I house-sat for a year near Schramsberg.

In four years of rigorous

pruning, Larry Turley fixed

decades of neglect of the old

olive trees on his property.

The Valley was different back then—very, very quiet. There was no fine dining, no nothing. No traffic, either. I was working a lot and I'd just come home and cook. It was my refuge from work. ER was pretty hard in those days. There were no paramedics, no seat belt law, no helmet law.

Larry and his wife, Suzanne, live on a beautiful property near Calistoga with lots of old olive trees that Larry maintains. The trees were a disaster when he bought the place, but he has slowly brought them back into production (with his now-famous chain saw) and is making small amounts of wonderful extra virgin olive oil.

The day I bought the house, I came home and found a tent in my front yard, so I drove into the tent with my motorcycle and it was John Williams. I didn't know him from Adam, and I asked him what he was doing. He looked up and said, "Well, it's about time for a glass of wine." He had a bottle of wine under his pillow. I thought, this guy couldn't be all bad.

John knew my sister Helen from Cornell. She had told him that I had just bought a place in Napa Valley, but how he found it I'll never know. He moved in and helped me work on the house, and then we started Frog's Leap Winery in 1981. And we grew that business from seven hundred cases to thirty-six thousand.

In 1993, John wanted to grow the brand even more. But I had four young daughters and a young wife and I wanted to spend time with them. So I sold the brand to John and he moved it to the Rutherford Cross Road. And I started Turley here with my sister Helen and Ehren Jordan. We had not a whole lot of aspirations, and the winery has done eight zillion times better than I would have ever thought. So I quit medicine in 1997. I would work all day here and then I would work all night in ER. I never realized how tired I was.

A lot of people probably wondered whether Larry could maintain the winery's reputation when Helen left after the first two vintages. Nobody wonders anymore.

What Helen did was open the door and say, "You can go through here." And you know, we went through and we never looked back. I've always sort of believed that you leap and the net will appear.

After we saw what *could* be made, I knew that was the right way to go. I've always loved Zinfandels, but people made them all over the board. You never knew if you were getting a sweet one or a raisined one or a light style where you could see through the wine. Occasionally, I'd taste a mountain Zin and say, "You know, there's something really special here."

I remember when Larry first visited my property with all its old, abandoned vines—a property that scared everybody who came near it. He walked through like a doctor doing triage. He looked for health in the vines, not for sickness. I think that's why he loves old vines so much—he likes the challenge of making something neglected into something productive again.

Old vines respond dramatically if you give them half a chance. Most of ours are over sixty years old. Our Duarte Vineyard is one hundred and four years old. Dogtown's probably seventy-five or eighty years old. Typically, a lot of

these old Zin vineyards went for white Zin, which is hard because it's all about large crop and you get paid so little for it. But at least it saved the vineyard.

We come in and put in a cover crop, and we prune very differently—for flavor, not for yield. Pruning is probably the most fun project of all winemaking. First you prune and nothing happens because the vine is dormant. Then in spring you come back and see what you did. Then at harvest you say, well, next year we'll do it a little differently.

When the old vines finally come around, they make a balanced wine, even at 28° Brix.

Larry has had to battle growers who want to pick the fruit at 23° Brix. Brix is a measure of sugar content and thus a sign of ripeness. It also determines how much alcohol you'll get when the grapes are fermented. Most wineries pick grapes at 23° to 24° Brix to get wines that are about 13 percent alcohol. To Larry, that's not nearly ripe enough. He wants to hang in there until the sugar gets to 28° or more—risky business if rain is threatening.

Pruning is probably the most fun project of all winemaking.

It did sort of startle some growers. They said, "Okay, it's 23." I said, "Great, call me in a week." "What?" "Okay, two weeks then!" We call it growers' goggles. They put on the glasses and, yup, the fruit's ripe.

Some people think I'm just shining them on when I say, "We picked that at 30° Brix." They say, "Yeah, right. That would give 17½ percent alcohol." And that's what it is. Europeans come here—my wife imports wine—and we get in big arguments. They think I said 7 percent. No, I said 17 percent.

I want my wines to have a lot of individuality. We make twelve Zinfandels and three Petite Syrahs [that's the Turley preferred spelling] and they're all different. If you go through and sample the fruit about a month before you pick, it's not very interesting. And it's still not very interesting when most people pick. When the fruit starts to get interesting, you wait until either the vineyard says, "I'm done," or you can't wait any longer. Then that's the taste you try to get into the bottle.

Rattlesnake Ridge is one of the highest vineyards here in the Valley. It's at eight hundred meters. When we bring the fruit down here, the smell is incredible. People come out of the winery and say, "Is that the Rattlesnake Ridge?" That's what we try to get in the bottle.

When people say, "Why do you make so many wines?" I give them a Dogtown Zin or the Hayne Zin or the Black Sears. These are very different wines, and they each have their staunch defenders. The fun for me is to show the individuality of an area planted almost one hundred years ago, when somebody said, "This is a good area for grapes."

To let the vineyard speak, Larry and Ehren do as little as possible in the winery. They don't even have a crusher to turn the grapes into juice. Instead, they do what's called "whole berry fermentation." The weight of the berries releases some of the juice, but mostly it's whole berries fermenting in the tank.

Nobody believes me, but we don't do anything. We put the grapes in the tank, leave them for a long time, check them constantly, put the wine in a barrel, and let it finish fermentation in the barrel. When you don't crush, you're getting a lot of whole berries. We probably get 80 percent whole berries in the tank. So when we press the wine, we

break a lot of berries that obviously haven't finished fermentation, so they release some sugars. So they finish fermenting in the barrel.

We don't filter, we don't fine. The wine is really made in the vineyard so we do a lot in the vineyard. We spend a lot of time there with cover crops. One of the nice things about organic farming is that it makes you a better farmer. You can't just drive by and do 'windshield' farming. You're out there looking for eggs or mites on the leaves. You can see the health of the vine, see how it gets through the summer.

He's also a proponent of letting the yeast that's naturally on the grapes start the fermentation, rather than adding yeast purchased from a lab. This is a controversial practice (see page 173), but he's convinced it's better.

We think we get much better flavors from natural yeast than laboratory yeast. Then you build up sort of a resident culture. Part of beer-making lore is that the secret is in the yeast. People would write to Heineken to get yeast for the home, and they would say, absolutely not! So then people would write to the brewmaster because they knew his office was in the brewery, and then they would try to culture the return letter. People say it's risky to use natural yeast. I don't think so. I think a lot of the individuality is in the yeast that's living with the fruit when you bring it in.

I have to believe Larry's risk-taking nature, his willingness to leap before he knows there's a net, explains part of his success.

My first week in the ER, I had a dentist and a chiropractor who had both just retired and had terrible strokes on the same night. It was just heartbreaking to hear the wives say, "You know, he worked so hard and saved, and we were going to do all these things." I never want to be in those shoes. I kind of overdid it for awhile, but I never want to look back and say, "I wish I had done that." Other people's opinions don't matter to me, which was the opposite of the way I grew up in the South. In a small town, everyone has an opinion on what you should be doing. I've mellowed a bit with that, but it's still my motto. Every day you should do exactly what you want to do because you might not have a tomorrow.

Just because he loves the way it tastes, Larry also makes Petite Sirah—what the old-timers called Petty Sarah. It's never really been a distinguished varietal like Cabernet Sauvignon, but Larry thinks it's underappreciated.

People used to use it to color up wines in lighter vintages, or to give perceived depth to a wine. But I enjoy it by itself. We have quite a few fanatics for Zinfandel, but multiply that intensity times ten and those are the people who want Petite Syrah [sic]. They've been lurking in the background and we get letters and poems and pictures. And I appreciate that very much because I really like the Petite Syrah. We planted some up in the hills; to me, mountain Petite Syrah will be very exciting.

For some, the sign of a good wine is that it improves with age. Larry doesn't have a lot of experience with how Turley wines age (he's only been making them since 1993) but he says the older ones have mellowed nicely. That doesn't mean he thinks they're better for it.

We have this discussion a lot, but it's sort of a nonissue. I mean, most people drink wines young. I certainly do. Robert Parker has been a very good friend of the wines. He comes out every year and we have the same conversation. He says, "This wine will age." And I say, "But will it have more fruit?" "Well, no." "Then why would you age it?" And it's never resolved. I say, "Do you think it gets better?" And he says, "Well, it changes."

When a wine needed aging, that to me was really a sign of an unbalanced wine. If you have to wait ten years to let the tannins get subdued enough to drink, then you're drinking flat wine because all the fruit's gone.

I like Larry for his frankness and his willingness to buck the tide. We always have a good time at the table, and I especially love it when he cooks. Sometimes, in the thick of harvest, he'll light the grill and make lunch for his crew. He had a machine shop jury-rig a mobile grill that can be rolled through the vineyards during winter pruning season. The prunings go inside to burn, and then Larry can cook on top. A typical pruning menu: grilled beef, tortillas, and salsa. A cold day, a hot lunch outdoors. Does life get any better?

It's phenomenal, really. People like the wine that I love to make. I'm lucky that my passion isn't some oddball white sweet grape that only ten people in the whole world like.

Pruners' Lunch

LARRY'S CARNE ASADA TACOS

FELICITAS'S POSOLE

*M*ost wineries prune their vines in winter, usually just after the first of the year. Larry Turley likes to wait until the sap is running in the vines, as late as March. He has no wind machines or other frost protection in his vineyard, so he doesn't want to encourage growth that could be killed by a late frost.

Even so, it can be chilly when Larry and his crew head into the vineyard with their pruning shears. To burn the prunings and keep themselves warm, the crew wheels a makeshift firebox through the vineyard. Based on a contraption that Larry's winemaker, Ehren Jordan, saw in Burgundy, the Turley low-rider consists of a fifty-five-gallon steel drum, halved lengthwise and pierced with holes, a steel frame, and an old motorcycle tire. The workers feed the prunings into the drum and burn them as they go, leaving a trail of ash behind. Larry's refinement was to add a flip-down grate so the workers can cook lunch over the smoldering vines.

A makeshift grill holds

vine prunings, the perfect

fuel for a vineyard lunch.

A garlicky marinade, a fiery salsa, and a wood-fired grill make these tacos hard to beat. Nobody wants to stop for long in the middle of winter pruning, so Larry brings the grill to the pruners. Once the ingredients are prepared, the tacos take only about two minutes to cook, and even less time to eat. Then it's back to work.

2 pounds boneless beef chuck

2 ancho chilies

4 cloves garlic, minced

3 bay leaves, crumbled

Olive oil

Sea salt, preferably gray salt (see Note on page 26)

16 corn tortillas

garnishes:

1 head iceberg lettuce, finely shredded

1 onion, finely chopped

Felicitas's Salsa (see page 271), or other homemade salsa

Slice the meat into ¼-inch-thick strips. The shape of the pieces doesn't matter but larger ones will be easier to grill. Remove seeds from chilies and toast the seeds in a dry skillet until lightly colored. In a spice grinder or coffee mill, grind the seeds to a fine consistency. Place meat in a large bowl and add ground chili seeds, garlic, crumbled bay leaf, and enough olive oil to coat the meat. Let rest at cool room temperature for 3 to 4 hours.

Prepare a hot charcoal fire. Season meat with salt. Grill on both sides until done to your taste. Set the meat aside while you grill the tortillas quickly on both sides to warm them. Tuck slices of meat in each tortilla and garnish with the lettuce, onion, and salsa.

MAKES 16 TACOS

FELICITAS'S POSOLE

Larry's housekeeper, Felicitas Chavez, makes large batches of her posole because Larry's daughters will happily eat it for days.

Vegetable oil

3 whole ancho chilies

4 pounds pork shoulder blade roast, in 2-inch cubes

2 pounds pork back ribs, cut into two-rib portions

Cloves of 3 heads garlic, peeled

4 quarts canned white hominy, drained

Salt

Large pinch of dried Mexican oregano

Freshly ground black pepper

garnishes:

2 onions, finely minced

2 lemons, in wedges

2 bunches radishes, quartered

1 head iceberg lettuce, finely sliced

Dried Mexican oregano

Felicitas's Salsa, or other homemade salsa

Heat a thin film of vegetable oil in a large pot over moderate heat. Add chilies and brown on all sides, then set aside. Brown meat thoroughly in the pot, in batches, adding more oil as needed. Set aside. Add 4 quarts water to the pot and bring to a simmer, then add browned chilies, garlic, hominy, and salt to taste. Simmer gently 1 hour. Add the browned meat, a large pinch of oregano (rub it between your fingers to release its flavor before you add it) and black pepper to taste. Simmer gently, partly covered, until meat is very tender, about 2 hours. Taste and adjust seasoning.

Serve the posole in bowls and pass the garnishes on the side.

Felicitas's Salsa

In a large skillet over moderate heat, toast 2 ounces chilies de arbol (80 to 90 chilies) until they almost smoke. Add 2 cups water, 1 clove garlic, minced, 1 teaspoon dried Mexican oregano, and a pinch of salt. Simmer gently 10 minutes, then blend in a blender until smooth.

SERVES 12

Napa's Mexican Accent

Vineyard workers in the Valley are, with few exceptions, Mexican—some migrant, but many permanent residents. In winery cellars, Mexican workers also help press, ferment, rack, and bottle the wine. The large Mexican community, which has grown along with the wine industry, adds diversity to Napa Valley's culture and culinary arts.

When Rosaura Segura's father, Enrique, came to Napa Valley in the 1950s, there were only a handful of other Mexican families. Enrique Segura was a *bracero,* an agricultural worker brought to this country by the U.S. Department of Agriculture. World War II had created a shortage of farm labor, and the bracero program helped close the gap.

Enrique Segura settled in the Valley, and today, his daughter, Rosaura, is a well-connected paralegal who provides help with immigration to the Valley's fast-growing Mexican community. Napa Valley is an estimated 20 percent Hispanic now, and that percentage is projected to rise.

"We're getting many new citizens," says Rosaura, a trend traceable to the amnesty for illegal aliens passed in 1986. The program awarded legal residency to many agri-cultural workers, who have since become citizens and been joined by family members from Mexico.

"It's a close-knit community," says Rosaura. "You have a party and three hundred people come." When her church held a fundraiser to buy an ambulance for her hometown in Mexico, hundreds attended. At Crane Park in St. Helena and at Kennedy Park in Napa, Hispanic families gather on weekends to celebrate baptisms and birthdays. The St. Helena Catholic Church holds one of its masses in Spanish on Sundays and the three-hundred-seat church is standing room only, says Sister Kathleen O'Shea.

"Most Anglos are Catholic only on Sundays," says Sister Katie, who works closely with the Mexican parishioners. "Mexicans are more integrated in their faith. You never see a car with Mexican men in it passing this church without seeing the hats tipped or them making the sign of the cross."

At harvest time, an estimated three thousand migrant workers—mostly Mexican—arrive in the Valley to help wineries pick the grapes swiftly. The annual influx solves a problem, but also creates a dilemma because the Valley has so few low-cost options for temporary housing. Concerned vintners are searching for a solution, including the possibility of a mandatory grower and vintner levy for farmworker housing. The grape boycotts of the 1970s are only a memory now, but local social worker Aurelio Hurtado says labor leader Cesar Chavez left his mark in making vintners more sensitive to workers' needs.

For those farmworkers who live in the Valley year-round, there is year-round work: pruning, ripping out old vineyards, planting new ones. Some start their own vineyard-management businesses, says Hurtado, who works for a nonprofit organization that provides education and training for area farmworkers. Others move from vineyard work into landscaping and gardening. The work of Mexicans "should be factored into the beauty of this valley," says Hurtado. "Who keeps up this beauty? The farmworker hasn't been recognized for his contribution, not in my mind."

Hurtado believes Napa's Mexican community is becoming more unified and politically active, partly in response to recent California ballot initiatives that were hostile to immigrants. He also sees a stable future for Mexicans in the Valley. "We're not going anyplace," he says. "We're part of this valley, and it's time for the rest of the community to see us as part of the community. When I looked in the most recent phone book for Napa, I couldn't believe the number of Spanish surnames."

Although migrant workers are essential to the wine industry, they no longer tell the whole story of the Mexican experience in the Napa Valley. The Hispanic community is here to stay—buying houses, building retail and service businesses, and sending children to local schools. "I hope they will always maintain their cultural family values," says Sister Katie, "because they are so rich—from birth to death."

Jim

Barbour

Jim Barbour is a duck-hunting buddy of mine and a much sought-after vineyard manager. When I bought several acres of neglected old vines in St. Helena, I turned to Jim for help in restoring them. I knew I could trust his advice, and I knew he'd let me participate. He's planted a lot of the greatest vineyards in the Valley over the years, like Grace Family Vineyard, and he's been working with Napa grapes since childhood.

In 1962, when I was about six, my parents bought the ranch in Rutherford where Sequoia Grove Vineyards is now. We moved up here when I was about ten. We had thirty acres of grapes, plus prunes and apples. There was a prune dehydrator in St. Helena and an apple dehydrator in Napa. We used to shuttle fruit back and forth.

Back then, you knew all your neighbors. I mean, you knew everybody. I used to ride my bike into Rutherford and it was all basically dirt sidewalks, and you'd never have one car pass you the whole way. My two stepbrothers and I did all the pruning on thirty acres, and we got two hundred and fifty dollars each, which was a lot of money then.

Jim wanted to be a parole officer but the job prospects weren't good, so he transferred to the University of California at Davis and got a degree in viticulture. That's when he realized that his dad, who was selling all his grapes to the Napa Co-op, was missing an opportunity.

At the end of the sixties, people started planting Chardonnay and they were getting a thousand dollars a ton or more for it. Well, that was unheard of. We were used to two hundred and fifty dollars a ton. So when I got out of school, I came back and said, "Dad, we've got to plant something we can make some money with. We've got to plant Chardonnay." Well, the old-timers didn't want to hear that. They didn't want to be told how to plant grapes. But I talked my dad into planting five acres of Chardonnay, and we made more off those five acres than we did off the other twenty-five.

After college, Jim went to work for one of the biggest vineyard management companies in the Valley, Frank Wood and Sons. He worked for Laurie Wood (Frank's son and successor) for seventeen years. The company specialized in developing hillside vineyards and over the years planted some of the most well known: York Creek, Cain, Barnett, Bella Oaks, Martha's Vineyard.

Laurie, now in his eighties, is a legend in the Valley for his skill at witching wells (see page 284). He witched my well and it came within ten gallons per minute of what he predicted.

Oh, it's amazing. He talks to his rods while he's walking. He'll say, "When I get to that tree, will I find water?" or "When I get to the tree, how many gallons will I find?" And supposedly these brass rods talk to him.

If you don't have water, let's face it, you're not going to plant vineyards. You've got to get the vines started properly, or they're never going to be right. Once they're started, you can start shutting the water off. But they need water in the beginning or they're not going to grow. You don't want to stress them early. Stress them later for quality, but not early.

It's a shame Jim's parents sold the Rutherford ranch in 1976. Today, it's worth about ten times the $285,000 they got for it. Their son could have been a gentleman farmer.

Instead, when Laurie retired, Jim struck out on his own. His clients now include many wealthy individuals who bought vineyard land in the Valley for the lifestyle. They want their name on a wine label, and cost isn't their first concern. Given the price of prime vineyard land in the Valley now—about $150,000 an acre and rising—the new arrivals may not see a profit in their lifetime, says Jim. But that doesn't deter them. They all want to be the next Grace Family Vineyard, selling their wine for $100 a bottle.

For a vineyard manager, every year is a new ballgame, but the basic routines are the same.

Usually you start the year by pruning and get most of it done in January and February. March and April is when you start to plant new vines, and in April the vines start to grow. March and April are also frost season, when you've got to get up at night and protect the vines.

Usually your best protection is sprinklers because they coat the vines with water, which turns to ice insulating the vine. Wind machines are next best. They only bring the temperature up three to five degrees, max. If it gets really cold and the wind machines aren't bringing the temperature up, you light the smudge pots [heaters].

When I was growing up, we used to put five-gallon buckets filled with diesel down the rows, and you'd just put a little gas on top and light the buckets and go. Or you'd have five tires stacked on top of each other. There was never a problem getting rid of tires in the valley because you burned them during frost season.

When I was a senior in high school, we got up twenty-eight nights in a row. I didn't like getting up every night with my dad, but they pretty much shut down school because everybody was doing it. You had to fill the pots during the day to get ready for the next night. Two-thirds of the crop was damaged. We burned tires every night, and the pollution was so bad you couldn't see across the street. That's when they said this is a little out of hand, and they invented the return-stack heaters, which burn their own emissions. They just throw out heat, not smoke.

RENEWAL

A lot of the old-timers talk about how cold the winters used to be. The weather must have changed in the Valley in the last twenty years. We still have occasional frost but it's rarely severe or prolonged.

The weather's really changed. We're picking earlier every year. When I first started growing grapes, we were picking until Thanksgiving every year, in the rain, with grape gondolas skidding through the fields because it was so wet. Now I'm done by October twenty-fifth or so.

Mid-April is when we start hillside work. The hillside ordinance [designed to prevent erosion] says you can't move any soil before April fifteenth or after October fifteenth. So April fifteenth we start clearing and doing any major movement of ground, and this continues into May. We're also training new vines, either tying them or putting up catch wires into July and August. We're irrigating young vineyards. And we're still planting up until harvest.

In September and October, we're wrapping up erosion control on new projects—seeding cover crops and mulching over the seed. We need to have this finished before the rains. And of course we're picking grapes. Once it starts raining in November, it's vacation time, although we're still out in the field monitoring new projects to make sure they're holding up to the rains. If a drain plugs up, it can cause a ton of erosion, which the county doesn't want to see.

Everybody asks me how Grace Family produces the grapes it does, but it isn't any one thing.

Napa Valley growers have really fine-tuned how grapes are grown over the years. They take so many more pains now than they used to—from pulling leaves to get more sun exposure to dropping crop: intentionally cutting grapes off so the fruit that remains is more concentrated. I wondered what new vineyard practices have had the biggest impact on quality.

I think it's people working together—winemakers with growers. Before, the winemakers were on one side and the growers on the other and they never really worked together. Also, new clones and new rootstocks are producing better wine. Everybody asks me how Grace Family produces the grapes it does. It isn't any one thing; it's a combination. The right rootstock, the right clone, closer vine spacing, the right type of soil. And tending to it. Making sure you pull leaves, so there's more sun on the buds and the fruit early on. If you do it late, your fruit isn't climatized and it will sunburn and dry up.

You also hear more talk these days about low yields. Growers boast about dropping fruit, and some growers are also planting vines closer these days to make the vines compete for nutrients. Supposedly, stress improves quality. (For another view, see page 77.) More vines per acre also increases yield. More yield, more wine, more profit—right?

We're still playing with that. I really think it depends on your location and your soil and how much crop the vine will set. If you're on rocky ground or hillsides, you're only going to have so much fruit. If you're on deep soil, you're going to have twice as much. With close-spaced vines, you could set six to eight tons to the acre, but I think you're

Even the small

Chiarello Family

Vineyard, managed

by Jim Barbour,

requires many hands

at harvest time.

not going to get the quality. I don't know that for a fact because no winemaker ever wants to take the chance, so we're always cutting fruit off. No winemaker wants me to leave more than four tons to the acre. You try to tell them that with close spacing, we've got five times the number of vines. We should be able to set more fruit. But they haven't quite changed their mentality.

Jim isn't taking chances with his own grapes, either. He has a few acres of Cabernet Sauvignon around his St. Helena house, and he says he fears he'd lose quality if he tried to get more than three tons per acre. (Consultant Heidi Barrett makes the Barbour Vineyards wine—all one hundred fifty cases of it—and it's worth seeking out.)

Lowering yields is just one step top growers like Jim are taking in their search for grape perfection. They're also picking in smaller bins than before, so the grapes aren't crushed before they get to the winery. They're hand-sorting to remove any underripe clusters or green berries. And instead of picking a whole vineyard or whole block at once, they're picking individual rows or half-rows to get the grapes at optimum maturity. That means they're going back over a vineyard multiple times during harvest—another reason fine wine costs so much.

It reminds me of Bart Araujo saying he tries to be 1 percent better in a hundred different ways. The best growers and vintners are always looking to improve. In some cases, no matter the cost. It must be a thrill to taste the improvements in the bottle.

The challenge is trying to make the best of whatever piece of ground I have. Each place is different, and I can't wait to taste that final product. You want to know what that wine's going to be like.

A guy with so many prestigious clients must have quite a cellar.

Oh, yeah. My daughter was born in 1990, which just happened to be a damn good year for Cabernet, so I started putting a lot of wine away for her. She's got an unbelievable cellar. When she was nine, I told her, "Eventually, you can either drink it or sell it. Hopefully you're going to sell some for college." And she said, "I'll decide that, Dad, when I get old enough."

Time in the Bottle

One of the reasons many people find wine more fascinating than, say, whiskey is that bottled wine continues to evolve over time. The beverage that goes into the bottle tastes different in six months, even more different in two years, and completely transformed—not always for the better—in twenty years. This transformation is the work of oxygen and the results are far from predictable, but winemakers are often asked to see into the future. First, winemakers have to decide when the wine is ready for release to the public. For their red wines, many will wait six months or more after bottling to see the wine through "bottle shock," an inexplicable phenomenon that temporarily changes a wine's aroma and taste.

"Bottling is a traumatic time for wine," says Daniel Baron, winemaker at Silver Oak Wine Cellars. "It has to be pumped out of tanks. Then it's often filtered. Then it's agitated as it comes out of the filter spout, and then I jokingly say that it's traumatized when the cork goes in. Two or three days after bottling, a wine is often very aromatic and showy. Then, a month later, it's just dumb as dirt. There are no aromatics. All you can smell is wood and all you can taste is tannin, and it takes a few months for the aromatics to come back."

Baron and Silver Oak owner Justin Meyer believe that it can take twelve months or more for the wine to be itself again.

"Imagine ripples in a pond," says the winemaker. "The further away you get, the smaller the ripples become. So you still have fluctuations, but after about a year in the bottle, they become acceptable. I often say a wine won't taste as good as it did its last day in the barrel until about two years after it's bottled."

That's why Silver Oak holds on to its wine so long before release—fourteen months after bottling for the Alexander Valley Cabernet Sauvignon, twenty months for the Napa Valley Cabernet Sauvignon. The additional aging also smoothes out the tannins, so that consumers who just can't wait to open a bottle will find a wine that's reasonably ready to drink.

More often, consumers want to know how long it will age and winemakers have to test their powers of clairvoyance. It's hard to say how a wine will respond to the slow oxidation that occurs over time, but it's clear that the wine will change.

"Everyone thinks that oxygen is the enemy of wine," says Baron, "but none of the evolution that we glorify in red wines would happen without it. If you leave wine in a stainless steel tank, it will taste the same as it did two years ago. The management of oxygen is crucial to what people, through the centuries, have written poetry and songs about—that wine improves with age."

Every two years, Baron tastes every vintage of Silver Oak since 1972 and writes tasting notes for the public, including some prediction about when the wine will be at its peak. But as well as he knows the wines now, he still has to revise his forecasts when vintages age slower or faster than expected. And as his winemaking practices change, the wines' aging potential will change, too, he says. He's picking grapes riper now, which should add longevity. On the other hand, he's no longer acidifying the wines, which may make them age faster.

"People are always asking winemakers 'How will this evolve?,'" says Baron, "but winemakers are used to tasting very young, raw wines. We can become completely blind to tannins. So a winemaker can drink a very young wine and take pleasure in it, where a consumer might find it rather rough. So sometimes we're the worst people to ask."

Napa Valley's Good Witch

Some people would say that the most important ingredient in wine is the grapes, but you could make a case for water. If you don't have water to irrigate your vines and rinse your barrels and tanks, you can forget about making wine.

Water is a scarce resource in some parts of Napa Valley. You can easily spend $20,000 digging a well and not find a drop. To improve their chances, some Napa Valley grape growers hire geologists to determine where the aquifers are. Others hire Laurie Wood.

Laurie is an old-time water witch—otherwise known as a dowser—with a success rate that makes you pay attention. I hired him to find water on my own property, and he found a stronger source than anyone expected. Doug Shafer says Laurie is batting a thousand on the wells at Shafer. Chuck Wagner at Caymus has used him, as have many others. Laurie himself claims he's 80 to 85 percent accurate, a record I suspect is better than the geologists'.

Since the 1940s, Laurie has managed vineyards in the Valley and his company has planted some of the most famous ones—Martha's Vineyard, Bella Oaks, York Creek, Grace Family.

One day, many years ago, Laurie saw two men walking through a prune orchard with a forked willow stick. "What the deuce are they doing?" he thought. One of the gentleman was a local witcher who taught Laurie how to use the stick to guide him to water.

Today Laurie uses two thin metal brazing rods that he says are more responsive. The rods bend like an L and Laurie holds them by the short side, pointing them straight out in front of him.

Witching takes a lot of concentration, so he does it early in the morning. He puts the rods in search position, then he asks permission. "You ask three questions: Can I search? May I search? Should I search?" says Laurie. "If I don't get a yes to all three questions, I don't go on the job that day." If the rods cross, that's a yes.

If he does get a go-ahead, he will walk the property with his rods, waiting for them to cross—"by what magic I do not know," says Laurie—to signal the presence of an aquifer. Then he swings a pendulum over the spot where the rods crossed, and the number of revolutions tells him the potential water flow. Lastly, he holds a single rod over the spot and watches intently as it starts to bounce. The number of bounces indicates how deep the well needs to be.

"People say, 'You're crazier than a bed bug,'" says Laurie, who is a very spry and genial 80-year-old. "I know this is way out, but I still believe in it."

Why wouldn't he? His dowsing talents are in great demand beyond the valley. He is paid in proportion to how much water he finds, and he has done well enough to establish a college scholarship fund at St. Helena High School, his alma mater. Probably these students will be taught in their geology classes that dowsing is a lot of bull, but then how do you explain Laurie Wood?

Bill

Harlan

I've known Bill Harlan since I came to Napa Valley in 1986. He's the landlord of the old stone building that houses Tra Vigne, and he's a partner in the restaurant. His first winery, Merryvale, is right across the street. Like a lot of successful

people, Bill is a gambler and an adventurer. He fared well in real estate development in the seventies and eighties because he has a huge appetite for risk and a sixth sense for timing. He's also the most patient person I've ever known. With Harlan Estate, he's realizing a dream he's had for thirty-five years.

I've been coming to the Napa Valley since the 1950s, when there were six or seven wineries where you could taste wine. It was beautiful and calm then, and the tasting was free. I came to the opening week of Bob Mondavi's winery [in 1966], and it triggered in me the thought that I could have my own winery—that sooner or later, I wanted to be in the wine business. By the early seventies, I began to look for a vineyard but I couldn't quite afford it yet.

Instead he and two partners bought the parcel that became Meadowood, today one of the loveliest country resorts in the world. The St. Helena property was near foreclosure because the owner had lost his permits for a subdivision. Bill saw its potential as a community resource and a wine country escape. For years, the Napa Valley Vintners Association met at Meadowood. The annual Napa Valley Wine Auction still takes place here, as it has since the auction began.

While he developed Meadowood, Bill continued to look for a vineyard that could create earth-shaking red wine.

I didn't want to buy someone else's vineyard. I wanted to carve something out of the land that hadn't been done before. During better than a decade of research, I was trying to find the common thread among the finest vineyards

Pages 290-291:

Mount St. Helena,

viewed from Harlan

Estate, rises above

a valley shrouded

in morning fog.

in the world. Why is this land more valuable than that land? I talked to farmers. I tried to get behind the brand to the land. I made a decision that I wanted to have hillside land, but not too far up.

I've spent a lot of my life gambling, and when you're a gambler, you've got to have the odds in your favor to win in the long run. And when you're planting vineyards, you don't really know what you have for twenty years. That's a big gamble—not only financially, but a gamble of a big chunk of your life. That's why I spent so much time trying to understand what things are common to the best vineyards in the world. I also wanted history on my side. Where was the best red wine produced in America over the last hundred-plus years? South of St. Helena and north of Yountville, on the west side of the valley, in the Rutherford–Oakville Bench area.

When he hadn't found his dream property by the early 1980s, he and his partners decided to buy grapes and make wine anyway. In just a few years, they created the successful Merryvale brand, building it to forty thousand cases. Bill is no longer part of Merryvale, but it got him launched in the wine business.

In 1984, he bought the forty-acre parcel that would become the foundation of Harlan Estate. Then he spent the next decade piecing together more property. Today Harlan Estate covers two hundred and forty acres, with about forty acres in vines. Located in Oakville, west of the famous Martha's

Vineyard, the property starts at a 225-foot elevation and rises 1,000 feet. But most of the vines are within a narrow band on the lower elevations.

For a man who can be brusque and intense in person, he's amazingly patient in business. He knows how long it can take a big bet to pay off, and he doesn't take shortcuts to get to the payoff faster. Watching him has been a great lesson for me.

I bought the property with the single purpose of creating a first-growth estate. We cleared the land in 1984, started planting in 1985, and made our first wine in 1987. But because the vines were so young, we couldn't make the quality of wine we wanted. We didn't release any wine until 1996, when we released the '90 and '91 together. So from the time we acquired the land until we released our first wine was twelve years. Twelve years without a nickel of revenue, let alone any profit, is a long time to wait.

Bob Levy, who used to make the wine at Merryvale, is Bill's winemaker now. From the start, the wines have gotten outrageous reviews, with two vintages—the 1994 and the 1997—getting a perfect 100 from critic Robert Parker. Tasters use words like dense, powerful, ripe, fleshy, and jammy to describe Harlan Estate. You have to wonder what steps they take to make not just a fine wine but a "first growth," the term for the top Bordeaux estates. I had heard that Harlan's workers hand-sort the grapes almost berry by berry.

Well, I think it really starts with the land. You can fight Mother Nature for a long time, but sooner or later, she wins. So I think that starting with the best land is by far the most important thing; and then recognizing what are the right varietals for that land, the right rootstock, the right clones, the right trellis system.

There are hundreds of little things that you do, but every year is different. Just because you did it last year doesn't mean you do it this year. Each varietal, each vintage is different. But I don't know of any winery any place that is more focused on each berry than we are.

For Harlan Estate, Bob skims the cream from the forty acres. He makes only about fifteen hundred cases a year, although he could make much more. Grapes that don't make the cut go into The Maiden, the winery's less expensive red wine, or they're sold off. A banker looking at Bill's business plan would probably think he's nuts.

Certain years we have less than a ton of fruit per acre. And not all of that goes into the final blend. The primary, overriding commitment we have is to create a first growth, in quotes—a first-growth wine-growing estate in California. To be a first growth takes many generations, but we have to start somewhere. It's important to produce quality and consistency, but most important is to bring out the character of the land. What does it have the potential to produce? Some years the vineyard wants to produce two and three-quarter tons per acre, some years one ton per acre. Some years are easy; years like

Twelve years without a nickel of revenue, let alone any profit, is a long time to wait.

Bill talks a lot about heritage, about creating something that will endure.

1998 are more difficult. We felt that we weren't going to get grapes to maturity in the time we needed to, so we dropped half of our fruit, which was basically a million-dollar loss.

In the short run it's hard to take, but we have to have the best wine every year, even if it means having a third of what we had the year before. People often ask how wine can be so expensive. But when we make decisions like this, they're expensive and very high risk. We didn't finish picking in 1998 until the second week in November, when almost every weekend the forecast called for rain. If we had had weekends of rain, we would never have gotten the quality we needed. So waiting for ultimate maturity meant taking the risk of worse weather, the risk of losing it all, and the risk of dropping half the fruit to ripen the rest. It did get warm and the fruit got to maturity, but there's all that judgment going on.

Maybe another reason for Bill's success is that he and Bob are never satisfied. They're always trying to find the little refinement in the vineyard or the cellar that will make a big difference—or even a little difference.

There were years that we thought we might produce better fruit if we dropped our crop really low. And we found that that isn't necessary. Our vineyard tends to want to produce at about two and a quarter tons per acre. Taking it lower every year doesn't mean it's going to be better. There are a lot of ways to make wine. There's no one recipe. With winemaking, the recipe that's right for one vintage is not necessarily right for the next one.

Another thing I've admired about Bill is how he looks beyond today. He talks a lot about heritage, about creating something that will endure. I think he's really building Harlan Estate for his great-grandchildren.

I've pretty much always followed what I felt like doing at the time. When I was younger, I was really living in the "now." And that, to me, meant working to a point of disequilibrium so you didn't know what was going to happen next. From big-wave surfing to motorcycle racing to big-stakes gambling to chasing girls—at a certain point, you don't know what's going to happen in the next second. When you're in that zone, it's a very exciting place to be, but it's also very fleeting. There's not much that's meaningful.

I didn't get married until I was almost forty-six, so I was able to travel. I spent time at sea. I spent time flying airplanes. I spent time racing. I swam a relay across the English Channel. I tried almost everything I wanted to do, but as time went on, I wanted experiences that had more meaning. I wanted things that had more 'lastingness' to them.

When you look at businesses that have been around for more than three hundred years, there are a few things they have in common. One is that they are based on the land. Another is that they're usually owned by a family.

Now the wine industry happens to be an industry that's based on land, where families get involved. In other industries, most businesses are there for the benefit of the stockholders, to make money. So businesses come and go with what the world needs at that time. That's why it's difficult to be in business three hundred years unless it's based on something that doesn't change. Land doesn't change.

Our kids are eleven and thirteen, and they've been coming to family board meetings since they were five. Their attention span in the early days was maybe five minutes or less, but at least they could sit in on the meeting. Will they want to be in the wine business? I don't know. This is my dream, not theirs.

What's important is that they understand the values of agriculture. If you want to have a crop in the fall, you've got to work in the winter, spring, and summer. They visit the countries where we have our wine, and they begin to learn about other cultures. So it gives them a global perspective and some idea of time and money and risk. Whatever they want to go into, this is a good education. My hope is that they will have a certain respect and appreciation for the estate and see it as a homestead for their children and grandchildren. But what's as important as passing on the physical plant and the property is passing on the values that go with it—the work ethic, the importance of relationships, the idea of doing things the best way, the right way. These are the principles that improve your chances of keeping an asset for generations.

Bill Harlan released his first Harlan Estate wine in 1996, the culmination of a dream nurtured from the early 1970s.

RENEWAL

Targeting Wine Sales

Napa Valley wines have become so sought-after worldwide that, for many wineries, the challenge isn't selling their production, it's allocating it. When demand exceeds supply, vintners have to decide how much of their wine to allocate to restaurants, how much to retail stores, and how much to their mailing list and tasting room. Mailing-list and tasting-room sales are desirable because the winery pockets more of the profit. But most wineries of any size have to look beyond those two avenues, and even the smallest wineries may choose to sell some of their production to restaurants and retailers as a way of building visibility for their brand.

"Our basic philosophy is, we'd rather see our wine in a nice restaurant because then we know people enjoy it in good circumstances," says Dennis Cakebread, vice president of sales and marketing for Cakebread Cellars, one of the country's most popular restaurant brands. "Usually you go to a nice restaurant with people you enjoy, or you're having a special occasion so you're happy to be there. The restaurant has a nice ambience and nice glassware, and you've ordered well-prepared food. We just think that adds to the flavor and feeling you get from the wine.

"What's more, when a table orders a bottle of Cakebread Cellars wine, typically several people share it and the diners at neighboring tables see it. That's great exposure," says Dennis, "especially compared to the retail customer who buys a case of wine and puts it in his or her closet."

As Napa Valley wineries proliferate, Cakebread Cellars has to work even harder to cement its relationships with chefs, distributors, retailers, and consumers. Once a year, the winery brings five different chefs from around the country to Cakebread Cellars for a culinary experience in wine country. Dennis, his winemaker brother Bruce, his parents Jack and Dolores, and his sister-in-law Karen spend many hours on the road at tastings for the trade, charity auctions, and winemaker dinners, trying to meet customers one on one.

"It's a consumer business with few parallels," says Dennis. Imagine people getting so interested in a particular manufacturer's shoes that they traveled long distances to tour the factory and take a few pairs home. Or imagine that when the shoe salesman went on the road, people paid money to go hear him talk about shoes, as people pay to attend winemaker dinners.

"I think people enjoy having insider access," says Dennis, whose winery, like many others, has launched a consumer club that gives people more of those "insider" opportunities and helps build loyalty to the brand. Club members may have first chance at limited-quantity wines or receive invitations to special events, such as a barrel tasting with the winemaker.

The difficulty for wineries like Cakebread Cellars that sell wine faster than they can make it is keeping customers when the wine is out of stock. Restaurants may turn to another Sauvignon Blanc producer if you can't supply them year-round. Wine isn't breakfast cereal, says Dennis. You can't just make more when the supply runs out.

Managing sales to keep customers satisfied may be an annual challenge, but all things considered, being sold out is not a bad problem to have.

A Chef's Herb Farm

One thing I've noticed about Napa is how many people live here because of a hobby gone wild. Probably most of the vintners in the valley started out in other businesses, but their interest in wine eventually took over their lives. It wasn't enough to drink wine; they had to make it, too.

When you see Linda-Marie Bauer's Lazy Susan Ranch in Calistoga, you get another view of where a passion can take you. On eighty acres of beautiful wooded countryside with views of northern Napa Valley, Linda-Marie has planted eight acres of culinary herbs in a sunny clearing and hundreds of roses on terraces constructed with stones from the property. The 120 citrus trees she inherited when she bought the place weren't quite enough, so she has also planted Kaffir lime trees.

Today, Lazy Susan Ranch supplies chefs in the valley and in San Francisco with hard-to-find ingredients like orange blossoms and lemon verbena for desserts; Kaffir lime leaves for Thai curries; lemongrass, Vietnamese *rau ram* (a fragrant herb), and Thai basil for other Southeast Asian dishes; *epazote* for Mexican cooking and *nepitella,*

a mintlike herb that Italians love.

"My real mission is to get people to use herbs that haven't been available commercially," says Linda-Marie. "It doesn't excite me nearly as much to sell someone English thyme as it does to introduce them to angelica."

As I said, another hobby run amok. Linda-Marie did not set out to grow herbs for a living, but she did own a restaurant in San Francisco, and chefs who ate there couldn't help noticing all the unusual aromatics she used—herbs she grew herself at her weekend home in Calistoga. They asked if they could have some, too.

Linda-Marie now lives full-time on the property, in a Victorian home built in 1879 for one of Calistoga's most prominent families. The estate, which used to be larger, had been a working farm in those days, but later generations gradually abandoned agriculture.

Today, there are wine grapes on the ranch again. New stone walls and terraces are giving the property definition and character. ("This property grows rocks," a previous owner told her. "You dig a hole,

and the next day there are rocks in it.") Linda-Marie has also undertaken a renovation of the house itself, paying close attention to period details.

The ranch is open to the public for U-pick on alternate Sundays, and Linda-Marie will show groups around by prior arrangement. Gardening groups visit often, and she is scheduling cooking classes in her home now that her kitchen renovation is complete.

When I see projects as ambitious as Lazy Susan Ranch, I'm awed by the creator's commitment. Linda-Marie says she didn't really know what she would make of the place when she bought it. From the start, she had only two goals: to create something beautiful enough to share, and to put the land back in agriculture. "It was obviously a farm," she says, "and it needed to be in production again."

Linda-Marie Bauer gathers
amaranth (above) and
Kaffir lime leaves (below)
for her chef clients.

Lyndsey and Sofia

Harrison

I know there are some former pilots in the Napa Valley wine business, but Lyndsey Harrison is the only flight attendant turned winemaker I know. When Lyndsey and her husband, Michael, bought forty-eight acres on Pritchard Hill

in St. Helena in 1988 (their winery neighbors are Chappellet, Bryant Family, and Long Vineyards, among others), Lyndsey found a new calling. Her high-intensity Cabernet Sauvignon and Chardonnay from the property have earned raves, and she now makes a little Zinfandel and Merlot, too.

A few years after Lyndsey and Michael moved here from New York, Michael's adult daughter Sofia joined them. Sofia and I became wild mushroom hunting buddies and our young daughters became best friends.

Michael Harrison was larger than life: a business genius, a food fanatic, and an amazing home cook. He and Sofia ended up starting a small packaged foods business, while Lyndsey took charge of the wine. When Michael passed away in 1999 at the age of sixty-one, the Napa Valley lost one of its true originals.

The Harrison wines are originals, too—massive, chewy Cabernets that seem to concentrate the essence of Pritchard Hill.

Lyndsey: The grapes are definitely mountain grapes. The wines tend to be longer-lived and they can be more austere if you don't manage the tannins. The soil is very, very rocky. I like to say we farm rocks with a few grapes in between. The wines are big, very big. Intense fruit and dark color. It's mostly red wine growing on this hill. We're among the few people who grow Chardonnay up here. We inherited it and became known for it so we are actually replanting four acres of Chardonnay. We should be planting Cabernet, but we don't always do things the "right" way.

The vineyard was actually planted back in the sixties, by a gentleman who ran into financial problems and committed suicide in my library. And, yes, there is a ghost in the house.

A boletus mushroom, the sought-after porcino, emerges from its forest bed.

Sofia: I used to live here and one night when I was watching television in bed, the door opened and you could feel cold air, then it closed and the door going to the bathroom opened and closed. What else could it be?

When Michael and Lyndsey bought the property, they had no intention of making wine. They just wanted a country place.

Lyndsey: I said, "Well, if we're going to get a country place, let's get a country place with vines because they're really cool to look at." Famous last words.

We spent a week in Napa Valley looking at places in the rain, and it was still beautiful. Then we walked in this house and saw the view and I said to Michael, "Let's buy it." And he said, "Let's find out how much it is first." The seller said, "Well, I have this magic number in my mind," and Michael said, "Do you mind sharing it with us?" No. We had to guess.

The first year we sold the grapes to Caymus and Raymond. Then Bob Long [of Long Vineyards] said, "You know, you shouldn't be selling those grapes," so I made a barrel of Chardonnay and Cabernet in my basement.

I was sort of in transition. I had been a flight attendant with Pan Am for twenty years, and Michael had been saying to me for years, "Why don't you get a real job?"

Sofia: Both Lyndsey and my father were already interested in wines and had a wonderful wine collection, and my father was a very accomplished chef. So you move to this valley where everything is about the land, the food, the wine, and all your friends are in the wine business, and you're constantly talking about making wine. And Lyndsey's a very smart woman and good with chemistry. It wasn't a difficult transition.

Lyndsey: The most incredible thing about this valley is that the people are so helpful. Coming from New York, we were skeptical about anything anybody said, thinking they must have an ulterior motive. They wouldn't really give us that information if that was how it really was. People just took my hand and said, "Look, here's my whole list of retailers and distributors. You should deal with this one but not that one. Be careful of this one—he doesn't pay so well." Everything was an open book; it gives me goosebumps to think about it. Everybody gives advice and tells you how they do things. There are no real secrets. I've never been in a business like that before. I've been involved in several and so had my husband, and he still didn't believe it.

Lyndsey soon moved the winemaking out of the house and over to Robert Pecota's winery in Calistoga. Bob Long looked over her shoulder for the first few vintages. But what really helped the brand is that Lyndsey knew how to sell.

Sofia: She was an absolute nobody with no reputation in the wine business, but she had this incredible list of restaurants and retailers that her friends had given her. They assumed she would call and make appointments to have buyers taste the wine, but in many cases, she would call up and say, "I have this really great wine, a 1989 Chardonnay, and it's very . . . expensive. This is how much it is and aren't you going to take it?" They weren't used to someone with such nerve.

Lyndsey: My first vintage was 1989, a vintage that was not well received by the press. It was released during the middle of the Gulf War, during a recession. The wine was expensive, and nobody had ever heard of it, so why would they buy it? But they did. I sold a lot of it in New York. At that time, there weren't that many winemakers who sold the wine themselves. But I knew all the restaurants that I wanted it to be in because those are the restaurants I liked to eat in.

In 1993, Lyndsey hired consultant Helen Turley to take her to the next level of winemaking knowledge. The two worked together for a couple of years.

Sofia: Helen was a wonderful teacher for all of us, and by that point we had moved our production to Chappellet, right up the hill. That gave Lyndsey an opportunity to be more hands-on with the wine. I think Helen taught her everything she knew and when we parted ways, Helen said, "You don't need to hold on to me anymore, Lyndsey. Go . . . you're fine. I'm just holding your hand anyway," a really sweet compliment. Lyndsey had absorbed everything Helen had to teach, but the most important thing was that it all starts in the vineyard.

The most incredible thing about this valley is that the people are so helpful. Coming from New York, we were skeptical about everything.

John Kongsgaard of Luna Vineyards consults with Lyndsey now, but she is confident of the Harrison approach. The grapes are picked super-ripe, fermented with indigenous yeast (see page 173) and aged in new French oak. The result is bold, brassy wine that is almost always more than 14 percent alcohol, with great depth of color and flavor.

I'd been curious about something else that seemed to be a Harrison signature. The Cabernet label has a zebra on it, their Jeep has zebra stripes, and I've occasionally seen Lyndsey in zebra-striped clothes. What's the deal with the zebras?

Lyndsey: It came from one of the first times my husband and I ever went away together. We were on an African safari and we had fun chasing around with zebras. When we came here, we went out very early one morning and picked up a couple of cans of spray paint and painted our Jeep.

Sofia: That's how they enticed me to come out. They sent me pictures of the zebra Jeep. "Look what we're doing out in California! We're painting stripes on Jeeps!"

Lyndsey: So when it came time to do the label for the 1989 Cabernet, Michael drew this incredible T'ang horse with zebra stripes. It's a mythical beast, as are all the others on all our labels.

Michael Harrison, a talented graphic artist, created the labels for his wife's wines.

Michael Harrison was an artist at heart, a wildly creative man who made his living in the direct-mail business. He and Lyndsey met in the ticket line at the Bangkok airport, when Lyndsey was on an around-the-world trip with her parents. When he heard they were on their way to Beirut, he changed his itinerary on the spot. They had their first date in Beirut and were married for twenty-six years.

Michael was the best amateur cook I've ever known, and he was fearless about cooking for chefs. He would do what he called "counter dinners," where all the guests sat at the island in their kitchen, and he cooked course after course, never sitting down. He'd have nine things going at once—usually Asian-inspired—and he'd be telling stories and mixing "saketinis." It was really something to see.

Michael knew he had a heart problem, so he became a vegetarian in his last few years. But that didn't change how he cooked. He always made menus with lots of meat and then he'd ask, "Tell me, have I got that right? Is that good?" He wouldn't eat it.

Lyndsey: He was supposed to do a dinner and a luncheon the week he died. We were coming back from France and Sofia still has the menu and the shopping list he made for her.

Sofia: The last time I ever talked to him on the phone, he said to me, "Okay, make it twelve avocados." That was the last thing he said. It was about food, you know.

He was inspired by restaurants, but he was always thinking, "Well, that's great, but what if I put a jalapeño in the center and wrap it in pancetta and then fry it in rice flour?" or whatever. And he would use us as guinea pigs.

The first thing my daughter said when my father died was, "What are we going to do about eating now?"

I wouldn't say he was a renegade, but he liked to push the envelope a bit and to shock and surprise people. As much as he loved the Valley, he sometimes thought that people here were too serious and should have more fun. One year, for the wine auction booklet, he dressed up in drag for his picture. I don't think anybody appreciated it but us, but that was just the type of person he was.

Sofia now runs the packaged food business that she and her father launched together. They started with Harrison olive oil, branched out to vinegars, then into mustards and salsas. They just had fun with it, and they couldn't care less about market research.

Sofia: Basically, my dad would come up with an idea for a product. You know, "I really like mangos and I like mustard and I like that sauce they put on the calamari at Tra Vigne. Let's make mango–honey mustard!" That's how things would happen. Sometimes he would develop a label before the product. A lot of it had to do with his design creativity, and what we felt like eating. The last line that we worked on before he passed away is a line of Asian sauces that I'm naming "Counter Culture" in his honor.

Michael Harrison worked hard but played harder, and he put a high priority on fun.

Sofia: We used to have a clam sauce cook-off. The first time was years ago with Lyndsey, my dad, my husband, and me; my father won hands down. Boom. No question. And he taught all of us how to make clam sauce, so they should have all been the same, but no, they were all totally different.

Years later, he decided we were going to have another contest. So I called Michael [Chiarello] and said, what do I do? He said, use butter. Of course! How perfect! And I won. I was very proud of winning the clam sauce cook-off, but my dad said I cheated because you never put butter in clam sauce. So then all of a sudden there were rules about how you can't use butter.

This was how we lived our lives. It was about us. It was about how we were going to entertain ourselves. We would be having dinner and Lyndsey would bring up some everyday wine and my dad would say, "This is garbage. Get the good stuff. This is for us!" That's the kind of person he was. He lived life to the fullest more than any person I've ever seen.

Well, if we're going to
get a country place, let's get a
country place with vines.

Creating this book has been an experience filled with enormous pleasure and gratification for me. In a small way, I'm trying to repay a deeply felt debt to Napa Valley for the encouragement its residents have always given me. My mission since the project began was to gather the stories of the Valley's wine people; my concern from the start has been how to convey the spirit of the whole Valley in the memories of just a few.

I chose the twenty vintners and growers profiled here because they are close personal friends who I believed had rich stories to tell—diverse experiences that covered a span of more than sixty years. Collected here, these reminiscences add depth and detail to Napa's modern history. But with more than two hundred vintners in the Valley, I'm aware that I have left many compelling stories untold. New ones are being written all the time by new arrivals, and the ones included here aren't finished yet.

Like a photograph, these interviews also capture a moment in time—in this case, a particularly prosperous moment for the Napa Valley wine industry as the new millennium debuts. What lies ahead? Probably more debates about if and how the Valley should grow, possibly more restrictions aimed at preserving its agricultural character. The demand for premium Napa Valley wines, so strong right now, could take a dive; the industry is notoriously cyclical. With local land and grape prices rising steeply, it's certainly more difficult than it used to be for a young person to start a winery here. But Napa Valley has always lured dreamers and doers, and I have no doubt that I'll be able to write a sequel in a few years filled with more fresh and inspirational stories.

M i c h a e l

*N*apa Stories is a book of reflections, a collection of stories told to me by friends old and new. I would like first to thank all the vintners of the Napa Valley, especially those whose participation in this project made it possible. I appreciate the many hours you spent with the book team, sharing your memories and expertise.

I particularly want to acknowledge some older members of the wine community, the modern pioneers who laid the foundation for the rest of us. Belle and Barney, thanks for all the stories you've shared; they inspired this book. Dorothy T., thanks for recounting André's story and your memories of life with him; I felt lucky to have known him, and I'm equally fortunate to know you. Barbara Eisele, grazie for your gracious support of all the good things that make up Napa Valley. Thanks to Robert Mondavi, Peter Mondavi, and their children for continuing to be such tireless spokespeople for wine and the good life.

To every vineyard worker who has contributed to turning Napa Valley grapes into wine, thank you. May your days be warm, filled with friends and family, and blessed with the respect you deserve. Steven Rothfeld, your heart and camera have captured the essence of Napa. I will forever remember not only your wonderful images, but also the friendship that each photo represents. I thank Stewart, Tabori & Chang and my editor and publisher Leslie Stoker for not just supporting this work but being a true partner. Janet Fletcher, your words open my heart. Thank you for your enormous effort, for all the research "above and beyond," and for keeping us on schedule. I have learned as much about Napa from you as from anyone. Barbara Vick, your design has framed these reflections in a way that gives the reader a lasting memory of each hero in the book. To GardenHome, our neighbors in St. Helena, sincere thanks for your continuing generosity.

To my team and partners of NapaStyle: A special thanks to Susie Heller, the creative glue that pulled together this dream. David Shalleck, our culinary director, has inspired me as much as any single chef in my life. David, you have captured the true flavor of these vintners in each and every dish. And thanks to the rest of the NapaStyle team for your support and your passion for wine. Never have I worked with such a great team.

To my daughters, Margaux (my sun), Felicia (my moon) and Giana (my stars), it is because of you that our home in Napa became a reality. My desire for you to grow up in a magical place led me to Napa and launched me on a mission to share the valley's way of life with others. I will always cherish you. To my love and partner Eileen Gordon: You have taught me what beauty is and how to see it in the most magnificent ways. Your creative thoughts, vision, and artistic nature are woven not only into this book but also into the fabric of me.

Janet

I would like to acknowledge the considerable assistance of the many people who contributed to this manuscript. For helping me understand the many decisions a winemaker or grape grower faces, I'd like to thank Daniel Baron, Thomas Brown, Dennis Cakebread, John Caldwell, Cathy Corison, Mary Hall, Ashley Heisey, John Kongsgaard, David Ramey, Jack Stuart, and John Williams. For taking time to share their stories with me, I'd like to thank Jeff and Sally Manfredi of Calistoga Pottery; Peter Forni, Lynn Brown, and Barney Welsh of Forni-Brown Gardens; Linda-Marie Bauer of Lazy Susan Ranch; Ernie Navone; Michael Adams of Music in the Vineyards; Amy Wend of Skyhill Napa Valley Farms; Jim Neal of Fusion Verjus; Dale Taylor of T&O Masonry; Laurie Wood; Rosaura Segura; Aurelio Hurtado; Sister Kathleen O'Shea; and Ray Particelli of Napa Valley Olive Oil Company.

I'm grateful to Lisa Harper for her able transcription services, to Alessandra Bocco for her rigorous copy editing of the manuscript, and to publisher Leslie Stoker for her genuine enthusiasm for this unusual project. My husband Douglas Fletcher spent many hours on this book, too—transferring digital recordings to audiotape, helping me through computer glitches and tirelessly answering questions about every aspect of winemaking and grape growing. I can't thank him enough. Finally, I'd like to express my deep gratitude to Michael Chiarello, who invited me to participate in this great adventure and who always wanted to make sure that the project was equal parts work and fun.

Steven

I feel as if I were summoned to Napa Valley six years ago to prepare myself for the task of creating the photographs for this book. Meeting and working with the people involved in this project has been an enlightening and inspiring experience—one that I will reflect upon and nourish myself with for many vintages to come. I would like to express my gratitude to Michael Chiarello for sharing his Napa passions, Leslie Stoker for her nurturing support and flawless intuition, Barbara Vick for her tireless patience and unparalled aesthetic, Janet Fletcher for her enviable organizational skills, and Susie Heller for her endless stream of ". . . I sure hope you're out there shooting because it's a gorgeous day. . . ." messages.

Thanks to the following individuals and businesses for their kindness and generosity: Doug Fletcher, Bob Gallagher, Terry Hall, Mindy Kearney and her hands, Nancy Light, Ray Tonella and his harvest knives, All Seasons Wine Shop, Beringer, and Nadalie.

Resource List

Across from Tra Vigne sits NapaStyle, Michael Chiarello's new expression of great foods and unique home furnishings. He creates Tuscan sauces and spice rubs, served on barrel staves from local vintage wine barrels, and cooks for television and radio shows.

NapaStyle
801 Main Street
St. Helena
1-866-776-NAPA
www.napastyle.com
Retail room with daily food tastings
Call for hours

Bale Grist Mill
Bale Grist Mill State Historic Park
Highway 29 between St. Helena and Calistoga
Open daily 10 a.m. to 5 p.m.
Milling four times a day on Saturday and Sunday
Call 707-942-4575 for milling times.

Calistoga Pottery
1001 Foothill Boulevard
Calistoga
707-942-0216
Open daily

Cantinetta at Tra Vigne
1050 Charter Oak Avenue
St. Helena
707-963-8888
For picnic provisions and wine

Dean & DeLuca
607 S. St. Helena Highway
St. Helena
707-967-9980
For picnic provisions, packaged foods,
housewares, and wine

Gordon's Cafe and Wine Bar
6770 Washington
Yountville
707-944-8246
For box lunches and sandwiches

Lazy Susan Ranch
P. O. Box 1152
Calistoga
707-942-0120
707-942-6232 (fax)
www.lazysusanranch.com
Open for U-pick herbs, flowers, and citrus on
alternate Sundays

Music in the Vineyards
P. O. Box 432
St. Helena
707-578-5656
www.napavalleymusic.org

Napa Valley Olive Oil Manufacturing Co.
835 Charter Oak
St. Helena
707-963-4173
Open daily
For Italian and Italian-style foodstuffs

Oakville Grocery
7856 St. Helena Highway
Oakville
707-944-8802
For picnic provisions and wine

Sunshine Foods
1117 Main Street
St. Helena
707-963-7070
For picnic provisions and wine

Index

(Page numbers in *italics* refer to illustrations.)